Customer Power

Customer Power

*How to Grow Sales and Profits in a
Customer-driven Marketplace*

David C. Swaddling
and
Charles Miller, Ph.D.

THE
WELLINGTON
PRESS

Design and layout by the Devereaux Bureau.

Printed in the United States of America on 100% recycled paper.

1   2   3   4   5   6   7   8   9   10

Cataloging-in-Publication Data

Swaddling, David C.
 Customer power: how to grow sales and profits in a customer-driven marketplace / David C. Swaddling and Charles Miller.
   p. cm.
 Includes bibliographical references and index.
 ISBN 0-9700879-4-2 (hardcover)

 1. Marketing-Management 2. Organizational effectiveness
  3. Customer services 4. Consumer satisfaction. I. Miller, Charles
  II. Title
 658.812-dc21   00-191028
         CIP

Table of Contents

Why Another Book about Customers?

It is the customer who determines what a business is. For it is the customer, and he alone, who through being willing to pay for a good or for a service, converts economic resources into wealth, things into goods. What the business thinks it produces is not of first importance – especially not to the future of the business and to its success. What the customer thinks he is buying, what he considers 'value,' is decisive – it determines what a business is, what it produces, and whether it will prosper.[1]

That says everything we want to say. So, why write a whole book? Or, more accurately, why write *another* whole book? There are more than 900 titles in the index of Books in Print with the word "customer" in them. What could be left to say about the importance of customers to a business?

Well, we believe there is quite a bit left to say. At the consumer level, we are confronted everyday with lousy customer service. In the business-to-business sector, many companies are struggling to reap their fair share of the unprecedented economic growth of the past decade and can't determine why they are having such a difficult time. Unfortunately, everyone has encountered companies that are still primarily product-focused.

The beginning quotation is from one of the most respected sages of American business, Peter Drucker. The only amazing thing about it is that it was written by Drucker nearly *50 years ago*! Being customer-focused is not at all a new idea. Still, many companies continue to struggle with the concept.

Our guess is that most managers know that the customer is important, but many don't know what to do about it. They can read book after book and hear speaker after speaker telling them that they have to become customer-focused, but that mantra has little relevancy when they must go back to their offices and deal with the complex problems and decisions that make up their real work days.

That is why we decided to write one more book about being customer-focused. Rather than providing another pep talk about how important the customer is and *why* something has to be done, however, we are hoping to help managers make the connection between customer perceptions and their own job responsibilities by providing some ideas about *how* to become more customer-focused. And we provide numerous examples of what that looks like when it is successfully done.

Because we believe this book is among the first-of-a-kind, it is necessarily an overview of the topics. We have emphasized the *breadth* of management issues that should be impacted by a customer-focus rather than going into depth in any one area. For example, an entire volume could be written about the customer's impact on strategic planning (and most any of the other topics covered), but that wasn't our purpose. Rather, this book was designed to provide an *introduction* to the different management decisions that should be driven by an understanding of how customers perceive value.

Of course, there are many other requirements for success in business, including such things as leadership, communication, people management, finances, engineering, technology, and hard work. But the primary topic of this book is about capitalizing on an understanding of customer perceptions. Besides being what we know best, we believe that learning about how customers perceive value, and making management decisions on that basis, is the quickest, safest, and most surefire way to increase the health of any business.

None of what we offer here is, as they say, rocket science. In fact, once the reader has thoroughly accepted the idea that the whole world of business revolves around the customer, much of what we say may appear to be simple, common sense. That's O.K. Simple doesn't mean unimportant, and the travails of today's product-focused companies indicate that what we have to say here may be very important. Because we know that not everybody is practicing all of the things we discuss in this book, it seems worthwhile to promote these common sense ideas.

We've organized our book into three sections. The first sets the table, the second provides the meat, and the third offers the dessert.

Section One consists of three chapters. In Chapter 1, we review the importance of a customer focus and place it into context with other major management themes. Our hope is that the reader is convinced at the end of this chapter that there is nothing more important in business than understanding customers.

Chapter 2 provides a more precise definition of what we call Customer Perceived Value (CPV). Here we differentiate the concept from others, such as customer satisfaction and customer loyalty. We describe the elements of CPV very specifically because they are used throughout the rest of the book.

Chapter 3 suggests a specific method of turning management intentions into action. We introduce a model called the CPV Delivery Cycle, which demonstrates the relationship of customer research, strategy development, process design, and management follow-through. This tool is referenced throughout the remainder of the book because it represents the way things get done in a business.

Readers who are already believers in the importance of a customer focus might not require Chapter 1 unless they need ammunition to convince others in their organizations. We recommend Chapters 2 and 3 to everyone, however, because they set up terminology and concepts for the remainder of the book.

Section Two deals with seven different applications of CPV. Chapter 4 is devoted to the process of making general business strategy and Chapter 5 to market segmentation. The next four chapters address each of the Four Ps of marketing: Product development, Pricing, marketing channels or Place, and marketing communications – that is, Promotion. The final chapter in this section deals with implementation – production and operations.

Throughout Section Two, we review many of the major theories and practices commonly used by managers. The intention is to provide a "checklist" that helps the manager find a starting place and a menu of choices for incorporating CPV into the respective process. We tried to stay at a level general enough not to exclude most readers but precise enough within each topic to allow the manager to take action based on the information provided.

Readers can pick and choose the chapters in Section Two in which they are most interested, based on their functional responsibilities or immediate needs. However, there might be value in plowing through the whole section to get the complete picture of how CPV plays on all of the aspects of running a business.

Finally, Section Three offers some ideas about turning the concepts into action. Chapter 11 describes the customer research tools for building a CPV Learning System. Chapter 12 explains why this should be done by examining the Return on Investment of understanding CPV.

Throughout, *Customer Power* is filled with numerous real-life examples that illustrate the various points we are trying to make. Most of these examples are from the consumer sector, even though the topics apply as much, or more so, to the business-to-business sector. In fact, this book is intended primarily for business-to-business managers, for whom the premise of capitalizing on a customer focus is sometimes newer and always more complex. Nevertheless, the examples we offer are mostly consumer-oriented because those experiences are more universal, and, therefore, we expect that more of our readers will readily relate to them.

We appreciate the contributions of the many people that helped us in so many ways in the production of this book. Our colleagues who read early versions of it and provided their insights and suggestions were particularly important, especially Charlotte Collister, Dave Ditmars, and Duane Gilbert. Kerry Pathy helped us with some of the more difficult literature research. Our editor, Deb McWilliam, helped turn our thoughts into intelligible prose, and Sharon Bierman was instrumental in turning that prose into a finished product.

The thoughts themselves came primarily from two sources. First, we were influenced by the professional literature created by thought leaders who have preceded us. In particular, we owe a debt of gratitude to Bradley T. Gale, the "father" of customer value analysis, Philip Kotler, for his prolific writings on all things marketing, David A. Aaker, a brilliant strategist and branding consultant, and Thomas T. Nagle, the pricing guru.

Our second source of ideas was the many clients we have worked with during the last two decades. The trust they demonstrated in us, by allowing us to work with them to improve their Customer Perceived Value, has been the greatest contribution of all to the creation of this book.

David C. Swaddling
Charles Miller

REFERENCE

[1] Peter F. Drucker, *The Practice of Management*, (New York, Harper & Row, 1954), pg. 139.

SECTION ONE

Understanding Customer Perceived Value

CHAPTER 1

It's the Age of the Customer

In a strange way, we like the word "disintermediation." It is a 7-syllable euphemism for "going out of business because customers no longer value what you do." It is a relatively new word in our language, required because customers have only recently gained the power to unilaterally decide who gets to remain in business. For those companies that fail to realize the shift in marketplace power from the suppliers to the customers, and therefore fail to change how they run their businesses, disintermediation is a sophisticated word that sounds less severe than "you failed to deliver superior Customer Perceived Value."

Major shifts in supply chain roles are occurring in many industries. In the consumer world, banks, travel agents, stock brokers, insurance agents, and many small retailers are all struggling with disintermediation. In the industrial sector, many traditional wholesaler/distributors are under the same pressure. No longer is the ability to aggregate a variety of products and ship them in smaller quantities adequate justification for these businesses. Powerful customers, armed with the technological capabilities of the Internet, are finding that approach to be of insufficient value and, therefore, a role to be eliminated. Many traditional wholesaler/distributors have been forced to learn new ways to deliver value to these customers or simply go out of business – disintermediation.

The largest wholesaler/distributor in the United States, however, clearly saw these changes coming and chose to change the way it does business – this was the only way it could ensure its survival. Ingram Micro ranked No. 41 on the 2000 Fortune 500 List with sales of more than $28 billion and profits of nearly $200 million. It was named by Business Week *as one of the 100 best-performing information technology companies in the world. By one writer's estimation, when someone buys a computer, or another electronic device, or business software, it has probably passed through Ingram Micro to get to that customer.[1]*

How is Ingram Micro avoiding the threats of distintermediation? By changing the way it delivers Customer Perceived Value to today's powerful customers. It is abandoning the traditional wholesaler/distributor role of buying computers and parts from big manufacturers and then reselling them at a higher price to retailers. Instead, it is adopting a "fee for service" model, offering its expertise in logistics, order fulfillment, and customer service to anyone and everyone. Instead of being squeezed out of business by the shift from bricks-and-mortar retailers to e-commerce portals and retailers, it is benefiting from it by being the best at delivering the physical product.

Even Dell Computer, one of the most visible and successful manufacturers leading the trend toward disintermediation of computer retailers through its direct-to-the-consumer approach, is a $1 billion customer of Ingram Micro. Ingram handles most of Dell's distribution and customer service functions. Some suggest that the program called "Dell Direct" should be renamed "Dell Direct Enabled by Ingram."

Optimists usually point out that change represents opportunity. Most markets are undergoing fundamental changes as customers gain information and power. That will cause the demise of many companies. The ones that can find new ways to deliver value to the customer, like Ingram Micro, will grasp that opportunity and prosper.

American business managers have faced many different challenges throughout the 20th century. Labor unrest was probably the first. Then production processes had to be invented. The 1930s saw lack of demand and the 1940s scarcity of supply. Dangerous economic inflation took the fun out of the 1970s and global competition was tough in the last few years of the century. But none of those was as difficult as what today's managers must deal with. Business is really tough now, because the customers have taken over.

HOW THE CUSTOMER CAME TO POWER

Even very recently, it was enough to simply put out a good product. That is the basis on which most traditional American businesses prospered for many years. If one foundry casting met dimensional specifications more often than the other one, it would sell. If the American automobile could offer the same 5-year, bumper-to-bumper warranty that the import carried, then it was competitive again. We now call that a *product focus*.

Surprisingly, many American businesses are still operating with primarily a product focus. Few will admit it, because it has become generally accepted that a product focus isn't enough any more. But careful examination will show that many businesses haven't done anything about that realization.

Then came what we now call the *service focus*. This engulfed more than just the pure "service" businesses, such as restaurants, banks, and barber shops. Even businesses that primarily built or delivered a physical product came to learn that they had to deliver that product with good service. The service requirements spanned the entire range of customer interactions, from selling, to order taking, to delivery, as well as follow-up support. By then, the line between product and service businesses had become an anachronism.

With this evolution, competition took on a different dimension. Because everyone was delivering good products and good services, the customer was able to begin demanding more. Now, the customer wanted to be listened to. The customer began to expect customized solutions to his unique needs. He began to evaluate product and service quality on a different scale – his own scale. The customer began demanding that the supplier focus not only on the product or service but on the *customer*. We entered the Age of the Customer. That's where we are today.

Why must businesses now focus on the external customer instead of just the products and services for which they are directly responsible? Because modern customers are able to require that they do. That's the nub of it. In just a very few recent years, customers have become much more knowledgeable and much more powerful than before. Advances in communications technology and information management have made most markets "more perfect" than they used to be, because customers have so much more information readily available to them about those markets. Reductions in communications and transportation costs are rapidly "globalizing" our economies and bringing totally new competitors into previously parochial markets. And those retailers – the Wal-Marts and the Home Depots – smart enough to see these trends and capitalize upon them by joining forces with those newly powerful customers, have added momentum to the movement by consolidating their voices into a powerful few.[2] The same consolidation of customer power has taken place in the industrial sector, of course, as witnessed by companies such as Intel, MCI Worldcom, and the entire consolidating banking industry.

What Customer Power Looks Like

What is the result of customers seizing power from suppliers? It means that successful competitors must do some things differently. If we're not competing on product quality anymore, and we're not competing on service quality anymore, on what *are* we competing? "Customer focus" is a good term but not explicit, complete, or robust enough to serve the purpose. We suggest the basis of competition today is *Customer Perceived Value*.

Others have talked and written about the simpler term "customer value" before, but we find its meaning is often confused. For some people, "customer value" means the same thing as "customer lifetime value" – the calculated total value of the business a customer will bring to a supplier during the life of that customer relationship. To others, "customer value" means the quantified value calculated by a customer (or the supplier's sales rep) of a specific deal or transaction. Some use the term "customer value" in much the way we use Customer Perceived Value, but each such user includes his own variations on some of the specifics of his definition. That's why we'll stick to the term "Customer Perceived Value" and define it this way:

> **Customer Perceived Value** - *the result of the customer's evaluation of all of the benefits and all of the costs of an offering as compared to that customer's perceived alternatives. It is the basis on which customers decide to buy things.*

We find it convenient to envision an old-fashioned balance scale to depict Customer Perceived Value (Figure 1.1). On one side of the scale, the customer stacks up all the perceived benefits of a particular offering. Those benefits will be tangible and intangible, product related and service related, external (product) and internal (process) oriented, and so forth. Actually, there are no rules for what goes on the balance scale – it is whatever the customer chooses.

Figure 1.1 - Customer Perceived Value Balance Scale

On the other side, the customer stacks up all the costs associated with the supplier's offering. Certainly, price is one of those costs, but only one. Required training, or changes in processes, or the uncertainty of a new supplier could very well go on the "negative" side of the balance scale along with the price. Again, there are no set rules – the customer judges what should go on this side of the scale.

The customer establishes a balance scale like this for each offering or alternative under consideration. Whichever one tips most toward the positive side is the customer's choice. That is who gets the business. And that is why it is important for suppliers to use this model and to manage for Customer Perceived Value. After all, as Billy the Kid has been often quoted as saying as to why he robbed banks, "That's where the money is!"

Benjamin Franklin advised a friend who was trying to make a difficult decision to set up two columns on a piece of paper. He instructed to list all the pros involved in the decision in one column and all the cons in the other. After pondering the two lists for a while, he suggested that the action to be taken would be indicated by the longer list! Although oversimplified, Franklin's approach is the essence of Customer Perceived Value.[3]

Returning to modern times, we find that many customers don't literally write a list on paper (although some formal purchasing systems require that very thing). In fact, they may not even consciously stack up benefits and costs at all. Nevertheless, some kind of evaluation of benefits and costs is being conducted every time.

The seller, therefore, wants to know what the benefits and costs being considered by the prospective customer are, and how the prospect will weigh them on her balance scale of Customer Perceived Value. Because that information exists only in the mind of the customer, obtaining it requires good marketing research. There is no other way to gain this understanding without talking with, or at least observing, customers. Once information about customer perceptions is acquired, the smartest seller will manage his offering to emphasize the most important benefits as perceived by the customer, and mitigate the perceived costs. That throws the buying decision to that seller's advantage which is, after all, the object of the game.

Consumer, Industrial, and Nonprofit Sectors

Understanding Customer Perceived Value is a fundamental requirement for success in every business setting, including quasi-business operations, such as nonprofits. In every case where there is competition for some kind of resource – be it the customer's purchase dollars, a supplier's attention and support, a distributor's favoring of a product line, or a benefactor's charitable contributions – a buying decision is being made on the basis of a Customer Perceived Value balance scale. The more the hopeful seller knows about how that buying decision is likely to be made, the more that seller can do to influence it to his advantage.

The consumer sector has historically been the most researched of any category of customer. Unfortunately, that research appeared easier than it is and often missed the objective of better understanding Customer Perceived Value. The most common error is testing only the *features* of an offering, rather than seeking information about the consumer's perception of *benefits*.

For example, working on the assumption that the key performance issue in the small package delivery business is timely delivery, UPS instituted a reengineering effort that affected many of its basic operational processes. That company reconfigured the interior of its delivery trucks, redefined adjacent routes, and automated the package hand-off procedure with wireless record keeping and signature collection. Upon completion of this work, UPS had significantly increased the amount of deliveries, and the timeliness of those deliveries, across its system. Unfortunately, it had failed to understand what the key performance issues were in the minds of its customers. Those customers were less concerned about how fast their delivery person worked and more concerned about the amount of personal interaction they could have with them. UPS redefined its processes and performance measures to permit *more* time to be spent by the delivery people interacting with customers. That was perceived as real value by the customers. And, that's the *only* thing that matters.[4]

Some of the issues are different in the business-to-business setting. A fundamental one is that buying decisions are often made by a *decision group* rather than an individual. That makes collecting and understanding the information collected in customer research more complicated. And, in business-to-business, the seller-customer relationship is usually a part of a *supply chain*, so identifying the customer and the seller is not always a simple matter.

The health-care business, for example, is a growth industry in America. It is also a complicated business for the manufacturers of pharmaceuticals and medical devices, however, because their products are usually delivered through distributors who carry a wide range of competing products. What should a manufacturer know about how the decision to buy is made by these distributors? Even at the point of use – such as a hospital or nursing home – it's not clear who the customer is. The product is prescribed by a physician, dispensed by a pharmacist, administered by a health-care worker, and purchased by a purchasing manager. Each of those people view the benefits and costs of the same product by different criteria. The best of these manufacturers have determined that all these people, including the distributors, are "customers" and the behavior of all of them needs to be understood.

Despite these complexities, the objective is the same – understand Customer Perceived Value better than competitors do and thereby gain a competitive advantage.

Finally, Customer Perceived Value is even important in quasi-business settings. Charities, government agencies, and service organizations advance their objectives by better understanding how their funding sources make "buying" decisions.

The General Services Administration sells office facilities, telephone services, computer equipment, and other infrastructure elements to all other agencies of the Federal government. In the current era of deregulation and privatization, however, those agencies are permitted to purchase such goods and services from anywhere they choose, so the GSA is competing for their business. To be competitive and, in fact, justify their existence, the GSA is seeking to better understand how other government agencies are now going to be making their procurement decisions. That means understanding Customer Perceived Value.

ALONG THE SUPPLY CHAIN

In spite of the complications that are created by multiple relationships, participants in the typical product supply chain can benefit greatly from using the Customer Perceived Value model. As always, the end user of the product is the "ultimate" customer and the "ultimate" object of efforts to increase Customer Perceived Value. To do that, there are times when the other supply chain members should be considered to be "customers" as well. In those cases, the position of each of the members in the supply chain must be used to determine how best to deliver that end-customer value.

Manufacturers

Manufacturers, for example, can add end-customer value in many ways. The challenge is to determine the best ways to do that, considering the strategies and capabilities of downstream distributors and retailers. For example, if a manufacturer's *brand* could add to Customer Perceived Value, then that is something the manufacturer can contribute that no one else can. Or if the product is one for which low cost truly is the predominate attribute for the end customer, then low-cost production could be the manufacturer's greatest contribution to the ultimate Customer Perceived Value.

Middlemen

Wholesalers and distributors, in most industries, are generally feeling pressure to find additional ways to contribute to Customer Perceived Value as a supply chain member. Because retailers have consolidated into giants that can now "break bulk-and-ship" as efficiently as the traditional wholesalers used to, many middlemen are being threatened with disintermediation. The solution to this very complex and revolutionary problem for wholesalers and distributors is to identify where they can contribute Customer Perceived Value better than other members of the supply chain. Perhaps it is by providing packaging services, or logistics expertise, or information management. Whatever the solution, it will most certainly lie in finding ways to contribute end-user Customer Perceived Value.

Retailers

One would think that retailers, who are the closest to the all-important end user, would be the most adept at measuring and managing Customer Perceived Value. Sometimes that is true, but not often enough. Many retailers are currently experiencing changes in their traditional roles that are as profound as those of wholesalers and distributors. The catalyst for those changes is the arrival of *e-commerce*. Given the capabilities of new communication technologies, many consumers are redefining their Customer Perceived Value equations and cutting out some of the traditional retailing functions in the process. Survivors in the retail sector will be those that understand their customers' Customer Perceived Value and are able to deliver their share of that value.

COMPETING FOR THE ATTENTION OF MANAGEMENT

The Customer Perceived Value model can be used to simplify life for senior management without reducing stretch goals or sacrificing performance. American managers are offered a continuous stream of management advice and "fads" by academics, consultants, and publicity seekers. Some of that advice is worthless. More, perhaps, is valuable. But the sheer volume of it can be debilitating. We suggest a primary focus on Customer Perceived Value can help cut through many issues and add support to those that are worthy.

Shareholder Value

Growing shareholder value was an important movement of the 1990s, and probably more executives than ever before are being compensated now on share price, Economic Value Added (EVA), or some related measure of shareholder value. Certainly, growing shareholder value is an admirable goal. Indeed, it must be accepted as the ultimate goal of every economic entity participating in the free economy. Success within our system requires the ability to attract and accumulate financial capital and the only way to do that is to deliver a competitive return to the source of that capital – the shareholder. So, growing shareholder value is the correct goal. Focusing primarily on growing shareholder value, however, can result in unintended and undesirable results.

When applying EVA at the individual project level, it can be said simplistically that EVA is a method of determining the "Return on Investment" required to attract and retain shareholder capital. This number is often determined by a company and then used as a "hurdle rate" for all capital investments. Say, for example, that a company determines its required ROI is 25 percent. Any project submitted for approval that fails to reach that hurdle rate is refused. That is a good way to ensure that the growth of shareholder value will be what is expected. But, if a specific project that is valuable to an important customer is turned down because of strict application of a ROI hurdle rate, the company might face losing much more than the calculated required return on an individual project.

An improvement on the focus on shareholder value would be a focus on Customer Perceived Value. Many studies have shown that companies which deliver superior Customer Perceived Value realize better financial performance than their competition. Bradley Gale, the founder of the Strategic Planning Institute and former manager of the famous PIMS database, has best described this correlation.[5] There is really very little room for debate. Focusing on delivering superior Customer Perceived Value is the surest and best way to deliver increased shareholder value.

Total Quality Management

Much of what we know today about delivering Customer Perceived Value came from the TQM movement of the 1980s. The underlying principles of TQM are customer focus, process management, and employee involvement. These are critical ingredients to business success, and we deal with each in the chapters that follow. TQM should be considered a precursor to focusing on Customer Perceived Value, but a dangerous distraction if incorrectly implemented.

Two of the outgrowths of TQM were the emphasis on reducing error rates and cycle time. As a result of a significant TQM initiative over several years, a leading manufacturer of commercial truck parts reduced its cycle time from customer order to delivery by more than 50 percent. But, at one of the six plants, the cycle-time measurements for one of the company's largest customers looked out of line. Specifically, the cycle time for this customer's orders was several days longer to deliver than the others. The plant manager came under considerable pressure to improve his TQM results until it was realized that this particular customer had requested that their parts be accumulated and staged into unique shipment packages. This plant manager had been accommodating that important customer by staging the parts on his loading dock floor before making shipment.

If implementers of reduced error rates and cycle times would read their TQM sources again, they would be reminded that those goals are only important in the context of what we are now calling Customer Perceived Value. Too often that context gets lost in the shuffle. Resources being spent today on reducing errors or cycle time, which do not contribute to increasing Customer Perceived Value, are wasted resources. It shouldn't happen, but it does.

Relationship Management

The theory here is that loyalty between customers and suppliers can be developed by becoming more "intimate" with one another and creating "strategic partnerships" whereby the parties engage in mutual planning, joint financing, and cooperative production processes. The underlying premise is a good one – the more suppliers and customers know about each other, the more effective they can be in delivering increased Customer Perceived Value. It is at the execution stage that focusing on developing such relationships and applying the balance scale model becomes critical.

Sometimes getting "closer" to supply chain partners can be very productive. In other cases, it is just as good or better for each player to tend to her respective business and execute clean "hand offs" to the next partner in the chain. It all depends on how the benefits and costs for each customer stack up on their respective balance scales. Relationship management is a good idea for those customers who place a high value on the information the supplier has to offer, or who know how to integrate supplier technologies into their processes, or who value the more intense personal relationships that often are a part of this approach. But, for those customers who are better off "on their own" (or, at least perceive that to be the case), it would be a less fruitful strategy to impose the idea of a "strategic partnership."

Advocates of relationship management strategies argue that customer loyalty is always increased when suppliers and customers work closely together. They might suggest that this approach supersedes the Customer Perceived Value balance scale model because those customers no longer will make such rational "pros and cons" choices when they have a "partner." Sometimes we wish that were so.

Wal-Mart is known to many would-be suppliers as a very tough customer. The clout it carries in consumer markets is certainly substantial. Wal-Mart's "strategic partnership" with mutual giant Procter & Gamble is well documented.[6] For many years, both companies gave speeches and published articles about how the two companies had "made the decision to change the way they did business together." They adjusted their respective organizational structures to make communication easier, they conducted joint planning sessions to explore possibilities together, and they entered into significant business transactions that increased the business these two companies did together from almost $350 million to almost $4 billion during the ten years since the 1987 decision to "partner."

Then, in the summer of 1999, Wal-Mart announced that it would introduce its own brand of laundry detergent.[7] Industry analysts struggled to decide whether Wal-Mart's brand would compete with P&G's premium brand (Tide) or nonpremium brand (Cheer). P&G didn't want to talk about it. It was another case of "so much for partnerships." In other words, it all depends on how the customer stacks things up on their own Customer Perceived Value balance scale.

Knowledge Management

The establishment of Knowledge Management as a discipline separate from others is a recent phenomenon. A few companies are beginning to appoint Chief Knowledge Officers (CKO) and several consultants have written books on the topic in the last couple of years.[8] The movement appears to be a reincarnation of the "learning organization" idea with greater attention to installing processes to ensure that organizational knowledge is protected and developed.

Specifically, Knowledge Management advocates describe three major components essential to any effort in this area: gathering, codifying, and transferring knowledge throughout the organization. For example, Hewlett Packard's Electronic Sales Partner project started with the gathering of every possible kind of information residing in the organization about its most important customers. This information includes technical product information, sales and marketing interactions, customer-specific account information, sales presentation templates, and so on. Having accumulated this information, the project leaders carefully codified it by "categorization and pruning." The information was then placed on a company intranet so that it was easily transferred to every sales representative who could benefit from the knowledge provided.[9]

The authors describing this project criticized it for dealing with more "information than knowledge," pointing out that only information which is supplemented by human experience and judgment becomes knowledge – a more powerful basis for organizational learning. We have no problem with that distinction, but prefer to focus more on HP's wisdom in selecting customer-oriented information as the starting place for its Knowledge Management initiative.

As with each of the management focal points described here, the discipline of Knowledge Management has the potential to improve business performance greatly if it is properly used. To us, of course, that means it must be used in the pursuit of delivering greater Customer Perceived Value. If it is not, it has the potential to be a horrendous waste of time and money.

We are concerned, for example, that the first criterion that Davenport and Prusak suggest for measuring the success of a Knowledge Management program is the "growth in the resources attached to the project, including staffing and budgets." In our view, that is too inward a view of why Knowledge Management should be pursued. Rather, Knowledge Management efforts should be evaluated as to the positive contribution they make to increasing the Customer Perceived Value delivered to customers. Because, after all, that is the only thing that matters.

E-Business

Everyone is scrambling to do business on the Internet. And well they should. E-business is clearly the most profound change of the 20th century in how the world conducts business. But, those that stay true to the objective of delivering Customer Perceived Value, and see the Internet as simply the most recent and powerful new tool to do that, are reaping the greatest immediate success.

Almost anyone can set up a website and display "brochureware" describing his company and product offerings. And many are doing just that. Keep in mind, however, brochureware sites do not provide competitive advantage, they are simply required to stay in business.

E-commerce goes a step beyond brochureware. It includes taking customer orders, confirming available stock, communicating delivery times and, usually, taking payment on-line. Many retailers have such capabilities in place and more business-to-business suppliers are also engaging in e-commerce. Customers are often finding this new way of shopping to be more convenient than traditional methods and, therefore, the trend toward more e-commerce continues.

The greatest opportunity for suppliers, however, is in those sites that represent true *e-business*. E-business goes beyond simply effecting transactions on-line. It includes delivering information, creating dialogues between supplier and customer, facilitating interaction among people with common interests, and every other method of providing more *Customer Perceived Value* to the customer, ensuring that he goes nowhere else.

Amazon.com, one of the first true e-businesses, is at this writing one of the best at it. Amazon.com tracks the customer's book purchases based on subjects, authors, and styles and from that makes recommendations for future purchases. It encourages readers to post reviews of books they have read so that other customers can use that information. Authors are also allotted space to explain their works to Amazon.com customers. And it sends e-mail messages to alert customers to new book releases in their reading areas of interest. For all of these features, and others, Amazon.com is one of the most frequently visited websites on the Internet.

How did Amazon.com rise from nowhere to become the leading bookseller in the nation? Although Amazon.com is considered one of the first "technology" companies to have built a commanding presence on the World Wide Web, it did not really get there on technology alone – lots of companies had access to the technology. It got there by delivering greater Customer Perceived Value. All e-businesses should keep that in mind.

THE FOUR CHARACTERISTICS OF CUSTOMER PERCEIVED VALUE

So, if the concept of Customer Perceived Value is so great, why isn't everybody using it? The answer is that it is not easy to do. Other business models, including those based on innovation, financial control, and employee relationships, provide more opportunities for management *control*. They are familiar – that's how America has always competed. As basic as it is, Customer Perceived Value is something new and less familiar and very difficult to measure and manage.

Specifically, Customer Perceived Value carries with it four attributes that reflect both its power and its challenge:

PERCEPTION
COMPLEXITY
RELATIVITY
DYNAMICS

Perception

Customer Perceived Value is in the mind of the customer. It originates *only* in the mind of the customer. Management, at its own peril, can guess at how the customer defines Customer Perceived Value, but without directly engaging the customer that is all it would be – a guess. Every business that conducts its affairs without the benefit of customer research of some type is operating only on guesswork. Because Customer Perceived Value is defined *only* in the mind of the customer.

The implications of this first attribute of Customer Perceived Value are two-fold:

1. Management decisions are always based on hypotheses about customer perceptions.
2. Good customer research is fundamental to improving the accuracy of those hypotheses.

Unfortunately, neither of those implications is simple. The obvious concern about the first one is the old argument that customers aren't very good at anticipating their needs. Most people agree that customers didn't initiate the idea for fast-food restaurants, or microwave ovens, or personal computers. So, the argument goes, we can't rely on customer research for developing new product offerings.

Not true, of course. Each of these innovations was based on the inventor's ability to understand Customer Perceived Value so well that they conceived an entirely new way of delivering those benefits. People were spending more time in their cars and sit-down meals were becoming less important – so Ray Kroc believed that a pre-cooked hamburger delivered at a drive-through window would carry customer perceived benefits. Recognizing that more working couples had less time to prepare meals and that the 5-minute preparation time of a microwave oven would be a customer perceived benefit was probably an easy call. And Steve Jobs foresaw, very accurately, the benefits that individuals would perceive in the ability to process computer programs independently of the remote, mainframe computer when he invented the first Apple microcomputer. Those products, with their various features, came from the minds of their creative inventors. They did not come from taking a poll of prospective customers. But, they were all based on guesses – and in these cases very good guesses – about what customers would perceive as benefits to them. And, in the end, customers made their buying decisions based on those benefits (and costs) of the offering. They based their buying decisions on Customer Perceived Value.

The second implication of believing that Customer Perceived Value exists only in the mind of the customer is that managers must, therefore, go to those customers to learn what those perceptions are. In other words, good customer research is a fundamental management tool made necessary because all buying decisions are based upon Customer Perceived Value and that value exists *only* as a perception of the customer.

The complication here is that not all customer research is *good* customer research. It is not easy to learn about customer perceptions of value when those customers are not even thinking explicitly about them as such. And, to make matters worse, management usually needs to know about those perceptions *before* they exist (which occurs when the buying decision is being made). That is difficult to do and, certainly, won't be accomplished with a simple "comment card" or customer satisfaction survey.

That these challenges exist, however, does not change the underlying premise that buying decisions are made upon Customer Perceived Value. It explains, perhaps, why more managers have not yet stepped up to the concept and begun using Customer Perceived Value as the central principle underlying their efforts. It just is not easy to do. But, some solutions have proven to be effective, and a heightened awareness of its importance will lead to more. Some of those that are available now are presented in the chapters that follow.

Complexity

The second attribute of Customer Perceived Value is complexity. We use this word to convey that customers can place anything they choose on both the Benefits and the Costs sides of their Customer Perceived Value balance scale. And, usually that is much more than just how well the product works on the plus side and how much it costs on the negative side. Often, the customer's balance scale holds both concrete and abstract benefits, primary and secondary costs, and items that are both typical of all customers in the segment and also unique to specific individuals and groups. It gets very complicated.

A few years ago, we spoke with the customer of a client who was a very prominent logistics executive in an internationally respected consumer products company. The interview was progressing nicely, covering various ways our client could improve product and information management capabilities to better serve the needs of this customer. All of a sudden, this executive swiveled in his chair and pointed to his mahogany credenza. There was a small collection of toy trucks given to him by the various trucking companies with whom his company was doing business. He became visibly agitated and exclaimed, "Do you see a truck there from your client? No! That shows you just how little they think of me!" Needless to say, we reported this incident to our client and that executive soon had another toy truck to add to his collection. But the lesson to be learned from this experience was more profound than that. It pointed out to us, once again, just how complicated this issue of Customer Perceived Value can be.

Think about the Costs side of the balance scale for a moment. It is easy to see that the price per unit for the offering belongs on this side of the balance scale. There are others, however, that are less obvious but are clearly associated with a particular product or service offering. Perhaps the customer's personnel will have to be trained to use the new product instead of the one that had been used before. Or, perhaps processes or physical equipment used in the customer's production process will have to be modified to use the supplier's new offering. These Costs are, perhaps, less obvious, but they are no less real and important if the customer characterizes them that way on her Customer Perceived Value balance scale.

And at a more detailed level, there are probably secondary and tertiary benefits and costs that belong on the balance scale in addition to the obvious primary ones. For example, the product or service that saves labor time for the customer saves not only direct salary costs (the primary benefit) but also employer payroll taxes and workers' compensation premiums, the hiring and training costs that accompany needing more employees rather than fewer, and the reduction in supervisory costs for the same reason (the secondary benefits). If hiring and training requirements are reduced, perhaps that puts less pressure on getting the new human resources database set up so management can divert those scarce IT resources to more direct Customer Perceived Value applications (a tertiary benefit).

On the cost side, perhaps the requirement to advise the labor union that fewer hours will be needed will have to go onto the Customer Perceived Value balance scale. That is an example of a "secondary" cost that might appear on the negative side of the balance scale.

Just how complex the identification of benefits and costs for the balance scale becomes is a function, of course, of the customer. As established in the first attribute of Customer Perceived Value, the only things that matter are what the customer perceives to matter. So, the level of complexity of Customer Perceived Value is totally controlled by how complexly the customer thinks about the relative benefits and costs of it all.

Psychologists have studied the complexity of human cognition for generations. There are numerous scholarly works, far outside the scope of this book, that address this issue directly. Usually, they deal with "chunking" data and "relating" information of one type to another. Suffice it to say here that the cognitive process that underlies a customer buying decision is usually more complicated than sellers wish it was. It is, indeed, a challenge to understand what attributes are on the Benefits and Costs trays of the balance scale and what sellers can do to improve the ratio of those attributes that the customer perceives in their offerings.

Relativity

Each of the four attributes of Customer Perceived Value defined here probably appear to be obvious, once they have been explained. But the actual behavior of most business managers today would indicate that they're not obvious, or at least not dealt with as often as one would expect.

"Relativity" means that customers are always choosing from among their available alternatives. Certainly, doing nothing is always one of their alternatives, but the others are usually represented by the offerings of competitors. This third attribute emphasizes the point that it doesn't matter how much an offering *satisfies* a customer except to the extent that it satisfies her more than her alternatives satisfy her.

Indeed, this is probably the greatest fallacy of the entire Customer Satisfaction movement. For more than a decade, businesses have spent kazillions of dollars to measure how well they have "satisfied" their customers. A few years ago, a major effort was undertaken to duplicate a Swedish "national" customer satisfaction study in this country. The resulting American Customer Satisfaction Index is an ongoing survey consisting of more than 50,000 interviews with consumers. The survey addresses offerings of more than 175 different consumer products and services. The results of this, as well as the individual Customer Satisfaction studies conducted each year by most large businesses, produce interesting results but very little of practical value.

While many have tried to prove it, there is scarce empirical evidence that high Customer Satisfaction scores correlate with any measure of successful business performance. Most interested parties admit that there is a significant theoretical gap remaining between what has traditionally been measured as customer satisfaction and the actual buying behavior of customers. Rather, the most informed studies show that high customer satisfaction is important to customers only until someone *else* satisfies those customers more. Then, their buying decision changes immediately.

In the automotive industry, the American Customer Satisfaction Index ratings are consistently in the 80 to 85 percent range. That's very high, even though repurchase behavior (a.k.a. "loyalty") is about 40 percent. It simply is not enough to "satisfy" customers if competitors or other alternatives "satisfy" them more. As one writer put it, "Loyalty is simply the lack of any better alternatives."

Dynamics

If the first three attributes of Customer Perceived Value weren't enough to make measuring and managing it difficult, the fourth one would do it. This is because customers' perceptions are constantly changing, so Customer Perceived Value constantly changes. If Customer Perceived Value is the target, as we believe it is, then we must acknowledge and deal with its being a moving target.

As the environment in which they operate changes, customer needs change. Competitors improve their offerings. Prices of alternatives change, both up and down. The customer's own priorities change as her customers make changing demands on her. So, when we measure Customer Perceived Value we are collecting, at best, a snapshot of that customer's balance scale. It will look different the next time we take a snapshot.

The implication of this attribute should be clear. We have established, already, that delivering Customer Perceived Value is the objective and, because it is all about customer perceptions, understanding it requires interaction with the customer. This fourth attribute would indicate that those interactions must be frequent and continual.

We were interviewing one of another client's customers who had, just three months earlier, appeared at the supplier's annual sales meeting to speak of the benefits and glories of an effective customer-supplier strategic partnership. Legend has it that the customer's presentation included the best of today's theatrical production elements, including background music from Sister Sledge's classic song *We Are Family*. We arrived at this customer's office expecting to gather a long list of items he had placed on the positive side of his Customer Perceived Value balance scale. Instead, we were informed that he was about to terminate this supplier relationship altogether! Several service failures during the last three months had built to such a level of frustration that he had decided that all "supplier partnerships" were worthless and that he intended to find a lower priced alternative to our client's offering. Of course we hurried back to plan with our client how to recover this customer relationship, and we succeeded in doing so. But, the very idea that this customer "partner" had essentially turned into a "lost" customer in less than three months' time was shocking. It verifies the point, however, that Customer Perceived Value is a moving target.

SUMMARY

We have reached the "Age of the Customer." Globalization, information management, and business consolidations have shifted the balance of power in the marketplace to a new, better informed customer. That customer is demanding more value in every purchase.

Surprisingly, many companies haven't responded to the requirements of this new age. For many years, they successfully competed on the quality of their products and, on that basis, saw revenues and profits grow over time. Some of those companies are now beginning to encounter stiffer competition and more demanding customers. They are wondering what has changed. They need to move quickly from their *product focus* to a *customer focus* to survive.

We offer the Customer Perceived Value model as a tool to help management address the changing requirements of this new age. The model is based on the work of many others who came before us – from Levitt's *Marketing Myopia* to Gale's *Managing Customer Value*. We simply deliver it here in what, we hope, is a practical description and with more practical suggestions for using it to change the way companies compete for customers.

Customer Perceived Value is best visualized as an old-fashioned balance scale, with all the benefits perceived by the customer from the offering on one side, and all of the costs on the other. The customer is seen as comparing the results of setting up such a balance scale for each of her alternatives and selecting the one that holds the greatest *net benefits* as compared to the others. That is what guides the customer's buying decision and, therefore, what must guide the supplier's efforts to win the business.

The simplicity of the model permits it to serve well as a guide for managers at all levels of all kinds of economic organizations. If they are striving to increase shareholder value, managers should focus on delivering superior Customer Perceived Value, because that will result in increased profits and increased shareholder value. If they are thinking about how to treat employees, then managers should focus on delivering superior Customer Perceived Value because that leads to happy customers, which leads to happy employees. If distributors are finding themselves being squeezed between manufacturers and retailers, then they should focus on Customer Perceived Value because doing so will ensure their earning a continual role in the supply chain. If companies are jumping on the e-business bandwagon, then they should do it with Customer Perceived Value as the website design goal because that will raise the effort above all the rest.

Because all of business originates and ends with the dollars that customers contribute to the business, the Customer Perceived Value model supports every effort of every organization to improve its business performance.

There is only one drawback to the value of the Customer Perceived Value model – it is not an easy task to manage.

Four attributes of Customer Perceived Value make it a challenging assignment. First, Customer Perceived Value is all in the minds of the customer. Management is only guessing about it unless it finds good methods to extract it from the customer. Second, it is complicated. Customers put all kinds of things on both sides of their balance scale, and some are easier to discern than others. Third, Customer Perceived Value is relative to the customer's alternatives. It is not enough to determine how "satisfied" the customer is unless it is determined how "satisfied" he is with competitors' offerings and his alternative of doing nothing. Finally, Customer Perceived Value is dynamic. It is always a moving target, so it's not easy at all to keep management's thumb on it.

Despite these challenges, however, the Customer Perceived Value model offers the best and most practical management tool in this new age of customer power. The concept is simple, widely applicable, and intuitively pleasing. The only thing standing in the way of its widespread and successful use is knowing where to begin and what specific action steps can be taken. We attempt to help with those things, at least in an introductory way, in this book.

REFERENCES

[1] Chris Farnsworth, "After Old-Economy Success, Ingram Micro Focuses on Dot-Com Growth," *Knight-Ridder/Tribune Business News*, March 20, 2000. Also see William Gurley, "Why Online Distributors – Once Written Off – May Thrive: The Evolving World of E-tailing," *Fortune*, September 6, 1999, pg. 270.

[2] James S. Keebler, Karl B. Manrodt, David A. Durtsche, and D. Michael Ledyard, *Keeping Score: Measuring the Business Value of Logistics in the Supply Chain*, (Oak Brook, Council of Logistics Management, 1999), pg. 20.

[3] Michael D. Johnson, *Customer Orientation and Market Action*, (Upper Saddle River, Prentice-Hall, 1998), p. 55.

[4] Carl McDaniel and Roger Gates, *Contemporary Marketing Research: Fourth Edition*, (Cincinnati, South-Western College Publishing, 1999).

[5] Bradley T. Gale, *Managing Customer Value: Creating Quality and Service That Customers Can See*, (New York, The Free Press, 1994).

[6] For example, see Roger Dow, Lisa Napolitano, and Mike Pusateri, *The Trust Imperative: The Competitive Advantage of Trust-Based Business Relationships*, (Chicago, National Account Management Association, 1998), Chapter VII.

[7] "Soap Opera at Wal-Mart," *Business Week*, August 16, 1999, pg. 44.

[8] See Nancy M. Dixon, *Common Knowledge: How Companies Thrive by Sharing What They Know*, (Boston, Harvard Business School Press, 2000); Jay Liebowitz, *Building Organizational Intelligence: A Knowledge Management Primer*, (Boca Raton, CRC Press, 2000); Annie Brooking, *Corporate Memory: Strategies for Knowledge Management*, (New York, Thomson Business Press, 1999).

[9] Thomas H. Davenport and Laurence Prusak, *Working Knowledge: How Organizations Manage What They Know*, (Boston, Harvard Business School Press, 1998).

CHAPTER 2

What is Customer Perceived Value?

Everyone has his own horror stories about traveling on any of the major airlines in the U.S. The most famous in recent memory was the Northwest Airlines plane full of people waiting for more than seven hours on a snowy tarmac at Detroit's Metropolitan Airport in January 1999. It had just landed from Fort Myers, Florida, but there was no gate available at the terminal to let the passengers get off the plane. There was no food on board, the passenger cabin reeked of foul air, and the lavatories were filled with waste and had to be closed. "The only reason we got off that airplane," one passenger said, "is that people stormed the cockpit and went berserk."[1]

That was not, however, an isolated incident. In 1999, the U.S. Department of Transportation received nearly 14,000 individual complaints from air travelers about poor service, up from only 4,500 just two years earlier.[2] Although some of those are probably complaints about the quality of the food or the courtesy of the flight attendants, many run to the very core of what the business is supposed to deliver - transporting a passenger and her belongings from Point A to Point B. Lost baggage, schedule delays, and cancelled flights are seemingly commonplace in this industry. Things have gotten so bad that Congress has considered legislation, known as "The Passenger Bill of Rights," for intervening in the aviation industry, which was originally deregulated in 1978.

Measures of customer satisfaction accurately portray passengers' frustrations with the airlines. The American Customer Satisfaction Index (ACSI), a quarterly survey by the National Quality Research Center (University of Michigan Business School), along with Arthur Andersen consultants and the American Society for Quality, carefully tracks the public's declining satisfaction with the airlines, which reached an all-time low score of 63 (on a scale of 1 to 100) in 1999. In this survey, which canvasses more than 50,000 U.S. consumers each year on the offerings of more than 200 companies, the airlines have fallen below almost every other consumer service, including the U.S. Postal Service.

Are the executives of the major U.S. airlines so incompetent that they can't improve their satisfaction scores above these dismal ratings? Well, measured from every other angle, they don't appear incompetent at all. Take Continental Airlines, for example. Revenue for fiscal year 1998 was $7.9 billion, up more than 100 percent in five years. In that period, net income increased from a loss of $39 million in 1993 to profits of nearly $400 million in 1998. Profits in 1998 provided a return of 32.1 percent on shareholders' equity.

Compare that to Toyota, with its high consumers' satisfaction ratings. (Toyota received an 84 percent satisfaction rating in a recent ACSI survey.) Although profit trends are up, revenues are down 7 percent from five years ago and 1998 return on shareholders' equity in 1998 was only 7.5 percent.

Airline executives aren't incompetent at all. They're simply not operating their companies on the basis of customer satisfaction. And why should they? Customer satisfaction isn't what puts paying customers in the seats. While those customer satisfaction surveys keep showing more and more dislike for the product the airlines are offering, more and more of us are flying every day.

What they are managing their companies on, however, is Customer Perceived Value. In limiting competitors' access to airports by controlling the number of gates available and fol-

lowing competitive actions closely so that no one breaks ranks and offers other attributes such as good food or comfortable seating, the airlines have trained the American travelers that they can choose only between a limited number of scheduled flight times to any particular location. That's all we're permitted to place on our Customer Perceived Value Balance Scale. So, that's what we do. We choose between the airlines based on the greatest Value we can find. Even if we're not "satisfied" with what we get.

THE CUSTOMER SATISFACTION TRAP

"Satisfying" customers – and then satisfying them even more (usually referred to as "delighting" the customer) – is an appealing concept. It certainly seems to make sense to try to make customers happy. The problem lies in what we have come to specifically label "customer satisfaction" and how we measure it. Traditional "customer satisfaction" misses the point.

Nearly every company does some kind of Customer Satisfaction measurement. Perhaps it is only a comment card inserted in the delivered package or a 1-800 telephone number to receive customer complaints. Most often, it is some kind of periodic survey that attempts to register how the customer feels about the product offering. Usually, that effort fails for several reasons.

Asks the Wrong People

Customer satisfaction surveys ask *customers* what they think. Only customers. Because they ignore the noncustomers that looked at the catalog and decided not to order or met with the salesperson but never bought anything, the survey respondents include only those prospects that found the offering to be attractive and decided to choose it over that of the competitors. That's a very biased sample.

Retailers frequently make this mistake. When per-store sales are down, or simply not growing fast enough, they'll often increase their efforts to talk to customers about the problem. "Intercept surveys" are conducted with greater intensity, asking customers as they enter or leave the store about their buying attitudes, their likes and dislikes, the store's product offerings, and the service level they received. Unfortunately, this survey only permits addressing *one* of the store's problems – average dollar sales per visit to the store. The bigger issue, total sales, is more dependent on getting people into the store in the first place. Asking the customers that are already there about that problem doesn't help very much. Current customers are not the ones to ask about why other people aren't customers.

It is not surprising that most customer satisfaction scores are relatively high, even for struggling companies and offerings. Customers who have just completed a purchase naturally want to ratify their decision-making process by reaffirming that they made the right choice. If they know that the survey is sponsored by their current supplier, they don't want to hurt its feelings. And, most of the time, those customers truly *are* satisfied. We knew that *before* we conducted the satisfaction survey, because they bought the product!

Asks the Wrong Questions

Too often, traditional customer satisfaction measurements ask about things that are too general to provide much useful information for management or ask about things that really don't matter to the purchase decision.

Although some seem to be getting better recently, most large hotel chains have been asking the wrong questions for a long time. Typically, the comment card found on the pillow lists six or eight aspects of the hotel's service offering, such as check-in, room cleanliness, room service, and staff courtesy. The traveler is asked to rate each of those aspects on a scale of, say, *1* to *5* (with *5* being the highest). So, what do they do when the room service question is marked with a *1*? It's not clear. Was the food cold? Late? Poor menu? Poor presentation? Unless the traveler offers that kind of information in the couple of blank lines at the bottom of the form, it must be very difficult for the hotel management to extract anything useful from the survey data.

Or, as described in the opening story to this chapter, what if airline travelers do not like how close together the seats have been placed? Should management take some seats out of the planes and reduce the amount of revenue each flight can generate, to improve satisfaction? The answer to that is probably "no," not if prospects will not (or cannot) make buying decisions based on whether they can comfortably fit into those seats.

Compares the Wrong Things

Traditional Customer Satisfaction measures how well the offering matches up against the customer's *expectations*. That's why "delighting customers" has become synonymous with "exceeding their expectations." Delighting customers has been established by many companies as the objective for product quality and service levels. That is not an appropriate goal, however.

Traditional customer satisfaction surveys usually ask the question, "Overall, how satisfied are you with this offering?" Typically, the customer is asked to put a number on their satisfaction level – perhaps on a scale of *1* to *10*, with *1* being *extremely dissatisfied* and *10* being *delighted*. Usually, it turns out, the answers come back in the range of *7* to *10*. So, what if the customer rates it a *9*? What does that mean?

By itself, a satisfaction rating such as that means very little. Perhaps that customer is *satisfied*, and maybe that customer has even been *delighted*. But what if that same customer was asked to rate his satisfaction with the competition? And what if he gives the competitor a *9* as well? That gives the rating he gave in the first instance a whole new meaning. This customer may be satisfied, but if he's just as satisfied with the competitor's offering, then from whom will he buy? Traditional customer satisfaction measurement does not help very much with that most important question.

Surprising prospects with performance that is better than they thought could be delivered is a good thing, as long as that performance is worth something to the customer and is perceived as being better than what he could get from someone else. What we really want, after all, is not "surprised" customers but "repeat" customers.

WHAT ABOUT "LOYALTY"?

After Customer Satisfaction came Customer Loyalty. Fred Reichheld's important book, *The Loyalty Effect,* gave managers the evidence they needed to begin to focus more on customer *retention.*[3]

Retention Drives Profitability

Although primarily based on research in the retail banking industry, Reichheld showed convincingly that repeat customers deliver greater profits to the supplier's bottom line than do new customers.

We need look no further than to the marketing and sales functions within any company to identify the greatest cost attributed to new customers, which is the cost of acquiring them in the first place. Consider the salaries, travel expenses, support services, and advertising budgets that are dedicated to identifying and acquiring new customers. In almost every business, those amounts are staggering. It is easy to see that customers who spend money without the seller having to invest in marketing and selling expenses are very much more profitable.

Actually, five profit enhancers were identified by Reichheld as the result of repeat customer business. In addition to the reduction in new customer acquisition costs, the research found that repeat customers spent more with the seller, probably as a result of increasing confidence in the seller's capabilities, as well as increased knowledge and understanding of all of the offerings of the seller. Repeat customers are also usually less expensive for the seller to service. Repeat customers know how the seller's processes work and conform better to how the seller can take orders, track deliveries, help with installation, provide after-the-sale service, and deal with returns and warranties issues. Repeat customers are more likely to tolerate premium prices from the seller. This is because the repeat customer has experienced the offering before and, therefore, has a better appreciation for the overall value delivered by the seller. Finally, repeat customers make referrals, allowing the seller to acquire additional customers with less customer acquisition effort and costs.

Most managers knew it intuitively before Reichheld did his research. But the results confirm it. Repeat customers are more profitable than new ones.

Loyalty versus Retention

So, it is obvious that managers want customers to keep buying from them. But why would customers do that? What is "loyalty?"

Most of the automobile industry enjoys a relatively high level of Customer Satisfaction. In the recent ACSI survey described earlier, Cadillac was near the top with a solid *85*. Nevertheless, fewer than 40 percent of Cadillac owners will buy another Cadillac the next time they need another car. Clearly, there is not much "loyalty" among car buyers. In fact, a recent syndicated research study conducted across many industries determined that 70 percent of the respondents to that survey did not recognize a clear benefit from being loyal.[4]

"Loyalty," then, is probably a misnomer. What businesses are after is repeat buying behavior from its customers. Managers needn't be as interested in how their prospects *feel* as how they are likely to *behave*. Of course there is a connection between feelings and behavior, but focusing primarily on those feelings will not necessarily lead to an understanding of likely behavior. There are too many variables and too much uncertainty connected with that linkage to rely upon it as the path to improved business performance.

BUYING BEHAVIOR

The study of buyer behavior is a science all of its own. Significant textbooks have been devoted to understanding the psychological motivations that drive buyer behavior.[5] A complete review of those works is beyond the scope of this book and would likely be of little interest to our readers anyway. We find it sufficient, for our purposes, to describe here only the practical aspects of understanding buyer behavior and to relate those to our model of Customer Perceived Value (CPV).

In that regard, we envision a continuum of issues, from the most abstract to the most tangible, consisting of the following:

> PERSONAL NEEDS
> BUYING NEEDS
> BENEFITS
> FEATURES

Personal Needs

Underneath all human behavior, including taking the necessary actions to buy a particular product or service offering, is human motivation. Why do people do the things that they do? Fundamentally, they do them because of "what's in it for them." They satisfy some kind of "need" by taking that action.

As most of us will recall from studying Maslow's model in our college days, the categories of needs build upon one another in a set sequence. First, basic needs such as food, clothing, and shelter must be met. When this has been done, the person moves on to the higher level needs, such as socialization, ego, and "self-actualization" needs. Above the very lowest level of needs, a company could encounter a prospect at any of these possible levels of need satisfaction.

Precisely identifying the level of psychological need that the prospect is seeking to satisfy is a very difficult undertaking. Fortunately, it is rarely necessary to do so.

Buying Needs

Among other things, personal needs drive buying needs. And, buying needs are getting closer to what the manager needs to understand to know how to deliver CPV. The prospect may have a child about to attend an expensive college and does not want to lose her current job, but what is more practical for the seller to understand is that she is, therefore, under a great deal of stress to meet her operating unit's budgeted profit goals. That prospect's underlying buying need is to increase profitability.

Buying needs, like personal needs, exist at different levels. In fact, they form a continuum from fundamental and general to quite specific. Perhaps the prospect's fundamental need is to increase profitability. A more specific need may be to reduce costs, and beyond that, the prospect may have determined that an even more specific need is to cut labor costs, for example, in the warranty fulfillment function. Now we're getting much closer to something to which the selling manager can respond.

Benefits

Generally speaking, prospects go shopping for *benefits* to fulfill their needs. Benefits are the results that customers realize from the use of a product or service. To rephrase McKenna's famous reference, people don't buy drill bits, they buy the ability to make holes. Making holes is the "benefit" that drill bit manufacturers are selling.

Notice that benefits are definitely related to a specific offering. In the example we have been developing here, the prospect may perceive that an improved computer system would save time in the warranty fulfillment department and, therefore, help to meet the need of cutting labor costs. In that case, the benefit perceived by the prospect would be "saving workers' time." A temporary services firm, however, might offer the same prospect a method of reducing labor costs by reducing the costs of hiring and administration of employees. In this case, the benefit of the offering is "reduced overhead costs." Both solutions address the prospect's need to reduce labor costs, but present very different perceived benefits designed to meet that need.

Features

Finally, then, are the *features* of the product or service. Features are those aspects of an offering that create the benefits. The drill bit's feature is that it has very sharp cutting edges. Those edges enable the benefit of making holes better, faster, and cheaper.

Continuing our example, features of the improved computer system for the warranty fulfillment function may include an intuitive user interface and extensive use of keyboard function keys. Both of those features would contribute to the benefit of saving workers' time. Other features might be the ability to create an extensive customer history and multilingual capabilities. Those would be features of the product, which might be attractive but do not directly contribute to the benefit of reducing workers' time.

The difference between the features of an offering and the benefits perceived by prospects is an important one – one usually taught at an early stage in every salesperson's training regimen. This is the point of transition from a product-focused organization to a customer-focused one. Companies produce product and service features, but prospects buy product and service benefits. That is why benefits are the entry point for understanding CPV.

THE STRUCTURE OF CPV

Understanding the differences among needs, features, and benefits, we can now look at the specifics of the CPV model.[6] What specifically goes on that CPV balance scale and how those things stack up can be addressed.

Attributes

The basic building block of a CPV model is the *attribute*. We define an offering attribute as follows:

> **Attribute** – *benefit or cost, as perceived by the customer, of a specific product or service offering.*

As described earlier, customer-perceived benefits go on the left side of the CPV balance scale and customer-perceived costs go on the right side.

Benefits

Yes, these are the same benefits we have discussed in the context of addressing customer needs. We've found that benefits are usually the best point in the customer needs continuum around which to conduct conversations with customers because they represent customer-oriented perceptions but are close enough to supplier-oriented features to permit that linkage to be made by the seller.

AirNet Systems operates a 100-plane fleet of small business jets and twin-engine propeller-driven aircraft primarily serving the banking industry by moving documents overnight from one institution to another. The company's service *features* include late-night departure schedules with early-morning delivery, 6-hour access to all the major money markets in the country, and a ground delivery network coordinated with the airline. The banks' buying *needs* are to clear the cash represented by millions of cancelled checks into their own accounts as quickly as possible. The link between those features and those needs are the customer perceived *benefits*. In AirNet's business, those benefits include matters such as how well the airline's schedule matches the bank's check processing procedures, the speed of final delivery, and the reliability of the service. These are the benefits that would appear on these customers' CPV balance scale.

It is possible to simply ask customers what benefits they perceive an offering provides and get a fairly lengthy, and accurate, list of attributes. Usually, in fact, this is the very approach that is used to begin to construct an image of CPV. Some care is necessary, however, to be sure that a complete list is obtained because some of the benefit attributes may not be foremost in the prospect's mind at the time of the interview. Sometimes some "homework" by the researcher (prior observation of or preliminary research with the prospect) is necessary to enable skillful and unbiased extraction of complete information from the prospect.

Costs

There are also attributes, of course, on the right side of the CPV balance scale – all of the *costs* associated with the offering as perceived by the prospect. The most obvious of those costs is the purchase price for the offering, but there are many more.

When the natural gas industry was deregulated, the existing distribution companies were required to announce to their customers that they now had a choice of from whom to buy their gas. New entrants for that business sprang up everywhere and mounted major promotional campaigns to attract this business. And the price advantage to consumers was clear – the new companies charged less for the same commodity fuel. After several years, though, most consumers still purchased their natural gas from the traditional distribution company. Why? Because there was a "hassle" involved in switching to a new supplier. There were forms to be completed and the uncertainty of knowing which of the new companies to select. Those consumers had placed another item on the right side of their CPV Balance Scale, which is often called "switching costs." In many cases, it offsets the weight of the incumbent seller's higher price and any other benefits the new entrants could suggest that might go on the left side of the scale.

Some experts exclude price from the attributes of an offering, leaving all of the benefits and other costs to define "quality" of the offering, and then compare that quality to the price. We don't see the advantage in doing that. Although it is almost always an important attribute, price is no different in any other respect from other benefit and cost attributes. We prefer to envision the prospect's evaluation process as stacking all of the attributes, including the price attribute as a "cost," onto the CPV balance scale. This way, we ensure that the purchase price is managed as just another product attribute and not mistakenly assumed to be the primary focus of the prospect.

Importance Weights

A thorough investigation into all of the possible benefits and costs perceived in an offering by a prospect will usually result in a lengthy list of thirty, forty, or many more such attributes. Even small transactions will involve numerous attributes that a buyer might consider.

We recently observed a company buying a small telephone system for a remote office location. The price of the most expensive of the alternative systems under consideration was significantly less than

$10,000. The buyer had identified 31 attributes to be compared, some of which had numerous, complex characteristics. The attributes included such characteristics as price, subsequent upgrading prices, service prices, expandability, availability of training, and payment terms – in addition to product features, such as programmable keys, LED displays, number of speed dials, separate volume controls, voice mail ports, message storage capacity, and so on. This was not a complex purchase decision – the phone systems in their price range were actually all pretty much alike. Still, the number of attributes to be considered were many.

It is well established that a large number of variables is usually beyond the reasonable capability of most people to process. Most prospects, therefore, will probably place only the most important attributes, in their own judgment, onto the CPV balance scale. Identifying those and weighting them as to relative importance among them is both more descriptive of how the prospect is thinking about the buying decision and more practical for the seller to consider for his own decision-making process.

There are basically two kinds of attribute importance weighting data: stated importance and derived importance. In the first instance, the customer is asked directly about the relative importance of each of the CPV attributes. In the second approach, the importance weights are determined from indirect statistical analyses. Either approach provides important information about customer perceptions and the choice between them rests primarily on technical matters concerning research methods and costs.

However it is accomplished, the objective is to arrive at customer-perceived attributes and place them on the CPV balance scale according to customer-perceived weights of importance. What this provides the manager is a customer-oriented statement of the company's own "value proposition." It says, "Here are the benefits and costs we offer our customers, each weighted according to its respective importance to the customer." Any manager who cannot state his "value proposition" in this way, with such specificity and confidence that it represents how the customer sees it, needs to start right here.

Life Cycle of Attributes

A caution about reducing the multitude of attributes down to the most important few is in order. It should not be assumed that all attributes rated to be of lesser importance by customers can be dismissed as unnecessary. There is another dimension to CPV attributes, referred to as their *life cycle*, that must be understood (Figure 2.1).

Figure 2.1 - CPV Attribute Life Cycle

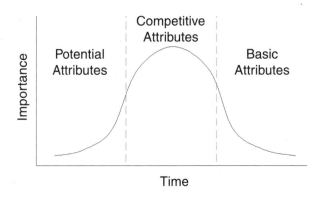

Potential Attributes

Before any supplier is able or willing to provide a desired attribute, it remains to the customer a *potential* attribute. These are the attributes in the category of "I wish someone would offer me this benefit." (For example, we wish an airline, going where and when we need it to go, would offer greater space between the rows of seats.) Such attributes might appear on a prospect's CPV balance scale, but do not actually come into play in the decision between suppliers because not one of them offers it.

Theoretically, potential attributes could even be benefits that are unstated and unrecognized by the prospect and, therefore, aren't even yet on the prospect's CPV balance scale. They would be there, however, if an aggressive supplier was to find a way to deliver them. Potential attributes, then, are the basis for supplier innovation.

Competitive Attributes

As soon as they are introduced through a product or service offering, and accepted as such in the perception of the marketplace, potential attributes become *competitive* attributes. These are the most obvious attributes to the prospect and the ones upon which buying decisions are currently made.

In the commercial airline industry, which airports are served and the convenience of flight schedules represent the principal competitive attributes. The availability of discounted fares may be another. These are the things that customers actively compare and evaluate to decide from which carrier to buy a ticket.

Competitive attributes represent the current competitive arena in connection with a particular product or service. They are the areas in which competitors are attempting to outdo one another.

Basic Attributes

As competitors continually improve their offerings, delivering better and better as well as more similar attributes, those attributes begin to fall into the category of *basic* attributes. These are the benefits and costs of a product or service that are the same across all of the prospect's alternatives.

Continuing the example of attributes in the commercial airline industry, a basic attribute would be the safety with which each airline carries its passengers. Because these matters are regulated by the Federal Aviation Administration, the maintenance and safety practices of most airlines are the same and the perception of flyers is, usually, that one commercial airline is just as safe as another.

Basic attributes may appear on the CPV balance scale, because they remain important to the prospect and customer. They are not a basis on which the buying decision hinges, however, because everybody offers the prospect the same thing in connection with this attribute. Unfortunately, because the customer has come to expect and accept the attribute as something deserved, sometimes it won't even be rated as very important. This is a deception, however, that must be uncovered.

An unfortunate example of underestimating the importance of basic attributes is the tragic story of ValuJet Airlines. Investigators into the crash of ValuJet's Flight 592 into the Florida Everglades determined that the financially struggling airline had scrimped a bit on maintenance procedures, apparently reducing the safety level of their operations. Safety, which was a *basic attribute* in the airline industry until that fateful day in May 1996, suddenly became an important *performance attribute* when ValuJet failed to provide it. Since then, at least for some time, safety was a prime consideration of buyers of airline service and most chose to take their business to other airlines. Soon thereafter, ValuJet officially went out of business.

Basic attributes are the "necessary evils" of competing suppliers. Although they carry a cost to the supplier for delivering them, they do not provide any competitive advantage at this late stage in the life cycle of CPV attributes. Nevertheless, they cannot be eliminated from the offering without reducing the value in the perception of the customer. They are "ante" to play in the competitive game.

Relative Performance

Even a completed CPV balance scale, with benefits and cost attributes well defined, weighted for importance, and stacked up on both sides, has limited utility. What it portrays is how the prospect is likely to behave if he has no alternatives other than to buy nothing else at all. In that case, if the balance scale tips toward the benefits side (the left side) then the purchase is likely to be pursued. It may also be useful in that management can use it to understand its "value proposition" for the first time.

In most cases, however, the prospect is selecting from among several offerings. When that is the case, the CPV balance scale for the manager's own offering is meaningful to the manager only when it is placed next to a comparable CPV balance scale for those competitive offerings. It really doesn't matter if one offering is very attractive to a prospect. To predict buying behavior, it *only* matters that the offering is *more* attractive than the prospect's alternatives.

As discussed earlier in connection with traditional customer satisfaction measures, a determination by a customer that an attribute performs *well* isn't as important as that it performs *better* than that of his alternatives. Hyatt, Marriott, and Hilton all compete at the high end of major city hotels. Most travelers would probably rate any one of those hotels as more than satisfactory. What matters the most, however, is which one of those chains the traveler rates the *best* in meeting his needs on any particular day.

With relative performance ratings added to the list of importance-weighted attributes, the conceptual CPV model is complete.

GENERAL CPV ANALYSIS TOOLS

We would not leave our readers, however, with only a conceptual model. That has no value (read CPV!) without a familiarity about how a manager can make use of it.

The CPV Construct

When we complete an investigation into CPV for a specific company's specific offering to a specific market segment, we like to stack the information up into a diagram similar to that shown in Figure 2.2. This gives the complete description of the CPV *construct* – the attributes, their relative importance in the buying decision making process, and their status in the attribute life cycle. This construct is the most important information that a manager can have about his business. Almost every decision the manager is called upon to make can ultimately be related back to this simple CPV construct. In fact, doing that very thing is the subject matter of the major portion of this book – Chapters 4 through 10. There are just three cautions, or clarifications, necessary in working with the CPV construct.

Figure 2.2 - Example of a CPV Construct

Attribute	Benefit or Cost	Importance	Life Cycle
Product life	Benefit	20%	Competitive
Ease of calibration	Benefit	15%	Competitive
Purchase price	Cost	20%	Competitive
Process changes	Cost	25%	Competitive
Warranty service	Benefit	10%	Basic
Field training	Benefit	5%	Basic
Billing accuracy	Benefit	5%	Basic

Only as Good as the Research

Explaining what someone else is thinking is, at best, a difficult task. At times, not even the person thinking it can explain it. The CPV construct is subject to all of those uncertainties. Good research methods and execution can substantially reduce the extent of error in a depiction of customer perceptions, but not even those things can totally remove it.

New Coke represents one of the most colossal new product failures in the history of consumer marketing, and it befell one of the greatest marketing companies in the world. Of course Coca-Cola conducted extensive research about their plan to reformulate their flagship product. Consumers told the people at Coca-Cola that the Pepsi ads were correct – Pepsi tastes better than Coke. So, Coca-Cola asked, "What would you do if we gave you a product that tasted better than Pepsi, but still was a Coke?" The consumers answered, "I would buy it." So, New Coke was introduced and the public reaction was immediate and overwhelmingly negative. Within 77 days of the new product roll-out, it was recalled, and Classic Coke was reintroduced to the marketplace. How could this have happened to a sophisticated consumer marketing company like Coca-Cola? According to Coke's marketing guru, Sergio Zyman, the mistake they made was that they didn't ask the *right* research question. As careful as they were, they forgot to ask, "If we took away Coca-Cola and gave you New Coke, would you accept it?" It is easy to see that now, but it was not that obvious at the time.[7]

Nevertheless, the difficulty of the research task should not prevent the manager from addressing it. Because benefiting from the customer's buying behavior is the ultimate goal of every manager, knowing more about that behavior (rather than less) is always preferable. And, *good* marketing research can deliver an incredible amount of information that is useful to the astute manager.

A Snapshot in Time

We mentioned earlier that CPV is a fickle thing. People change their minds. In fact, given the astounding rate at which more information is becoming available with the emergence of the Internet, people seem to be now changing their minds about everything at an increasing rate. Accordingly, any individual CPV construct is likely to change rapidly as well.

When gasoline supply is ample and prices are low, for example, drivers probably think most about which gasoline station is the most convenient, which one's convenience store has what they need that day, and where they can get in and out most quickly. Let supplies dwindle, however, pushing prices up, and suddenly it's a whole different ball game. Now, long lines at the cheapest dealer are seen on the evening news. Many drivers will go several blocks out of their way to save a few cents on gasoline.

The answer to this concern is the same as for the previous one: Nobody said this was going to be easy. Still, more information about customers is better than less, and even a snapshot of perceptions at a moment in time is better than no picture at all. The challenge for the manager is to keep her pulse on these changing perceptions. We have more to say about this in Chapter 11.

The Customer's Limited Vision

Finally, the manager must avoid getting so caught up in the CPV construct to the extent that he starts to think it represents all of the possibilities for causing customers to buy something. What the construct *does* represent is the customer's current thinking about the value delivered. That is not the same thing as what the customer *wishes* he could have or would value highly if someone else thought of it and provided it to him. That is a different animal.

The design engineers at Chrysler are famous for reminding us that they "didn't get lots of letters from soccer moms asking for the minivan." In fact, customer research by Ford indicated that there was little interest in this type of vehicle, so Ford did not proceed with it. At Chrysler, however, they looked beyond the customer's restricted view of what was currently available and sought to understand how young families solved their transportation needs. Based on that information, they introduced the first of the minivans and led Chrysler out of near financial disaster with it. It remains, however, that the minivan, at that point in history, would not have been on the customers' CPV radar screen.

The CPV construct is a snapshot of current customer perceptions. That is a powerful basis, however, from which to investigate underlying personal and buying needs, as well as to project what the customer might be likely to value at some time in the future. The manager just needs to be aware of the differences involved.

CPV Analysis

There is no real limit to the ways in which a manager can take the information contained in a CPV construct and apply it to specific management issues. As a minimum, we like to present the information in a couple of different ways.

Relative Performance Ratings

A 2-part bar chart, representing the ratings on each CPV attribute for each of the competitive offerings is a good starting place. A sample chart of this type is shown in Figure 2.3. The bar chart on the right side of the diagram reflects the actual ratings (this time on a scale of

0 to *10*) on each of the CPV attributes of the seller's offering as well as that of the customer's "next best alternative." We show these absolute ratings because it is important, for some purposes, that the seller knows how well his offering, and those of his competitors, is meeting the expectations of the customer. This, however, is not a contradiction. These Customer Satisfaction-like data are a part of the picture – just not the entire picture. That is why we show it on the right side of the diagram and, then, depict the relative performance ratings on the left side.

Figure 2.3 - Example of CPV Relative Performance Ratings

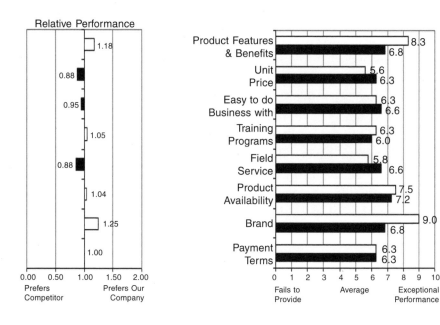

It is not difficult to convert the absolute ratings on the right side into relative ones on the left side. All it takes is some simple arithmetic to convert the actual ratings into a ratio. By doing this, we create a chart that is easy to read, because every bar on the right side of the vertical line means that the manager's product is out-performing the competitor's on that attribute, in the perception of the customer. Bars appearing on the left side mean that the manager's product is perceived as not performing as well on that attribute as compared to the competitor's. Where there is no bar at all, it means the customer perceives no difference in the performance on that attribute of the alternatives from which he chooses.

No one diagram gives the manager everything he needs to know about CPV, but each one contributes something different. The relative performance rating chart is the simplest chart a manager can use to convey how his offering stacks up against that of competitors.

The CPV Performance Matrix

This diagram, shown as Figure 2.4, incorporates the importance weightings of each attribute with the performance ratings, to help the manager make priority decisions about how to improve his overall CPV. In this chart, the vertical axis reflects the customer's importance weighting. The more important attributes will be found, therefore, toward the top of the matrix.

The horizontal axis reflects the relative performance ratings, right off of the relative performance rating chart just described. The attributes on which the manager's offering is perceived as performing better than the competition's will show up toward the right side of the chart, and those attributes where the manager's offering is at a disadvantage to competitors appear toward the left side.

McDaniel suggested labels for the four quadrants of this diagram.[8] He calls the attributes that fall into the upper left quadrant the "threats." These are the attributes that are more important to the customer, but the manager's offering is perceived as performing less well than that of the competitors. These are attributes that need to be improved to increase competitive advantage.

The lower left quadrant also contains attributes that are perceived as performing poorly in comparison to the competition, but they are

Figure 2.4 - Example of a CPV Performance Matrix

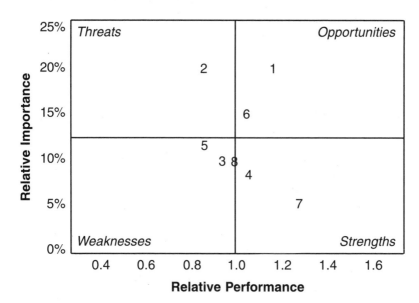

1 Product features & benefits
2 Unit price
3 Easy to do business with
4 Training & support programs
5 Field service & support
6 Product availability
7 Brand
8 Payment terms

less important attributes to the customer and, therefore, probably of somewhat less concern to the manager. This quadrant is referred to as the "weaknesses."

The right side of the diagram contains the attributes the customer perceives to be performing at a higher level than the competitors'. The lower right quadrant contains the attributes that are less important to the customer, so this quadrant is called the "strengths." These attributes probably should be maintained, but they will have less impact on CPV than the attributes appearing above them.

The upper right quadrant contains those attributes that are perceived as the strengths of the manager's offering and are more important to the customer. This quadrant is called the "opportunities," because these are the attributes that provide the manager with competitive advantage. If "leading with your strengths" is the strategy, then these are the attributes upon which the strategy may be based.

The two diagrams provided here are only the beginning of how CPV can be depicted. The important point is that CPV – a very complex, intangible, and transitory concept – can be described in very simple, tangible, and useful ways to help managers make difficult decisions. That process of simplifying and making tangible something that is so very complex is not to be taken lightly. It requires care, expertise, and judgment. Properly done, however, it provides management with a useful tool of immeasurable importance.

SUMMARY

Most companies track Customer Satisfaction, but few find it to be very useful to them. The problem with Customer Satisfaction, as it is traditionally measured, is that the research asks the wrong people the wrong questions about the wrong things.

A common criticism of Customer Satisfaction measures is that they do not seem to correlate with Customer Loyalty. Unfortunately, Customer Loyalty is another concept that has caused more confusion than clarity. While there is little evidence that customers are inclined to be "loyal," we do know that repeat customers are more profitable. In other words, the real objective is Customer Retention (rather than Satisfaction or Loyalty). The only valid objective is getting and retaining customers – getting them to *buy* from us. That logically leads to the need to understand why they do or do not buy.

The psychology of buying behavior is a complex matter and beyond the scope of this book. What managers really need to know is that human behavior is driven by satisfying needs, and that the most fundamental personal needs ultimately underlie most individual behavior. As a practical matter, however, managers do need to understand the *reasons* buyers make purchasing decisions. We call those "buying needs."

Customers satisfy their buying needs by seeking "benefits" that they perceive exist in a supplier's offerings. Suppliers deliver those benefits through the "features" they incorporate into the offerings, but customers don't buy features – they buy benefits. That's why *benefits* are the foundation of Customer Perceived Value (CPV).

CPV is made up of attributes, both perceived benefits and costs. Usually, the customer can identify a very large number of attributes used in the buying decision, so it is also necessary to understand the customer's relative importance weighting of those attributes. The customer's importance weightings allow the manager to focus on only the most important attributes of CPV.

There is a "life cycle" of CPV attributes that begins with "potential attributes" – those the customer desires or would perceive as valuable but are not yet being provided by suppliers. When companies begin providing these benefits, they become "competitive attributes." These are the perceived benefits and costs upon which different offerings compete. Eventually, everyone will provide many of the same benefits and those begin to look "all alike" to the customer. At this stage, they are considered "basic attributes." Although not usually rated very important by customers, basic attributes are "ante" required to be in the business and, therefore, cannot be eliminated from the offering without significantly decreasing CPV. Finally, CPV reflects the customer's perception of the performance of an offering's attributes, *as compared to* alternative offerings.

Summarized, then, the conceptual model of CPV consists of the customer's perceptions of how well an offering performs, compared to the customer's alternatives, on a set of benefit and cost attributes, weighted by importance to the buying decision.

That conceptual model becomes even more useful when it is supported by several practical management tools. The most basic is the CPV Construct, which is a list of the attributes, importance weightings, and life cycle stage for a specific offering to a specific customer.

The manager using the CPV Construct should be aware that (a) it is only as accurate as the research underlying it, (b) it is a snapshot of customer perceptions at a moment in time, and (c) it reflects only the customer's perceptions, not all possibilities.

CPV Analysis refers to graphical representations of the customers' relative performance ratings of the various attributes. These can be shown both as absolute values of the ratings themselves, and as a ratio of the rating of the manager's offering as relative to the customers' alternatives.

The CPV Performance Matrix is a 4-quadrant diagram that categorizes the attributes according to both the customers' ratings of importance and relative performance. This presentation is particularly valuable for managers to help them prioritize their actions.

REFERENCES

[1] *U.S. News & World Report*, March 15, 1999, pg. 45.

[2] U.S. Department of Transportation, Office of Aviation Enforcement and Proceedings, "Air Travel Consumer Report," for 1998 and 1999.

[3] Frederick F. Reichheld, *The Loyalty Effect: The Hidden Force Behind Growth, Profits, and Lasting Value*, (Boston, HBS Press, 1996).

[4] "Harte-Hanks Market Research announces results of customer loyalty study," *Direct Marketing*, July 1999, pg. 10.

[5] See Delbert Hawkins, Roger Best, and Kenneth Coney, *Consumer Behavior: Implications for Marketing Strategy*, 6th ed., (New York, Irwin, 1995); John A. Howard and Jagdish N. Sheth, *The Theory of Buyer Behavior*, (New York, Wiley, 1969); Hanry Assael, *Consumer Behavior and Marketing Action*, (Boston, Kent, 1987); James E. Engel, Roger D. Blackwell, and Paul W. Miniard *Consumer Behavior*, (Fort Worth, Dryden, 1994).

[6] Much of this material is adapted from Bradley T. Gale, *Managing Customer Value: Creating Quality & Service That Customers Can See*, (New York, Free Press, 1994).

[7] Sergio Zyman, *The End of Marketing as We Know It*, (New York, HarperCollins, 1999), pg. 57.

[8] Carl McDaniel and Roger Gates, *Contemporary Marketing Research*, (Cincinnati, South-Western College Printing, 1999).

CHAPTER 3

Delivering on CPV

In 1979, Wal-Mart was an also-ran. Kmart was the inventor of the "big box" discounting concept and, in that year, was enjoying its 1,891 stores and nearly $14 billion in annual sales. Wal-Mart, on the other hand, could boast of only 229 stores with per-store sales about half that of Kmart's.[1]

Within 10 years, however, Wal-Mart was showing its stuff. It was growing at an annual rate of nearly 25 percent, with the highest sales per floor space, inventory turns, and operating profit of all of the growing industry of discounters. Wal-Mart's 1989 pretax profits were nearly double that of Kmart.

Today, Wal-Mart is the undisputed king of retailing. It operates more than 3,500 retail outlets under the names of Wal-Mart Stores, Sam's Clubs, Wal-Mart SuperCenter Stores, Hypermart USA Stores, and Bud's Warehouse Outlet Stores.[2] Sales for the fiscal year ended in January 2000 were more than $165 billion, a growth rate during the previous year of more than 19 percent and average growth for the last five years of more than 20 percent. Kmart is still #2, but places a very distant second at only $36 billion in sales for the same year, up less than 7 percent from the previous year.

Wal-Mart is probably the most analyzed and written-about company in the history of retailing. So, why bring it up again here? Because this phenomenal success story is based on the principles of understanding what customers value and then doing the right things about it.

Sam Walton is famous for being a great motivator and making the customer the focus of his organization. That's a great starting point. But, clearly, there's much more underlying Wal-Mart's success than the charismatic power of its founder. The entire company had to become very skilled at putting into action the direction that Sam Walton set forth. And it did that extremely well.

Wal-Mart's market positioning of "Everyday Low Prices" isn't an easy thing to pull off. It requires a low-cost structure that permits the company to make a profit even after heavily discounting its retail prices. But, how does that low-cost structure come about? It's not from wishful thinking or simply an obsession with cutting out waste. That wouldn't be enough. Wal-Mart chose to base its "Everyday Low Prices" primarily on developing a logistics expertise second to none. Wal-Mart can move a product from the manufacturer to the consumer's shopping basket at a lower cost than can anyone else. It does that by very skillful management of transportation and information management processes.

Wal-Mart moves most of its inventory through its own warehouses, permitting more bulk purchasing and, thereby, lower costs. It practices a technique known as "cross-docking," meaning that much of the inventory never stops long enough to sit on a shelf. That results in more inventory turns and lower capital costs. And the entire logistics function is driven by an information management system that continuously provides point-of-sale demand information to Wal-Mart's 4,000 vendors over a private satellite-based communications network. That capability allows vendors to contribute effectively to Wal-Mart's low-cost delivery system.

Wal-Mart is certainly a wonderful success story based on understanding the customer perceived value of it targeted market segment. But even more than that, Wal-Mart is a story of "walking the walk." The managers of Wal-Mart know how to "make it happen" by designing, implementing, and con-

trolling business processes to deliver the customer value pre-scribed by its goals and strategies. For many others, that's a missing link that spells trouble.

MAKING IT HAPPEN

Almost everyone today is talking about "customer focus" in one way or another. Make no mistake, there are still exceptions to that – people who still believe that, if they make "a better mousetrap, people will flock to their door." But, more so everyday, most managers are accepting that the power has shifted to the customer. And they are certainly aware that competition for that customer has increased significantly. So, why are so many companies still operating the way they always have in the past? Why is the everyday service quality that we experience as consumers so bad? Why is the churn rate of industrial customers still as high as it is? Why don't more companies look like they're trying to deliver greater Customer Perceived Value (CPV)?

It's because this is not easy to do. Delivering CPV requires refocusing the entire organization on the customer. No longer is it possible that a few, visionary leaders can inform the organization about what to do – instead, we must be driven by what we learn that the customer needs. Because this is a radical change, all of the employees that have been successful and rewarded by the organization for doing it one way must be redirected and retrained to do it another way. Our business organizations have processes and other infrastructure that have, over time, become imbedded deep into what those companies are today. Performance measurement and compensation systems are just two parts of the usual infrastructure that require major overhaul to implement a CPV-based approach.

A giant information services company we know was recently certified as QS-9001 compliant. That means, among other things, that they have documented their intention to deliver high quality service to their customers and that they are seeking customer input on a regular basis. It doesn't mean they can do it, however. The director of research told us that none of the managers will pay any attention to her customer satisfaction data. The CEO complains that most of his people, "Just don't get it when it comes to the importance of customers." This QS-9001 certified company is "talking the talk," but hasn't yet learned how to "walk the walk." It hasn't learned how to put its intentions into action.

This chapter concerns *implementing* a CPV-based strategy. Well, actually, the whole book is about that. But, this chapter provides an overview of what it takes to "walk the walk" of CPV. Subsequent chapters, then, become more specific about managing each of the elements of the marketing mix and the company's traditional functional areas toward that end.

THE CPV DELIVERY CYCLE

We've spent most of our writing energy to this point attempting to drive home that "it all *begins* with the customer." And, as Figure 3.1 shows, it all *ends* with the customer as well.[3]

Figure 3.1 - CPV Delivery Cycle

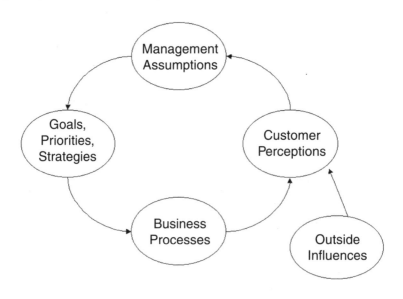

The CPV Delivery Cycle shows each of the steps that occur in between. The products and services delivered to customers, along with other outside influences on the customer, form the basis for CPV. ("Outside influences" include issues such as competitive offerings and actions and other things that influence customer needs.) The circle on the right side of the diagram, then, represents the set of customer perceptions that define CPV.

Management assumptions should come from, but are not necessarily the same thing as, customer perceptions. Recognizing this potential difference is an important first step toward getting improved, customer-focused results from a business organization.

We worked with a major mutual fund company a few years back that sold its financial products through national brokerage firms such as Merrill Lynch and Paine Webber. The retail brokers in those firms were the company's immediate customers. The company had operated for many years on the assumption that the attribute of their offerings of most importance to those brokers was the financial performance of its funds. After some structured discussions with them, however, it was determined that what really separated the various mutual fund companies in the eyes of those brokers was the quality of the supportive sales materials provided by the company. That understanding was a fundamental mind shift for the managers of the mutual fund company.

When Management assumptions are sound, the next step in the Cycle can be engaged. Goals, Priorities, and Strategies must be established by the organization. It is not enough that leaders know where they want to go. It must be clearly communicated to the rest of the organization – those people who will ultimately be responsible for making it happen.

The mutual fund company shifted its attention to providing superior supporting sales materials to its broker customers. It allocated resources for an entirely new department, to be called Broker Service and Support. Some of its best people were assigned to this new role. And it communicated clearly throughout the entire organization that it was committed to being the very best in its industry at supporting the selling effort of the retail brokers.

Moving on to the next step in the Cycle, then, management must develop processes, systems, and infrastructure required to carry out the Goals, Priorities, and Strategies. This is a matter of converting "what" the organization is going to do into defining "how" it is going to do it.

In our example, the original leaders of the Broker Service and Support function started out by designing "processes" to service the retail brokers. It was decided, at that time, to base those processes on inbound 1-800 telephone service requests from the brokers, with the requested information and services delivered outbound to the brokers via facsimile transmission. Appropriate equipment was purchased and installed, qualified people hired and trained, and processes documented and practiced.

The final challenge is to ensure that the Business Processes developed are executed properly and that the end result experienced by the customer is what was intended. This is what most of us think of when we refer to follow-up and follow-through.

At the mutual fund company, performance measurements were implemented from the first day, tracking how well the new Broker Service and Support function was meeting the needs of the retail brokers. Incentive compensation programs were developed to ensure that those involved were motivated to carry out the company's strategy. And customer feedback systems became the backbone of a follow-up and follow-through management approach to delivering the best possible service.

And so goes the CPV Delivery Cycle. Customers perceive, management infers, goals are set, and processes are executed to deliver CPV to the customers, which they perceive, and so on. The idea has characteristics of TQM's Plan-Do-Check-Act cycle, except that the TQM model did not explicitly include the customer. That's a big difference, of course. In fact, it is the whole point.

POTENTIAL GAPS IN THE CPV DELIVERY CYCLE

If it's just a matter of one-two-three-four, as this discussion suggests, what could go wrong? Extending the model, as shown in Figure 3.2, shows the four gaps between each of the nodes in the previous diagram. Let's look at each one of those gaps.

Figure 3.2 - Potential Gaps in the CPV Delivery Cycle

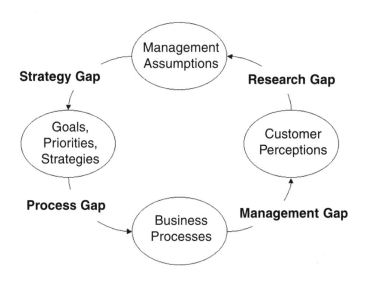

The Research Gap

Because CPV exists only in the minds of the customers, management is always making assumptions about what it believes those customers are, or will be, thinking. There is no way to avoid this problem. It is fundamental to our free-market system that buyers and sellers are operating at arm's length, and one is always trying to understand the other. Therefore, good customer research is the only tool we have to reduce some of the guesswork required of the supplier. That is why we call the potential gap between Customer Perceptions and Management Assumptions "The Research Gap." The

Research Gap occurs from either failure to conduct adequate customer research or conducting flawed research.

Lack of Research

Good marketing research is expensive and time consuming, so it is not surprising that some managers try to avoid it. Professor Kotler summarizes this situation in his classic marketing textbook:

> In spite of the rapid growth of marketing research, many companies still fail to use it sufficiently or correctly, for several reasons:
> • A narrow concept of marketing research: Many managers see marketing research as a fact-finding operation. They expect the researcher to design a questionnaire, choose a sample, conduct interviews, and report results, often without a careful definition of the problem or of the decision alternatives facing management. When fact-finding fails to be useful, management's idea of the limited usefulness of marketing research is reinforced.
> • Uneven caliber of marketing researchers: Some managers view marketing research as little more than a clerical activity and reward it as such. Less competent marketing researchers are hired, and their weak training and deficient creativity lead to unimpressive results. The disappointing results reinforce management's prejudice against marketing research.
> • Late and occasionally erroneous findings by marketing research: Managers want quick results that are accurate and conclusive. Yet good marketing research takes time and money. Managers are disappointed when marketing research costs too much or takes too much time. They also point to well-known cases where the research predicted the wrong result, as when Coca-Cola introduced the New Coke.

- Personality and presentational differences: Differences between the styles of line managers and marketing researchers often get in the way of productive relationships. To a manager who wants concreteness, simplicity, and certainty, a marketing researcher's report may seem abstract, complicated, and tentative.

  Yet in the more progressive companies, marketing researchers are increasingly being included as members of the product management team, and their influence on marketing strategy is growing.[4]

None of these reasons for management reluctance to use marketing research changes the basic fact – the objective is to learn what customers will perceive as valuable and that the best way to do that is to ask them and observe them. The difficulties involved in conducting good marketing research must be overcome, rather than avoided.

Flawed Research

Bad marketing research is even worse than no research at all because the manager is usually not aware that the research information she is using is not valid or reliable. And there are many things that can go wrong in the research process to bring about that result. Figure 3.3 lists many of the types of technical errors that can occur in the course of conducting research.[5]

A large financial institution, for example, included a customer satisfaction survey in its regular monthly statements mailing. Hundreds of surveys were returned, so a considerable amount of data was collected. The response rate was very low, however, representing less than 1 percent of the surveys mailed. An analysis of the surveys returned revealed that a large proportion of them – 20 times more than the general population – came from retired people. (Apparently, they had more discretionary time to complete the survey form.) This "measurement error" caused the survey's results to be highly questionable.[6]

Figure 3.3 - Common Market Research Errors

Random Sampling Error
Bias
    Sample Design Error
        Selection Error
        Frame Error
        Population Specification Error
    Measurement Error
        Processing Error
        Instrument Error
        Interviewer Bias
        Surrogate Information Error
        Response Error
            Response Bias
            Nonresponse Bias

With good research information, the manager's assumptions about how to deliver superior CPV should be in relatively close alignment with the perceptions of the target market. One remaining caveat here, however, is a reminder that customers are very fickle. Because of changing information availability, competitors' offerings, and circumstances driving wants and needs, how customers perceive value is constantly changing. To keep the Research Gap closed, it is necessary to remain vigilant with good, ongoing customer research.

The Strategy Gap

Of course, it is not enough for top management to have "figured out" what the customer needs. The rest of the organization must understand what it is they are supposed to do about it. That is the challenge of developing strategy and communicating that strategy to the organization. The failure or inability to do that is referred to as the Strategy Gap.

Chapters 4 through 10 of this book are devoted to the various aspects of creating strategy, starting with basic strategic issues in the next chapter, targeting customers in the one after that, and then followed by chapters on each of the elements of the Marketing Mix. We won't cover in this book those parts of a business strategy that are less directly related to customer needs, such as finance or human resources management. Those are left for specialists in those fields. But, in summary, most of this book is about using an understanding of customer needs to make strategic decisions. "Walking the walk" of CPV is largely about making such decisions.

Surprisingly, not many managers, even some who profess to understand that their success depends on meeting customer needs, are very good at making or communicating strategy. We know of a national manufactured parts distributor that proudly displays its Mission Statement on a plaque in the lobby of its headquarters building. It reads:

> Our mission is to furnish superior products and services to our customers on a continuing basis, while at the same time provide an excellent return on investment for our shareholders and share our success with our dedicated associates.

At first glance, this sounds pretty good. It contains all of the important words, such as "customer" and "superior" and "return on investment." Unfortunately, it does not indicate that a single strategic decision has been made by this company. Who are the targeted customers? What is the nature of the solutions this company offers? How is the company going to deliver CPV to its customers? Virtually any company in America could say this Mission Statement applies to it, and that's the problem. To successfully close the Strategy Gap, management must make some choices and communicate those choices to the rest of its organization.

Because this book is all about making strategic decisions, we'll only add a few more comments here about communicating those decisions. Communicating strategy is more than telling people about it. In our experience, we've found that three things are of critical importance in closing the Strategy Gap:

A Consistently Clear Direction

We have heard senior executives complain that "nobody listens to me." In fact, the real problem is that *everybody* is listening to top management all of the time. And they're listening in more ways than those managers usually expect.

Common in the heyday of TQM was the senior executive who would profess allegiance to "quality" in his weekly staff meeting and then go out on the plant floor and ask how fast the next order could be produced and shipped. Usually, workers would learn to ignore the speeches and go with what they inferred from the personal encounters with the boss. If that was the boss' intention then that interpretation was appropriate, but usually it wasn't.

Few companies send consistent messages to their employees, but when they do it is extremely powerful. Nordstrom department stores is legendary, of course, for the stories of retail employees going beyond normal expectations to solve customer needs.[7] When a regular Nordstrom customer, for example, accidentally laundered a pair of suit pants and shrunk them beyond recognition, he called the Nordstrom store for help in finding another pair. When he couldn't, the salesperson refunded the customer's money for the price of the original suit because, according to the salesperson, a suit coat without the pants was of no value to the customer so he shouldn't have had to pay for it! How many companies would actually reward and encourage such extravagant behavior from its employees? Not many, we expect.

In fact, extravagant customer solutions are probably not a good idea for most companies. Hopefully, there is a way to earn customer respect and trust without such wanton disregard for corporate profits. But, that is Nordstrom's philosophy, it works well for that company, and they do an exceptionally good job of behaving consistently with their strategy.

Relevant Performance Measures

A basketball game would not be very interesting without keeping score. And then, when the score is kept, most of the other statistics don't matter as much. The objective is to score more points than the other team, so that is where the focus lies. Like it or not, most people take goals seriously and try to "win."

It is critical, therefore, that the performance measures that are established at every level of an organization are consistent with the strategic decisions that have been made by managers. Tell that basketball team that "we only want to take good shots at the basket" and "we've got to win this game," and the results near the final buzzer will be quite predictable. The more easily measurable objective is whether they score more points than the other team, so watch out for the half-court shot if that's what it takes.

We worked with a major telecommunications company to improve the service level of their customer call center. This company spent millions of dollars on excellent training programs for their front-line staff concerning product knowledge, courtesy, handling irate callers, etc. The education requirements and pay levels were even increased in an effort to improve service quality. Unfortunately, the primary performance measure in the call center was "average minutes per call." Knowing that customers didn't want to wait for an agent for very long, the center's answer to that need was to make sure each agent could handle more calls, more quickly, to get on to the next waiting customer. Clearly, this performance measure drove behavior from the telephone agents that was contradictory to the company's stated strategy of providing high quality service.

This example of the length of calls in a customer call center as an inappropriate performance measure is an old one, and most competent call center managers have solved this problem by now. It is still a good example, however, because it is representative of the simplicity of this problem. Usually, performance measures are right out there in the open, where everyone can see them. It doesn't take much to look at them in the context of the company's intended strategy and make sure they are consistent.

Consistent Compensation Systems

One of the primary reasons performance measures are as inconsistent with strategy as they are is because of the impact of established compensation systems. Often, such compensation systems have been in place long before companies developed the awareness level that they have today. And compensation systems are the hardest thing in any organization to change.

Since the beginning of commerce, in all likelihood, salespeople have been compensated on some form of commission scheme. Because the objective of most salespeople is to ensure the customer buys from their employer, it seems quite natural that their rewards (primarily "compensation") should increase the more the customers buys. That makes sense, and thus was born the percentage commission. The salesperson receives, for example, a fixed percentage of every revenue dollar.

Unfortunately, it is not as simple as it appears. For what period should the revenue and commission payments be measured, i.e., is it important to get the customer to buy more this month, rather than next? Most commission systems encourage that very thing. Does it matter whether the sale helps solve a problem for the customer? Most commission systems can't comprehend such subjective factors. But, if the company's strategy is to develop long-term, value-based relationships with its customers, the traditional commission system is probably the worst possible way to compensate salespeople.

So, why not just fix the compensation systems? There are two problems with that. First, compensation systems are inherently complex and there is *no* single best solution to a compensation problem. There are always trade-offs encountered in the design of a compensation system – each method is good for some reasons and bad for others. The design of a compensation system is, in fact, a search for the "least worst" solution. It is very difficult to design a system that maximizes the appropriate motivation factors while consistently communicating the strategic objectives of the company.

Second, compensation systems are the most sensitive of all matters of employee relations. And most people don't like *change*. Therefore, it is important for management to move slowly in changing the way it pays its people. Although some would disagree, we recommend that companies make changes to compensation systems as one of the last of the required moves to align an organization's business systems around its chosen strategy.

More specifically, we recommend that management move aggressively to remove the obvious discrepancies between its strategies and its compensation systems, but very cautiously beyond that. This is not easy for us to say, because it is well established that compensation systems are critical to driving organizational performance. And, after all, our objective here is to close the Strategy Gap between its own understanding of CPV and the strategic direction the organization is pursuing. With that understood, we believe the greatest impact of compensation systems on the delivery of superior CPV is to eliminate the obvious contradictions in those systems.

The Process Gap

Up to this point, by examining the Research Gap and the Strategy Gap, we have been dealing with *directional* issues. Deciding and communicating *what* the organization will do to successfully deliver superior CPV. Finally, at the Process Gap, the focus moves to *how* the work will be performed. This is because, after all, all work gets done as a result of cross-functional processes.

The management of processes emerged as a central part of the TQM movement popular in the 1980s and 1990s. As are most good ideas, process management is both a simple and an elegant concept. Simply stated, process management means to determine the best way to combine individual tasks and activities to best get the job done and then manage that set of tasks and activities accordingly.

We address the topic of process management in Chapter 10 in connection with managing Operations. Here, we merely highlight the primary steps required for closing the Process Gaps. Those are:

DEFINE THE PROCESSES
NAME PROCESS OWNERS
ESTABLISH CONSISTENT PERFORMANCE MEASURES

Define the Processes

Processes are in place, delivering results to customers, whether or not those processes are recognized as being there at all. If those processes are not identified, defined, and documented for all involved to understand, the work and its results are not really being managed.

A few years ago, we helped a major telecommunications company examine its process of handling written customer inquiries. By interviewing the participants and observing the work taking place, we developed a detailed *process map* of how it was being done. In doing so, we discovered that every single piece of paper, amounting to thousands of documents each week, was moving into and out of a cardboard box located at the feet of one employee named Joe. Investigating further, we found that this "answering inquiries" function, years ago, consisted of just three people in a small room. When one of them was about to go on vacation and was replaced with a temporary worker, that worker was instructed to put all of the mail into this box and then work out of it. Now, with more than 40 people working in the department and the work volume increased several orders of magnitude, that instruction had survived. "Joe's Box," as it had become known, was the central point of the current workflow and a terrible bottleneck.

That story seems so simple that most managers would probably deny a problem like this could occur in their shop. And, perhaps, now that business processes are better understood by most managers, it couldn't happen today. But, the company involved, back then, was a successful, sophisticated company – one of the *Fortune 100*. The problem existed because they were so busy getting the work done that they failed to examine and document *how* it was getting done. We find that that happens often.

Name Process Owners

Processes are almost always cross-functional. That is because we define processes as those sets of tasks and activities that produce results, and we are defining results as those things that customers ultimately perceive. That usually takes the combined effort of many different parts of the organization. It takes cross-functional processes.

Take, for example, the delivery of an accurate invoice to a customer. That certainly sounds like something the accounting department alone could take care of, not a cross-functional effort. But, looking at how an invoice actually comes together shows otherwise. The shipping department must transfer accurate information about when a shipment took place and what was in it. The freight carrier, probably an outside vendor, must get the word back to accounting if the shipment didn't happen as expected. The people in sales must have accurately documented the selling price and payment terms agreed upon with the customer and communicated that to the accounting department. And the mailroom must know what to do with the document produced by the accounting department if they are to get it to the customer properly. Even at this simple level of analysis, it is clear that several functional areas of the company must coordinate their efforts to get the desired results for customers.

The traditional organizational structure, however, does not provide for that coordination. Each functional area has its own management and control methods, and any problems almost invariably occur in that "uncharted" area between those functions. That is when "finger pointing" begins – the accounting department blaming sales for not getting the prices to them correctly, or sales blaming the accounting department for having to send out an invoice correction to the customer for more money. It seems like a simple thing to avoid. But, it happens with frequency in every business organization.

One answer to the coordination problem is for the company to identify a "process owner" who is responsible for the performance of a properly defined process. Some companies have reorganized so that all the resources necessary to perform the process are reporting directly to the process owner. This is an extreme approach, however, and requires the complete transformation from a functionally-organized company to a structure organized around processes. This approach may or may not be the best thing to do. Other companies have simply appointed a process owner with "dotted line" reporting to the resources involved in the process. This requires greater skill from the process owner, because formal authority is now replaced with the need to persuade, argue, and cajole. But it is a structure that has worked well for some.

Regardless of the overall organization structure, *someone* must be ultimately responsible for the performance of each critical cross-functional process to make sure it's working. That's a process owner. We have more to say about Process Owners in Chapter 10.

Establish Consistent Performance Measures

This recommendation, made here in talking about the Process Gap, appears redundant with our discussion of performance measures in connection with the Strategy Gap, for a very good reason. Performance measures are powerful in defining goals and objectives. Assume the company wants to do a better job in keeping its customers informed about the status of its orders. But what exactly does that mean? Does it mean that every customer should have on-line access to her order status information? Does it mean that such information should be updated every day or every hour? Does it mean that the website must be "up" 24/7, or is it O.K. if it is taken down on Sundays for maintenance? Establishing these performance measures goes a long way toward helping everyone involved understand what "a better job in keeping its customers informed" really means.

Developing consistent performance measures is a matter of "cascading" the definitions from the more general strategic level to the very specific process level (Figure 3.4). Doing this is critical to closing the Process Gap.

Figure 3.4 - Example of Cascading Performance Measures

Level	Measure
SBU Leader	Sales, profits, overall CPV
VP, Operations	Costs & CPV of Support Services
Director, Call Center	Costs per call & CPV of Call Center Services
Call Center Supervisor	Minutes per call & CPV per call
Call Center Operator	Minutes per problem & CPV per problem

A medical services company providing independent medical examinations for workers compensation insurance companies decided it was important to get the medical reports to its customers more quickly after each examination was conducted. A part of their strategy was to "Get the reports to the customer faster than the competition can do it." It set about, therefore, to examine the underlying processes that were involved in producing and delivering the reports. The company organized a task force of employees who very nicely documented how the process worked and even suggested some process improvements for helping it to do a better job. The company named a process owner, who was eager to assume the responsibility for implementing the proposed improvements and measuring the process' performance.

Only one thing went wrong. In developing performance measures, the process owner decided to keep track of the elapsed time between when the medical examination was conducted and the placement of the finished report in the mailroom out-basket. That was a reasonably good performance measure for the process as she had defined it, but it didn't conform closely enough with the original strategic intent - which was to get the reports to the customer faster. The out-basket of the company's mailroom was not the same thing as the desk of its customer's claim analyst. Upon further analysis, this company found that the unreliable mail service in their community was impacting its ability to "get the reports to the customer faster," so it included the final delivery task into its process and began measuring the speed of its report all the way to their customer. They decided, in some cases, to use a private courier to deliver critical reports. Initially they weren't measuring the correct thing at their process level to ensure that their strategic goals would be attained. To properly close the Process Gap, it is important that the performance of the processes be measured on the same basis as measures used to define the organization's strategic intents.

Management Gap

The last gap, the Management Gap, is a more straightforward challenge. Closing this gap means assuring the *conformance* of the final output of the company's processes to the performance goals it had previously established for itself. Because those goals were built upon understanding customer needs, closing Gap Four means making sure the organization is, in fact, meeting those needs.

Because Gap Four is the point at which the company interacts with the customer, it is imperative that management is fully aware of, and actively managing the outcomes for, every one of those interactions. Jan Carlzon, CEO of Scandinavian Airlines, coined the term "Moments of Truth" for these interactions in his 1987 book.[9] We like to call them Value Opportunities, because it is in each of these interactions that the company has the opportunity to deliver greater value to the customer than its competitors. What goes on with the customer at all other times is outside of the company's control, so these Value Opportunities provide the company its *only* opportunities to succeed or fail. They are worth management's attention.

To demonstrate the number and variety of Value Opportunities in most companies, in Figure 3.5 we have listed many of the Value Opportunities of a traditional manufacturing company. Sometimes we find it useful to begin with defining Value Opportunities as a starting place for understanding CPV. We can then work either forward or backward through the CPV Delivery Cycle to (a) better understand Customer Perceptions that result from Value Opportunities, or (b) trace performance problems in the Value Opportunities back to the processes that need to be improved to correct that unacceptable level of performance. This is just one more exercise to help companies better understand CPV.

The point of the exercise, of course, is that many Value Opportunities are seldom adequately considered by suppliers. For example, a natural gas distributor in the Southwest served several large gasoline refiners in Arizona and western Texas. These were important customers to the distributor, so they strove to find ways to add to the CPV they provided. Providing a true commodity such as natural gas, this distributor had few opportunities to deliver value and, by finding additional ways to do so, set itself apart from the refiners' natural gas supplier alternatives.

Figure 3.5 - Value Opportunities for
a Component Manufacturing Firm

Promotional information in trade magazine, on
    web site, at trade show.
Product information in response to prospect
    inquiry & questions.
Meeting(s) with prospect.
Offer proposal & quotation.
Contract negotiations.
Credit application.
Order entry - new order.
Order entry - repeat order.
Rush order negotiation.
Order clarification.
Handling of order status inquiries.
Handling of order change (customer initiated).
Handling of order change (company initiated).
Order cancellation.
Product delivery.
Product performance in application.
Handling returns & rejects.
Invoicing.
Resolving customer invoicing problem.
Handling invoice corrections.
Response to technical inquiry.
Response to general customer inquiry.
Response to customer complaint or problem.
Problem resolution communication.
Problem resolution visit.
Relationship management meetings.
Technical design engineer meetings.
Account review meetings.
Product quality reports.
Customer newsletters.
Credit memo negotiations.

The distributor set about to inventory its Value Opportunities with these refiners and, in the course of doing so, uncovered a negative one that they hadn't before contemplated. The distributor provided natural gas, so it promoted the use of natural gas whenever possible.

One way in which it did that was to own and operate natural gas-powered automobiles for its own car fleet. These cars were painted in colors meant to attract attention and lettered with the slogan, "Powered by clean, natural gas." When asked, the refiners told the distributor they didn't appreciate the competition. The distributor had never realized that it was also a competitor to these refiners, even though they were also its largest customers. The realization helped both supplier and customer, in this case, to better define the intended relationship and find other, more appropriate ways for the distributor to deliver CPV to these important customers.

Every company should develop an inventory of its Value Opportunities – probably one for each offering to each market segment. If it has already done so, that inventory probably needs updating by now. Understanding all of the places at which a company interacts with its customers, even some of the less obvious and more obscure ones, will help the company improve its ability to see things as its customers see them. And that, after all, is where the CPV Delivery Cycle both begins and ends – with Customer Perceptions.

SUMMARY

More managers talk about the importance of delivering CPV than have done much about it. And it does take concerted effort on the part of managers to improve the CPV they deliver. It doesn't happen just by talking about it. We think that is the level most management teams achieve today. Ready and eager to compete on CPV, but not exactly sure where to start or how to make it happen. And to add to the problem, what they need to do is not easy.

This chapter provides an overview of the sequence of management activities that must occur. Specifically, it introduces a model called the CPV Delivery Cycle that shows the progression from Customer Perceptions to Management Assumptions to Strategy and finally, to Processes. The Processes, of course, are what deliver the results to the customer, thereby coming full circle to Customer Perceptions. The key for management is to be aware of, and close, the gaps between each of those phases.

The Research Gap can exist between Customer Perceptions and Management Assumptions if management doesn't thoroughly learn what its customers are thinking. Because CPV exists only in the mind of the customer, management has no idea what to aim for if it doesn't know precisely what the customer is thinking.

The Strategy Gap can occur between Management Assumptions and Strategy if management fails to decide, and explain to the rest of the organization, what should be done to meet the customers' needs. Section Two of this book deals primarily with the various aspects of developing strategy that is consistent with customers' perceived needs.

The Process Gap can exist between Strategy and Processes if management's strategic decisions are not translated into well defined business processes that describe *how* the strategy of the organization will be carried out. Processes already exist in every organization and fully account for the quality of the output delivered to customers. Many processes have not, however, been aligned with the current strategy of the company and this disconnect prevents any chance of delivering superior CPV.

The Management Gap is where the "rubber meets the road." It can exist between Processes and Customer Perceptions if those processes aren't delivering to customers what is intended or desired. TQM directly addressed many of these performance issues because they are primarily matters of "compliance," i.e., producing results according to agreed upon specifications.

Allowing any of these Gaps to exist will result in the failure to deliver superior CPV. The CPV Delivery Cycle is simply a description of each of the activities that must be carried out by management to make a difference in its company's performance. It is the answer to the often asked questions, "Where do I start?" and "What do I have to do to make it happen?" It's how to "walk the walk."

REFERENCES

[1] George Stalk, Philip Evans, Lawrence E. Shulman, "Competing on Capabilities: The New Rules of Corporate Strategy," *Harvard Business Review*, March-April, 1992.

[2] CorporateInformation.com, a division of the Winthrop Corporation, *Company Research Report: Wal-Mart Stores, Inc.*, January 6, 2000.

[3] We were influenced by the earlier work into service quality of Valerie A. Zeithaml, A. Parasuraman, and Leonard A. Berry, *Delivering Service Quality: Balancing Customer Perceptions and Expectations,* (New York, Free Press, 1990).

[4] Philip Kotler, *Marketing Management: The Millennium Edition,* (Upper Saddle River, Prentice-Hall, 1999).

[5] Carl McDaniel and Roger Gates, *Contemporary Marketing Research: Fourth Edition,* (Cincinnati, South-Western College Publishing, 1999), pg. 168.

[6] McDaniel and Gates, pg. 172.

[7] Ron Zemke, *The Service Edge: 101 Companies That Profit From Customer Care,* (New York, New American Library, 1989), pg. 65.

[8] See, for example, H. James Harrington, *Business Process Improvement: The Breakthrough Strategy for Total Quality, Productivity, and Competitiveness,* (New York, McGraw-Hill, 1991); Geary A. Rummler and Alan P. Brache, *Improving Performance: How to Manage the White Space on the Organization Chart,* (San Francisco, Jossey-Bass, 1990); Rohit Ramaswamy, *Design and Management of Service Processes: Keeping Customers for Life,* (Reading, Addison-Wesley, 1996).

[9] Jan Carlzon, *Moments of Truth: New Strategies for Today's Customer-Driven Economy,* (New York, Harper Collins, 1987).

SECTION TWO

Using Customer Perceived Value

CHAPTER 4

CPV and Business Strategy

In 1985, CompuServe was the world's leading consumer information service provider. That was before the Internet was widely available beyond government and academic institutions, so CompuServe's service at that time was called videotext, and it was delivered over a private telephone network. Even then, the leaders of CompuServe knew that big changes were coming and they wanted to get started addressing those changes. CompuServe's parent company, the tax preparation giant H&R Block, was reluctant to move too quickly, so the top three executives of CompuServe left to start a new venture called Discovery Systems.

The new company would use an emerging technology, CD-ROM, to deliver information in full motion video and sound. At the time, that represented a huge leap forward from the one-line-at-a-time text-based service that CompuServe then provided. Discovery Systems would deliver a CD-ROM, full of software programs, newsletters, and databases monthly to its consumer subscribers. To deliver that service on time and accurately, management decided it needed to develop its own capabilities to produce everything – from the information gathering to manufacturing the compact disc itself.

On the basis of that concept, $8 million (a respectable start-up fund in those days) was invested by a syndicate. Within 9 months, almost 300 people were recruited into the *company, a complete clean-room manufacturing facility was constructed, and all the infrastructure was put in place for a successful launch. Just one problem arose. There weren't any customers for the new business.*

Consumers didn't own CD-ROM drives in those days. It was clear that the CD-ROM would eventually replace the floppy diskette for high-volume data storage, but that day hadn't yet arrived. The only compact discs that consumers were familiar with in 1986 were those they bought at the music store to play on their stereos. So, to "buy some time" until CD-ROMs reached the consumer marketplace and Discovery Systems' business concept could be introduced, the company used its manufacturing plant to make CDs for the music industry. But, there was a problem with that, as well.

The executives from CompuServe knew a lot about the business of publishing electronic information. Unfortunately, by being forced into the business of making compact discs for the music industry (even as a stop gap measure until their intended market developed), they found themselves in a commodity-like, low-cost manufacturing business. Competition was fierce. In less than 2 years, the manufactured price of a CD dropped from almost $2.25 to less than $.75. The company wasn't able to deal with those economics, and it was forced into bankruptcy proceedings in the summer of 1988.

How could this have happened to such competent and successful businessmen – the same ones that had founded and built CompuServe to its leading position? Some might say that "these things will happen" in leading edge technology businesses. If anything could have changed the ending to this story, however, it would have been a better understanding of the potential market demand for CD-ROM technology. Like so many aggressive entrepreneurs, the executives at Discovery Systems were confident that their intuitive "feel" for this developing market was adequate. They didn't see a need to test their strategic plans against information obtained from the marketplace.

WHAT IS STRATEGIC PLANNING?

The term "strategic planning" means different things to different people.[1] In most electric utility companies in the United States, strategic planning has been a staff function where full-time specialists make plans for the next 30-year planning horizon. At Taco Bell, on the other hand, it includes a crew huddling in the kitchen to plan how to handle the busload of customers that just arrived on its lot. To encompass these disparate approaches (which is appropriate to do, because they *are* all part of strategic planning) and limit our interest in strategy to the world of business, we offer this definition:

> **Strategic planning** – *the activity of predicting what will be required to induce customers to buy at a profitable price.*

This simplistic definition is not intended to be irreverent but, rather, accurate and practical. It includes the development of both high-level *business* strategy and more tactical *functional* strategies for marketing, finance, and operations. Figure 4.1 provides an overview of some of the various types of management decisions that we include under the heading of strategic planning. This chapter addresses the kinds of strategy decisions that are made in connection with the organization's business strategy, and the next several chapters address each of the marketing strategy topics. Financial and operational strategy decisions are outside the scope of this book.[2]

Figure 4.1 - Examples of Strategy Decisions

Business Strategy	Marketing	Financial	Operational
• Markets	• Product	• Capital Structure	• HR
• Needs Served	• Promotion	• Planning Methods	• Integration
• Organizational Structure	• Distribution	• Management Controls	• Technology
	• Pricing		

Strategy is Predicting

Two of the terms in our definition deserve special attention. The first is the admission that strategic planning involves *predicting* what should be done. Wise managers know that all strategies are only hypotheses. When Wal-Mart first decided to pursue efficient logistics, that represented a hypothesis on Wal-Mart management's part that the resulting everyday low prices would draw large volumes of customers to their stores. Subsequent history has demonstrated that their hypothesis was correct. Similarly, Sears' decision to expand beyond its traditional hardware-oriented offerings and emphasize, instead, soft goods such as fashion apparel was a hypothesis by Sears management that this would draw new attention and large numbers of new shoppers to Sears. That hypothesis turned out to be less accurate. Strategic planning is always about making predictions about how customers will define Customer Perceived Value (CPV) and what they will do as a result. It is always filled with the uncertainty inherent in any prediction of the future.

Strategy is about Customer Behavior

The other term of most importance in our definition of strategic planning is "induce customers to buy." Ultimately, that is the *only* thing that's important to a business. If customers perceive sufficient CPV to cause them to purchase a company's offering, the company realizes cash from that sale – which is necessary to survive and prosper. What it really boils down to is this – without the cash coming in, the company ceases to exist.

So, what's the big deal about the terms "predicting" and "induce customers to buy"? If strategic planning involves "predicting what will be required to induce customers to buy at a profitable price," then it becomes clear that successful strategic planners will want to know everything there is to know about why customers buy things and what might make them do more of that in the future. That means thoroughly understanding CPV. Unfortunately, many managers involved in strategic planning never bother to investigate CPV at all.

OTHER STRATEGIC PLANNING CONCEPTS

When they don't have useful information from the marketplace on which to base strategic decisions, many managers rely on other concepts to guide their planning efforts. Usually those come from some type of internal perspective, because that's what they *do* know about.

Driving Force

This strategic planning concept suggests that managers identify the *driving force* of an individual business and do everything possible to build upon that. The driving force might come from a myriad of possibilities, including a company's proprietary technology, or unusual marketing channels, or even intangibles such as culture or vision. In effect, identifying a company's driving force is simply a matter of looking at the "strengths" in the traditional SWOT (strengths, weaknesses, opportunities, and threats) analysis and selecting one to be the foundation for all strategy decisions.[3]

One of the possible driving forces of a company is the "product concept." General Motors' strategies, for example, are based on the driving force of its experience in manufacturing automobiles. Similarly, Boeing is driven by its expertise in making airplanes. How that product concept is defined and leveraged in the context of CPV, however, is critical. In the 1980s, for example, IBM made an almost fatal strategic mistake by considering its driving force to be mainframe computers. Only when it redefined that driving force, in the face of CPV, to include other types of computing (including personal computers) did it turn the necessary corner to remain viable.

The driving force concept is a useful tool for organizing the strategic planning process. It remains useful, however, just as long as it doesn't get in the way of understanding that it all boils down to CPV. It won't matter how good a company's driving force is if its prospective customers fail to perceive the compelling CPV that will cause them to buy its offerings.

Stretch and Leverage

Professors Hamel and Prahalad introduced another thrust in strategic planning when they suggested that companies should establish goals beyond what can be easily accomplished (stretch) and should manage scarce resources by using them more efficiently instead of only reallocating them (leverage).[4] These principles, they said, better explained how companies such as Toyota, CNN, British Airways, and Sony were able to overtake their then much larger competitors GM, CBS, Pan Am, and RCA. This made much more sense than attributing those successes simply to the nimbleness of smaller companies.

There is a danger, however, in focusing solely on the principles of stretch and leverage in the strategic planning process if that focus overlooks CPV. Hamel and Prahalad, for example, described the "products of stretch" as "a view of competition as encirclement rather than confrontation, an accelerated product-development cycle, tightly knit cross-functional teams, a focus on a few core competencies, strategic alliances with suppliers, programs of employee involvement, consensus." No mention of customers. It is safe to say that the successes of Toyota, CNN, British Airways, and Sony had much to do with their understanding of what customers would value and decide to buy (CPV), in addition to the principles of stretch and leverage.

Strategic Business Units

Since Sloan reorganized General Motors in the early 1920s into 14 operating divisions, the idea of breaking a company up into separate components, each to develop a separate "strategy" for its respective business, has been widely used.[5] Strategic business units provide a way for corporate management to simplify the strategic planning process for themselves and, perhaps even more importantly, to measure, manage, and reward the resulting disparate business activities.

The danger with SBUs, however, is that they can easily turn into the dreaded "silos" that prevent the effective horizontal cooperation and information flow necessary to best serve customers' needs. Where the distinction is clearly based on differences in requirements for

CPV, such as the Lexus division of Toyota, the separation of business units works well. When that distinction gets fuzzy, however, it probably just gets in the way of aggressive and efficient customer service. It is significant that Toyota's product line covers all of the possible customer segments without copying the multidivisional model of General Motors.

WHY SOME MANAGERS DON'T USE CPV IN STRATEGY

Of course, it's all a matter of emphasis. The concepts of driving force, stretch and leverage, SBUs, and most of the other organizers of the strategic planning process each have something valuable to contribute. The primary risk in using any of these tools is in allowing it to become more important than understanding CPV.

If it is that straightforward, why do so many managers fail to gather information about CPV to use in the strategic planning process? It is usually one or the other of two reasons – the first one is sometimes legitimate and the second one is never so.

Lack Time and/or Money

At times, a manager is required to make a strategic decision "under the gun." There's no time, or budget, to gather the kind of information that is needed to thoroughly understand CPV. Theoretically, that information should have been gathered at some earlier time so that it would be available now, when it is needed, but it is too late for that. Management is always making decisions without complete information, and the lack of relevant marketplace information is simply an extreme case of the necessity to do that. If there is no ability to alter or improve the decision by adding good marketplace information to the decision mix, whatever the reason for that circumstance, then the "show must go on" without it.

"We Know What They Want"

Much more often, however, the reason for the lack of CPV information in the strategic planning process is because management believes it "knows what the customer wants." These managers don't *choose* to take the time or money that is available to obtain marketplace information because they don't believe the benefit gained from that information will exceed the cost of obtaining it. (Notice that this is just another CPV issue, turned around on the manager!)

Managers who have previously had a bad experience with customer research are especially prone to this error. It is understandable that a manager who committed a large portion of his discretionary budget last year for a survey of customers – which resulted in a large number of "highly satisfied" customer ratings but no useful information about how to make strategic decisions – would be reluctant to repeat the effort and expense. He didn't learn anything from that research that added to his existing knowledge of how customers perceive CPV, so why bother? Just as with customers, if the benefits don't outweigh the costs of buying or doing something, it makes little sense to do it.

It is natural for most managers to believe they know what the customer wants because, in many cases, they are in frequent and direct contact with that customer. They are talking to one another all the time, so what else is there to know?

Managers who regularly gather and use good marketplace information, however, know better. They know that there are at least five ways that their own customer information can betray them:

Filtered Information

Where did the information the manager is using actually come from? Perhaps it wasn't directly from the customer, but from a sales representative, or it was inferred from an incident or buying pattern. Or it might even have come directly from the customer, but customers don't always tell suppliers partial truths or the whole truth. They don't want to hurt the seller's feelings or engage in the inevitable debate that would ensue if they registered a complaint.

Some managers believe that gathering information about customer perspectives is the responsibility of the company's sales representatives because, after all, "it's their job to understand customers." While that may be partially true, information brought in by sales representatives is often faulty for two reasons. First, customers are sometimes reluctant to share information with salespeople, who they may view as adversaries in a negotiation process. Second, sales representatives have their own interests at stake in reporting information to their company. Old products are usually easier to sell than new products, for example, so sales representatives are not highly motivated to deliver information that supports a change in product specifications or features. We have even encountered situations where customers want *less* involvement with sales representatives, preferring written specifications and Internet ordering capabilities. Traditional sales representatives are unlikely to want to deliver that kind of information to their employer.

Managers who are using their own sources of customer information should carefully consider the possibility that their information has been filtered by the time it reaches them.

Biased Information

Information can become biased, or distorted, in many different ways. Perhaps the information applies well to one customer or segment of customers, but when used in connection with a different customer set it becomes misleading. Or, any number of research design and analysis errors can produce biased information.

In the early 1980s, when customer satisfaction measurement work was emerging, the major automobile manufacturers conducted studies on new car buyers to evaluate the effectiveness of their various dealerships. These buyers were provided survey forms by the manufacturer and asked to rate the service and support provided by the dealer. Because the results of the surveys were used to grade the dealerships, the dealers had a great interest in the results and took every step possible to make sure they were favorable. Stories of favorable "deals" and direct cash incentives being given to customers for the promise of a good report back to the manufacturer became widespread. Until these practices were discovered, however, the manufacturers thought that they were receiving useful information about what we call CPV. Biased information is insidious, because it looks so much like useful information.

Inaccurate Information

This information is just plain wrong. Perhaps a faded memory has damaged the information, or other circumstances have made what once was valuable information now into dangerous misinformation. Or a researcher simply asked the wrong question.

A simple consumer survey many years ago, in the middle of the Watergate scandal, asked the question, "Should President Nixon be impeached and removed from office?" Only 30 percent of the respondents to that question responded affirmatively. The conclusion from those results could easily have been interpreted as support for President Nixon to remain in office, and it probably was used in just that way by GOP pollsters at the time. When the question was posed in a different manner, however, the results were very different. To the question, "Should President Nixon be tried and removed from office if found guilty?" 57 percent (nearly twice as many) of the respondents said, "Yes." Getting accurate answers from market research is a tricky business. Everyone knows they have to "get their facts straight," but sometimes that's not easy to do.

Facts Get in the Way

Information based on fact is not always useful when dealing with customer perceptions. The manager might have the facts but might also be missing what's actually important – understanding CPV. There's a big difference between these two kinds of information.

A manufacturer of truck trailer hitches had introduced a new, maintenance-free fifth-wheel that was expected to revolutionize the way truck tractors and trailers were connected. The reduction in required maintenance provided the new product with a decided overall cost advantage, even though the purchase price was a little higher. Soon after its introduction, however, reports started coming in from the field that customers were experiencing difficulties in easily disconnecting the trailers. Drivers were reporting that the new hitch required additional manipulation of the tractor, causing extra time and inconvenience in what should have been a simple maneuver for the driver. The manufacturer's engineering team jumped all over the problem and found that, in fact, disconnection difficulties were actually less than with previous models. Fortunately, this company knew that their "facts" weren't as important as the customers' perceptions, however, and launched a major education effort in their marketplace to explain why their new product was, in fact, superior to previous products. That effort reversed the negative reputation that the product had been developing and saved the company's advantage.

The customer may not always be "right," but how the customer defines CPV or is likely to do, is always what's most important.

Bad Inferences from Good Data

The difference between "data" and "information" comes from analysis and inference. Turning data into information is a difficult task, requiring complete objectivity, disciplined expertise, and a lot of good judgment. Not many people, especially those in the middle of stressful situations, consistently do it very well.

For example, when customers are asked directly about prices, they'll usually suggest that the price is too high. That was the data that a pharmaceuticals company collected from its institutional customers about one of its leading products. It was accurate data, because those institutions, caught in the middle of the national crisis over rising health-care costs, could think about very little else. The inference from this information that these customers would only be satisfied if the company lowered its price, however, was not as accurate. The customers were actually complaining about the entire CPV balance scale and would respond favorably to any addition of a benefit and every reduction of a cost. When this company found a way to repackage their product into a size that reduced the institutions' overall cost of administering it to their patients, it had the same effect that lowering prices might have had. To have inferred that a price cut was necessary would have been a major misstep.

Marketplace information used in the strategic planning process must be just that – information – not data. Sometimes the information that management brings with it has not made that transition well.

Management thinking that they "know what the customer wants" when they're actually misinformed is common. The amount of time and the expense involved to thoroughly understand CPV sometimes explains why so little quality marketplace information is utilized in the strategic planning process. It's not easy to do.

The reason these obstacles must be overcome, however, is the high stakes involved in these important strategy decisions. Almost by definition, strategic decisions are those that result in major directional moves of a company. Sometimes, large amounts of money and human resources are being committed to a direction that will be difficult to change very quickly. Whether recognized or not, strategy decisions often come under the category of "bet your company" issues. To make decisions with less than all the possible available information about CPV usually makes very little sense.

THE CPV ENVIRONMENTAL SCAN

The first step in strategic planning processes of any kind, then, is the gathering and analysis of general information about the environment in which the company will compete. We call this the CPV Environmental Scan, because the effort should focus on how the various environmental factors influence and impact CPV.

A CPV Environmental Scan is a fishing expedition where the objective is to cover a lot of water. Because of the nature of this, it can be a very inefficient and ineffective undertaking if not done properly. Finding little or no information that has a major impact on the company's planning process might be a valid result, but too often that happens because the scan was not properly focused or conducted with the necessary research discipline. Sometimes it is appropriate to conduct a complete environmental scan as a foundation for a major strategic planning effort, especially where decisions about major changes in a company's direction are to be considered. In some cases, however, the scan can be focused on areas of major change impacting the company or known information shortfalls. Best of all, of course, is an ongoing scanning effort to match the ongoing nature of dynamic strategic planning. The CPV Learning System described in Chapter 11 is an example of how that can be accomplished.

Whether formal or informal, ad hoc or ongoing, a proper CPV Environmental Scan will seek out information from the following:

THE TARGET MARKET
THE TARGET CUSTOMER
EXPECTED COMPETITORS
THE EXTERNAL ENVIRONMENT
THE COMPANY ITSELF

Market Information

The attractiveness of a current or proposed market is usually the starting point for the strategic planning process. Even before customers or competitors or other components of a market are analyzed, the overall potential of the market for all participants is determined. This is accomplished by investigating these market factors:

CURRENT SIZE
PROJECTED SIZE
COSTS AND PROFITABILITY
KEY SUCCESS FACTORS

Current Size

The first step in evaluating a market, including estimating its current size, is deceptively difficult. The difficulty arises because in this first step what is really emerging is a definition of the target market itself. Decisions must be made to include or exclude various related offerings, substitute products, alternative solutions, etc. This process of precisely defining the market is often a fundamental step in the development of the company's strategy.

Once these definitional questions are resolved, the task of putting numbers to the current size estimate is usually relatively easy. The Federal government publishes an astounding quantity of statistics about the U.S. economy, often with enough specificity to aid in the market sizing exercise. Trade associations and publicly available research are also sources for this kind of information.

Projected Size

The next step in the process is to identify the key trends taking place in the market to adjust the current market size estimate and turn it into a projection. Identifying key trends is, of course, the challenge here. Projecting a potential market is almost always much more complicated than simply projecting historical figures using statistical techniques. Our world is rapidly changing in so many ways that discontinuities are the norm. Discontinuities are the "key trends" being sought.

According to a study described by David Aaker, Europeans buy only 25 percent as much breakfast cereal per person as do Americans.[6] Analysts have ascribed this difference to the lesser availability of shelf-stable milk products in Europe, making consumption of cereal and milk away from home less convenient. Product stability and safety is of particular concern to institutions, such as restaurants, schools, and day-care facilities. In estimating the potential market for breakfast cereal products in Europe, then, the likelihood of breakthrough practices in the packaging of milk products would play an important role. Historical U.S. cereal consumption statistics, population and lifestyle studies in Europe, as well as an evaluation of trends in milk products packaging would make up the elements for a useful near-term projection of the overall cereal market in Europe.

Costs and Profitability

The current cost structure of the industry, and the reason for it, are of vital interest to the strategic planner. Until recently, it was generally understood that a market would have to meet certain profit potential standards to be attractive.

At this writing, exceptions to this rule are the various Internet-based companies that are valued at billions of dollars but have never attained profitability. Amazon.com is currently the most infamous, having recorded more than $1.6 billion in revenues in its most recent accounting year and more than $390 million in losses. Critics have accused Amazon.com of "losing money on every book it ships." All of the many investors in this publicly funded company (recent market value of the company was $26 billion) are apparently betting that Amazon.com has some profitable cost structure in mind. Hopefully, it has something to do with attaining a large market share, because that is obviously what the company is focusing on at this time.

Amazon.com has all of the elements for a projected cost structure readily available. The costs of raw materials (books), handling (warehousing costs), distribution (shipping charges), customer service (call centers), and promotion (advertising) are easily obtained from analysis of traditional book selling and other mail order businesses. Time will tell if its desired cost structure can be attained.

Key Success Factors

Golfers "go to school" on players who try the putt before them. Watching the ball roll across the green is much easier than trying to imagine how the ball might roll. Companies who examine others' strategies and analyze what worked well and what didn't are taking advantage of a relatively inexpensive way to "go to school."

In the late 1980s, Schneider National, the nation's largest long-haul trucking company, decided that providing accurate load status information for its customers could be a strategic advantage. To do it right, the company decided to install a satellite-based tracking device in every one of its truck tractors. This was a huge gamble, because its fleet consisted of more than 10,000 tractors, and the tracking devices were not cheap. It executed its plan, however, and gained national recognition in the logistics industry as the leader in using technology to provide enhanced CPV. Not long after that, however, several of its smaller competitors came out with similar tracking capabilities and, now, virtually everyone in the industry has these devices. It must have been a much easier decision for those smaller companies, even though their investments were even more significant to them, because they had been able to "go to school" on Schneider's success.

Eventually, all of the key success factors in a market will become apparent to the rest of the industry, but the trick is to gain such information at an early stage when it is still useful. That requires a vigilant "ear to the ground" and, probably, a proactive research effort designed to track the significant events in an industry and the successes and failures of the main players.

Customer Information

The objective of using customer information for strategic planning is to identify individual or groups of customers with needs that the company can profitably serve. The process is called market *segmentation*. It has two important parts to it. The first is to decide how these groups should be defined, and the second is to be able to recognize members of each group when they're encountered in the marketplace.

Market segmentation is one of the most important elements of a strategic plan. That's why we've dedicated the entire next chapter of this book to it. Here, however, we'll explore the underlying information needs for segmentation, namely the understanding of customer needs and motivations.

Kotler has described the sequence of actions taken by customers, both consumers and business buyers.[7] As shown in Figure 4.2, those sequences contain somewhat different terminology, but are very similar in their progression. The objective of the Customer Information phase of the environmental scan is to determine *trends* about the perceptions of target customers that might alter the way they define CPV and approach each of these buying steps.

Problem Recognition

Demographic, social, and technological trends certainly impact cus-

Figure 4.2 - Summary of Customer Actions

Consumers	Business
Problem recognition	Problem recognition
Information search	General need description Product specification
Evaluation of alternatives	Supplier search Proposal solicitation
Purchase decision	Supplier selection Order specification
Post-purchase behavior	Performance review

tomers' needs. For example, the aging population in the United States is a well documented phenomenon that impacts nearly every business. While consumer eyeglass manufacturers are busy increasing their attention to bifocals and stylish reading glasses, industrial concerns are becoming more sensitive to the size of the typeface they use for technical documentation. The less obvious demographic trends (such as shifting geographical populations, economic buying power, and the profitability of various consumer industries) are equally important to strategic planning. Suppliers to the health-care industry today, for example, must be cognizant of the economic turmoil being experienced to understand what problems customers will be seeking to solve when defining CPV.

Information Search

Developments in information technology lead the way in helping to understand how customers are searching for solutions to their needs. Companies in every industry are struggling to determine what role their presence on the Internet will play and how to capitalize on this relatively new source of information for everyone. Understanding the customers' level of connectivity to the Internet, as well as being able to predict how that connectivity and utilization will evolve, is fundamental to many of the strategic decisions most companies are facing. When customers search for professional services such as lawyers and consultants, for example, where are they likely to look for those service providers? One young company, PENGroup of Boulder, Colorado, is betting they will go to the Internet. While many people believe that these kinds of personal services are less applicable to the benefits of e-commerce, PENGroup is investing millions of dollars in the creation of their website and the infrastructure to support it.

Evaluation of Alternatives

The question of which CPV attributes customers will evaluate to select their purchases, and how they will make those evaluations, is the most important of the competitively-oriented customer trends. A new oil production crisis might, for example, change the attributes that consumers use in selecting motor vehicles. Evaluating the likelihood that such a crisis would occur is probably an important strategic planning step for makers of the popular sport utility vehicles, which have, to date, escaped the government's gas mileage regulations. For a different example, the growing Spanish-speaking population in the United States will likely have significant impact on most companies. They'll find it increasingly important, for example, to provide bilingual instructions with their products and to devote more of their promotion budgets to using that language.

Purchase Decision

The trends underlying how customers will select their suppliers and commit to purchases are critical to understand. The technology revolution led by the growth of the Internet appears to be key in predicting how this buying step may occur in the future. Many companies are investing heavily in creating *communities* of customers at their websites to facilitate transactions and reward loyalty. Electronic payment processors, such as CheckFree of Atlanta, Georgia, are betting that the trend toward a cashless economy will continue and not be seriously interrupted by a rash of fraud or accounting errors that might scare potential customers away. And, of course, predicting consumer confidence in the continued health of the global economy is fundamental to every company's strategic planning process.

Post-Purchase Behavior

This is simply a fancy term for customer satisfaction. Understanding what macro-trends are likely to influence the level of post-purchase customer satisfaction, however, is not a simple matter. For example, will most customers *expect* free telephone customer support for all of their household purchases because they've experienced it with their personal computer equipment? The producers of Butterball brand turkeys apparently think so, because they're already providing it on Thanksgiving Day, even after the turkeys have been sold and, sometimes, carved.

Gathering macro-level customer information leading to an understanding of CPV may involve nearly all of the research methods available. Primary research, in the form of focus groups, in-depth interviews, carefully constructed surveys, and anthropological observations are sometimes appropriate. These methods are relatively expensive, however, so secondary sources of this kind of information should usually be exhausted first. The government, industry associations, academic institutions, and libraries are valuable sources for information of this nature, with the major challenge being to find and interpret it. As with all research, danger exists in poorly designed and executed efforts that fail to produce useful management information. The *major* danger, however, is that management will conclude that the information simply doesn't exist and, thereafter, decide not to pursue it.

Competitive Information

As discussed in Chapter 2, CPV is a relative matter. Every customer purchase decision results from the customer comparing the value of one offering against the value of his alternatives. (Alternatives consist of competitors' offerings, substitutes, or buying nothing at all.) As obvious as this point is, it is very important. Therefore, the strategic planner must understand and anticipate the customer's alternatives. This is accomplished by understanding what causes the customer to choose to buy anything at all (as discussed in the preceding section), and direct investigation into the intentions and capabilities of competitors.

There are, however, two very important steps in gathering competitor information: (1) identifying the competitors, and (2) learning about those competitors. The first step is every bit as important as the latter, and it is too often overlooked in the haste of making strategy.

Identifying Competitors

The traditional approach to identifying competitors has centered around understanding *industries*. This approach is based on looking for companies with common strategies, target markets, capabilities, and objectives. Most managers can easily name their competitors when they are defined in this way. The problem with this approach, of course, is that it ignores the customer viewpoint. And it is, after all, *only* the customer who defines CPV and, therefore, who will be considered to be a seller's competitors.

From their slowness to react to the new competition, it seems clear that Barnes & Noble, Waldenbooks, and Borders would have named each other as competitors in an industry analysis but missed Jeff Bezos, the founder of Amazon.com, as their real competition. A few years ago, the Bell operating companies would probably have failed to name the cable television giant, Time Warner, as a direct competitor for their "last mile" access to the nation's residential community. New competitors are coming from every direction in most industries today.

The Amazon.com example, however, highlights that customers often cannot directly describe who the competitors are or will be. It is unlikely that many consumers could have been any more farsighted than were the major bookstore chains in seeing Bezos' solution to their needs coming. But thoroughly understanding book purchasers' CPV, combined with vigilance about the Internet, might have enabled the bookstore chain companies to have been better prepared. The customer couldn't have told them about Amazon.com specifically, but she could have told them that she often is just looking for a title and wants it quickly at a low price. She might also have told them that she'd appreciate recommendations for new books based on her past purchases, and that she'd enjoy reading the reviews of books offered by other customers just like her. They might, then, have seen Bezos coming.

So, the primary source for identifying competitors is the customer. It is always wise to check the customer's perspective about where he would find alternatives or substitutes to a proposed strategic plan.

Understanding Competitors

When competitors, both present and potential, are identified, it is a relatively easy task to learn about them and try to understand them. The objective, of course, is to anticipate what competitors will do in reaction to another company's strategic plans.

Figure 4.3 provides a list of the issues of interest about most competitors.[8] The extent to which valuable information in each of these categories can be obtained is a matter of the effort and cost invested. The amount that is "right" will, of course, vary for each company and each strategic situation confronting it.

A better understanding of the current and past strategies of the Japanese automakers in the 1970s might have allowed the U.S. Big Three to avoid some of the damage done to them. For many months, the American companies remained confident that their customers wouldn't accept the lower-cost, "foreign" cars being introduced here by Honda, Toyota, and Datsun. In hindsight, it can easily be seen that a better appreciation for the Japanese strategies of continuous

Figure 4.3 - Information about Competitors

- Current and past strategies
- Size, growth, profitability
- Organization and culture
- Entry and exit barriers
- Relative cost structure
- Image and positioning strategy
- Strengths and weaknesses
- Opportunities and threats

quality improvement and long-term investments in new markets should have put the American companies on high alert.

Secondary data sources (newspapers, trade journals, specialized websites, etc.) are usually the most important sources of information about competitors. Public companies, in particular, are required by U.S. securities laws to make available a vast amount of information that is of strategic significance to their competitors about both their own successes and problems. In addition, primary research can be conducted with the competitors' customers and suppliers to augment the information available from secondary sources. In some cases, observational studies can be conducted on or around the competitor's premises to determine apparent volume levels, employment trends, etc. Sometimes ethical questions arise concerning investigations into competitors' activities, but experience has proven that a vast amount of useful information is available from entirely legitimate sources.

External Information

Examination of the environment in which a market exists, external information, moves the strategic planner one step away from the current realities of that marketplace. It is an important one step, however, because it provides insights into factors that potentially could have significant impact on how that market ultimately evolves and defines CPV. Most analysts organize these external factors into four major categories: technological, governmental/regulatory, economic, and cultural.[9]

Technological

Recently, technology advances seem to be a primary topic of conversation. Computer science, communications, medical, aerospace, and pure science breakthroughs are occurring everyday at a seemingly increasing rate. For our purposes, the trick is to keep track of these advances and apply them in strategic planning for both defensive and offensive competitive advantage.

There is certainly more art than science to projecting the application of technology advances to a specific business. A disciplined tracking system can be established, recording the advances as they occur and then presenting a timeline of advances to the planning team. This often helps the planner make the necessary projections and facilitates the "what if" thinking that sometimes leads to valuable insights. The major difficulty in doing this is in drawing the line between what are relevant technological advances and what are not. Drawing the line too closely to current offerings and capabilities might limit creative thinking, but going too far afield is simply confusing.

Governmental and Regulatory

The potential for regulation exists for some aspect of most every business. As the business world crosses more political boundaries each day, the number of potential regulatory jurisdictions increases and makes the planner's job ever more difficult.

The issue of jurisdiction is at the heart of one of the most complex taxation issues that has arisen for many years. This is the question of how retail transactions on the Internet should be taxed. To date, state and local governments hold sales and use tax authority, with "interstate commerce" exempted from such taxes. Because of the huge and growing value of retail transactions on the Internet, nearly all of it "interstate," that taxing structure is now under active review. It seems inevitable that either an acceptable method of imposing sales and use taxes on Internet sales will have to be developed, or another form of taxation will have to be created to replace the lost tax revenues the local governments are experiencing.

Tracking and understanding such developments is an important responsibility of the strategic planner. For example, for the sake of its investors, one would hope that Amazon.com's targeted cost structure (discussed previously) includes the possibility that it may someday lose the tax-favored status of its retail transactions.

Economic

A few decades ago, tracking economic trends was as simple as predicting next year's rate of U.S. currency inflation. That's no longer true, of course. While many in this country continue to watch the Fed's efforts to contain inflation, the globalization of so many markets makes international economics a topic of even greater concern.

At this writing, the U.S. is experiencing another run-up of the price of crude oil from the oil producing cartels of the world. Intensive international negotiation is apparently underway to influence the cartel's decisions about future production capacities, and Congress is examining its own taxing policies on refined petroleum products. Meanwhile, the transportation industries are facing economic conditions that they haven't seen since the late 1970s. Major strategic decisions are being revisited by companies in these industries.

Tracking these global economic trends is not too difficult – government agencies spend billions of dollars every year producing reams of data on every aspect of the world's business affairs. What is difficult is projecting futures and turning the data into information that is useful to a specific business for the planning process. Scenario planning (a full explanation of which is beyond the scope of this book) is particularly useful in attempting to make sense of this important information in the planning process.[10]

Cultural

Identifying the major trends in our society's likes and dislikes is the stuff of "futurists." John Naisbitt made a business of himself nearly 20 years ago when he published his first book, *Megatrends*, which included Naisbitt's list of his top 10 major trends.[11] Other authors, such as Faith Popcorn, have also contributed insights about major changes in our culture. These sources provide valuable "food for thought" for strategic planners.

To make practical sense of major trends and their impact on a specific business probably requires the process of reducing them to a few important trends. For example, in Naisbitt's second book, *Megatrends 2000*,[12] megatrend number two was "a renaissance in the arts." That was probably of much less importance to Nike, when that company was built to capitalize on a global supply chain, than was Naisbitt's sixth megatrend, "the rise of the Pacific Rim." For Nike, it was particularly important to track the emergence of the Pacific Rim to identify where and how to source the manufacture of its products. That manufacturing capability has been a cornerstone of Nike's strategy over time.

Internal Information

The final piece of the CPV Environmental Scan puzzle leading to effective strategic planning is information about the company's own performance. Certainly, every company must evaluate its successes and failures to identify where its most likely future opportunities lie.

Traditionally, these internal measures of success have been financial. Sales records are scrutinized to determine what the company has been most successful in selling. Sometimes, profitability analyses have been introduced, but these are usually fraught with problems resulting from traditional product-oriented accounting methods. Most companies know what the fully allocated profitability of each of its products is, but few understand how much each of its customer relationships is worth or which of them is profitable. And very few companies know how well they are currently performing in the areas that are necessary to deliver value to its customers.

Consultants Robert Kaplan and David Norton provided the necessary tools for internal performance measurement for strategic planners with their now famous Balanced Scorecard.[13] The Scorecard's value was in its urging that multiple measures, mostly those beyond financial measures, be used to evaluate a company's own performance. Specifically, it prescribes that there should be a measure for financial performance, another for performance from the customer's perspective, a third for measuring the performance of critical internal processes, and the last for indicating the company's investments in its employees. The Balanced Scorecard is both intuitively appealing and surprisingly useful.

Our primary interest, of course, is in the measurement of a company's performance from the customer's perspective to understand CPV. Specifically, Kaplan and Norton propose that a company evaluate its market share trend, rates of new customer acquisitions, customer retention rates, customer satisfaction measures, and customer profitability analyses. All of this information, except for the customer satisfaction measures, comes from the company's own accounting records. Certainly, some careful analysis beyond what is traditionally done with accounting data is necessary to make this information useful to the strategic planner, but many companies by now have developed, or found outside, some capabilities to do that. Customer satisfaction measures have also become a part of nearly every company's internal data set, but many are sorely lacking in credibility and usefulness. We examine ways to correct those deficiencies in Chapter 11.

USING CPV IN STRATEGIC PLANNING

To a large degree, understanding CPV and the environmental information necessary to do so for strategic planning purposes is a forest-for-the-trees problem. In their haste to get to more of the specifics and more of the issues within their own control, many managers fail to allocate the time and resources necessary to take a good look at the bigger picture. The fear that looking at the forest will produce only vague and generic information of little value can be resolved by focusing the effort on understanding CPV.

SUMMARY

Every business conducts strategic planning, whether it does so formally in periodic meetings, or informally on the work floor, or something in between. What's important is that the company is *predicting* what should be done to *induce customers to buy* at a profitable price. That being the case, it should be valuable for every company to know as much as possible about CPV and the environmental issues that impact it.

There have been many different concepts introduced regarding strategic planning and most of them have something valuable to offer. The common denominator, however, is maintaining a focus on CPV in any of these planning approaches. When that focus is lost, the entire strategic planning process becomes suspect.

A surprising number of managers fail to gather and incorporate an understanding of CPV into their strategic planning process. Usually, that's because they either lack the time or money to do the required research, or they simply think that they already know what the customer wants. Unfortunately, these managers are usually being misled because the customer information they are using is filtered, biased, inaccurate, confused by facts, or they are simply making bad inferences from the good data they do have.

What is necessary as a foundation for effective strategic planning is a CPV Environmental Scan. Such a scan incorporates information gathered from five sources: the general marketplace, customers, competitors, government and regulators, and internal performance data. Gathering and analyzing all of that information requires a significant effort and awareness of various techniques and pitfalls to avoid. Success in doing so, however, leads to more effective strategic planning.

REFERENCES

[1] See Clayton M. Christensen, "Making Strategy: Learning by Doing," *Harvard Business Review*, November-December 1997, pg. 141-156. Also, Henry Mintzberg, "The Rise and Fall of Strategic Planning," *Harvard Business Review*, January-February 1994, pg. 107-114.

[2] For additional resources on strategic planning, see Dan R.E. Thomas, *Business Sense: Exercising Management's Five Freedoms*, (New York, Free Press, 1993); Henry Mintzberg, *The Rise and Fall of Strategic Planning: Reconceiving Roles for Planning, Plans, Planners*, (New York, Free Press, 1993); Liam Fahey and Robert M. Randall, editors, *The Portable MBA in Strategy*, (New York, John Wiley & Sons, 1994); Michael E. Porter, *The Michael Porter Trilogy: Competitive Strategy, Competitive Advantage, the Competitive Advantage of Nations*, (New York, Free Press, 1998).

[3] Michel Robert, *Strategy Pure & Simple: How Winning CEOs Outthink Their Competition*, (New York, McGraw-Hill, 1993).

[4] Gary Hamel and C.K. Prahalad, "Strategy as Stretch and Leverage," *Harvard Business Review*, March-April, 1993, pg. 75-84.

[5] Alfred P. Sloan, Jr., *My Years with General Motors*, (Garden City, Doubleday, 1963).

[6] David A. Aaker, *Strategic Market Management*, (New York, John Wiley & Sons, 1998), pg. 80.

[7] Adapted from Philip Kotler, *Marketing Management: The Millennium Edition*, (Saddle River, Prentice-Hall, 1999), pg. 179 and 203; and Roger Blackwell, Paul Miniard, and James Engel, *Consumer Behavior, 9th Edition*, (New York, Harcourt, 2001).

[8] Adapted from Aaker, pg. 58-77.

[9] Aaker, pg. 99.

[10] See Alan S. Cleland, *The Market Value Process: Bridging Customer and Shareholder Value*, (San Francisco, Jossey-Bass, 1996), Chapter 4.

[11] John Naisbitt, *Megatrends: Ten New Directions Transforming our Lives*, (New York, Warner Books, 1982).

[12] John Naisbitt and Patricia Aburdene, *Megatrends 2000*, (New York, Avon Books, 1990).

[13] Robert S. Kaplan and David P. Norton, *The Balanced Scorecard: Translating Strategy Into Action*, (Boston, Harvard Business School Press, 1996).

CHAPTER 5

CPV and Market Segments

Avis CEO Joseph Vittoria has described the companies in his own industry as "probably the toughest competition in the world."[1] During the last five years, Avis and Alamo have lost millions of dollars. Ford, a major investor in Budget Rent-A-Car, wrote down its investment by $700 million. Only Hertz has reported consistent profits, although it is believed those come primarily from its European operations and an equipment-leasing business. So, why would anyone want to be in the rent-a-car business? And if one did, how could he possibly expect to make money?

The company that has done that consistently for 42 years is Enterprise Rent-A-Car. A privately-held company based in St. Louis, Enterprise was originally a car leasing company in the basement of a Cadillac dealer. Five years into that business, founder Jack Taylor responded to customer requests for rental cars by starting with a fleet of 17 vehicles. In 1996, it officially surpassed Hertz in the size of its fleet and became the world's largest rent-a-car company. By the late 1990s, it managed a rental fleet of nearly 500,000 vehicles from almost 4,000 rental offices and reached $4.7 billion in total revenues. Current CEO Andrew Taylor, son of the founder, likes to point out that there is an Enterprise rental office within a 15-minute drive of 90 percent of the U.S. population.

How did Enterprise elbow its way to the top of the heap

of powerful companies including Hertz, Avis, National, Budget, Alamo, Dollar, and Thrifty? Actually, it reached the top by not doing any elbowing at all! Enterprise defined a unique target market consisting of prospects who (1) need a car because of an accident, mechanical repair or theft, or (2) want to take a short business or leisure trip, or have a different car for a special occasion.[2] Ignoring the obvious $9 billion airport rental car market, it grew to a $5 billion company by defining its own target market.

The company's unique market is attractive for more reasons than simply avoiding the competition at the airport. The personal car replacement market provides Enterprise with:[3]

- *Cheaper sites. Most of Enterprise's office locations are in suburban strip shopping centers in the residential neighborhoods. Meanwhile, airport rental companies are paying up to 10 percent of their gross revenue to their airport landlords.*
- *Longer rental periods. Enterprise's typical rental period is 10 to 12 days, the length of time it usually takes for their customer's own car to be repaired at the body shop. It is thought that the airport rental companies usually rent for three days at a time. This means Enterprise's fleet is on-the-road, generating rental revenue, more of the time.*
- *More consistent demand. Enterprise points out that fender benders happen all of the time, in boom times and in recession. They are not affected much when discretionary travel is on the decline.*

Interestingly, Enterprise has recently established rental facilities at 95 of the top 100 airports in the continental United States, but not to take on the "big guys" directly. Rather, Enterprise says its loyal customers from the own-car-replacement market have requested the travel-related service. The company intends to continue to focus its attention on its unique market segment. As evidence of that, it announced a promo-

tion of its own. Instead of the typical frequent-travel program of the traditional airport rental companies, Enterprise is conducting a contest to gather the best travel war-stories from inexperienced travelers. Ever true to its own target market, Enterprise has claimed trademark rights to its InFrequent Flyer Rewards Contest.[4]

WHAT IS MARKET SEGMENTATION?

Focusing on a portion of a larger market is something that is always being done, whether or not the manager is aware of it. Some companies, of course, recognize that market segmentation is one of the first steps in a strategic plan. Others, however, are employing market segmentation on an implicit basis when they first decide what features to include in their offering, where to provide it, and how to promote it. Unfortunately, these managers are probably making many wrong and inconsistent decisions because of their failure to first fully understand their market segmentation opportunities and the impact they have on the rest of their marketing mix decisions.[5]

Even the manager who bravely proclaims that he is a "mass merchandiser" and refuses to target less than all of the population is actually segmenting the market every time he makes a marketing decision. Because, in the long run, all resources are scarce, certain parts of the total market are being prioritized when the manager selects a store location, decides on meta-tags for his website, or puts promotional material into the mail.

This implicit segmentation is so often wrong because it is based on decisions made about the wrong issues. Often, companies evaluate their own strengths and weaknesses and then seek customers that might match up with those capabilities. While that may be a necessary part of the strategic planning process, it is not the first step in segmenting markets. Rather, it is more important to first understand customers' needs and Customer Perceived Value (CPV).

A small telephone equipment company, for example, concluded that although their equipment was very sophisticated, they lacked the service capabilities needed to serve very large companies. Therefore, they targeted the new SOHO (small-office, home-office) market where, they reasoned, they could dazzle these prospects with the features and capabilities of their line of equipment. Unfortunately, they had not taken the time to fully understand this potential market segment from the customer's viewpoint. Sales never took off because these prospects did not feel the need for sophisticated features. Consequently, these prospects certainly could not justify the higher price tag this equipment carried. Generally speaking, this market segment was quite satisfied with the simple, inexpensive systems available from Radio Shack.

To continue this discussion, then, we offer this definition:

> **Market Segmentation** – *the identification of groups of buyers with differing views of Customer Perceived Value who will, therefore, likely respond differently to different offerings or marketing strategies.*

The significance of this definition is the focus on customer perceptions as the basis for segmentation, rather than basing segmentation solely on differences in a company's capabilities or shortcomings as a supplier.[6] Such internal strengths and weaknesses might drive which segments are most attractive to a company, but they do not define what the market segments are or how they are likely to behave.

LEVELS OF SEGMENTATION

Most experts agree that there are four basic levels of segmentation. These levels constitute a continuum from the most inclusive to the most exclusive:

MASS MARKETING

SEGMENT MARKETING

NICHE MARKETING

INDIVIDUAL MARKETING

Mass Marketing

Some companies have, in the past, attempted to make an offering to everyone. Coca-Cola, beginning in 1886, sold their single product in a 6.5-ounce bottle and made their brand image ubiquitous throughout the United States. Clearly, this worked very well and successfully established Coke as the best selling soft drink in the world. In more recent years, however, this strategy has made way for products and promotional campaigns targeted at more narrow segments of the market. Now, for the weight-conscious there is Diet-Coke, for the health-conscious there is Caffeine-Free Coke, for the sports enthusiast there is Powerade, and for non-cola drinkers Coca-Cola distributes Sprite, Citra, Barq's, Mellow Yellow, Surge, and many other soft drinks. Coca-Cola's market segments are clearly huge, but they are also distinct and targeted.

The attractiveness of true mass marketing is that it does not eliminate any part of a market from the attention of the marketer. Aggressive entrepreneurs are often reluctant to declare their segmented market focus out of fear of missing an opportunity with an excluded market segment. The failure to admit a narrow focus, however, has usually resulted in wasted resources and the negative effects of diffused marketing efforts.

Segment Marketing

One step more focused than mass marketing, segment marketing identifies large groups of prospects from the total market and separates those groups into segments. Coca-Cola, as described above, has evolved to a segment marketing strategy.

The advantage of segment marketing is that it provides a degree of customization in the offering to different, identifiable groups within a total market.[7] Usually, this is done by offering a "basic" offering to everyone, with "options" targeted at different segments. The major airlines exhibit this approach by offering everyone a seat on their scheduled flights, carrying up to two pieces of luggage in the plane's cargo space, and a free soft drink on board. For the segment of travelers who value them, they also offer alcoholic beverages and, on longer flights, an in-flight movie for a small extra charge. For the segment of travelers who value greater space, service, and dignity, they offer First-Class service. For the segment of travelers who travel most frequently, they offer free flights.

Segment marketing is under attack, however, as customer demands grow and more customers expect even more personalized service than segment marketing offers.

Niche Marketing

An even more focused approach to target market identification is niche marketing. Here, more specific groups are identified from within the segment as having similar buying needs, characteristics, or behaviors that are distinct from the others. While this continual narrowing of target markets reduces the apparent total size of the market, it facilitates greater focus in all of the company's activities.

Enterprise Rent-A-Car, described earlier in this chapter, is a master niche marketer. Cleveland-based Progressive Insurance has also done quite well by focusing on a narrow segment of its potential market.[8] Although it has recently expanded its offerings to become a "full line" insurance provider, its roots were in providing expensive, "nonstandard" coverage to drivers who had poor driving records. Although nonstandard insurance accounts for only 15 percent of the total automotive insurance industry, Progressive became the country's fifth largest auto insurer, largely on its niche marketing approach.[9]

Niche marketing is just one step away from the most extremely focused of the segmentation strategies.

Individual Marketing

The ability of companies to *profitably* deal with customers on an individual basis is the primary constraint to the use of an individual marketing strategy. Otherwise, every marketer would like to satisfy the needs of each individual customer on an individual basis.

In its truest sense, national account marketing as practiced by many industrial firms is the best example of individual marketing. At a major computer software development company, for example, two well-paid professionals are assigned to serve only five large customers. These professionals, or account executives, are dedicated to uncovering and understanding the needs of these few customers and then ensuring that their company delivers appropriate solutions. If the software needed by one of these customers isn't currently "on the shelf," the company will assign software analysts and programmers to develop it. Usually, each solution delivered by the company is individually negotiated, priced, and evaluated with the customer.

Consultants Don Peppers and Martha Rogers became famous by coining the term, "one-to-one marketing." This concept is related, but different from what we are here calling individual marketing. Both are based on the objective of meeting the unique needs of individual customers. Individual marketing, however, accomplishes this by creating and delivering offerings on a completely customized basis for each customer. It is always a "job shop" type of approach. One-to-one marketing, on the other hand, contemplates the creation of capabilities and processes to adapt basic offerings to the needs of different customers. The economics of one-to-one marketing are very different from those of individual marketing, thereby allowing the former to be applied to market segments and niches where individual marketing cannot be applied.

Peppers and Rogers described a program conducted by MCI to promote its use of customized solutions for individual business customers.[10] The Proof Positive program was developed to ensure that each customer was utilizing the best possible rate structure available from MCI. The program involved proactively contacting each customer, an analysis of that customer's telephone usage patterns, and the determination of the customer's current rate. With that information, the MCI marketer analyzed the company's array of rates and set the customer up with whatever structure minimized the customer's long-term costs. This program is impressive as an example of one-to-one marketing. But notice that it was still based on segment marketing to business customers.

SEGMENTING ON CPV

Professor Roger Best of the University of Oregon refers to a common problem in segmenting markets as "The Demographic Trap."[11] This occurs when managers use demographic information, which is usually readily available, to define their target markets. For example, minivan manufacturers might characterize their target market as "married couples, 30 to 40 years old, living in the suburbs." It is relatively easy to find individuals that meet these demographic criteria. It is probably not, however, the best effort those manufacturers could make at defining their optimal target market.

What all marketers should strive to do is to identify prospective customers who are the most likely to actually buy their product. Identifying those prospects requires understanding what makes people buy things. And, what makes people buy things is their perception of CPV. It is not the couple's age of 30 to 40 years old that puts them in the market to buy a minivan – it is the benefits of size and capacity that such a vehicle offers for easily transporting a growing family. It is not their suburban address that causes them to shop for a minivan – it is the benefit of having a private vehicle to get places when public transportation is not readily available or commonly used. Understanding CPV is the real basis for effective market segmentation.

It is often helpful to look for fundamental forces that create or influence the way customers define CPV. Professor Best identifies three categories of such forces that shape the views of both consumer and business-to-business CPV (Figure 5.1).

Demographics include the familiar matters of age, income, marital status, etc. Similarly, the business-to-business equivalent, firmographics, includes issues such as sales volume, number of employees, SIC code, etc. Notice that these are considered issues that might *influence* how customers define CPV – they do not provide the definitions. There are many 30- to 40-year-old marrieds out there who wouldn't consider driving a minivan.

Lifestyle and corporate culture are analogous factors that sometimes influence how CPV is defined by consumers and companies. Consumer lifestyle issues include attitudes, values, interests, and

Figure 5.1 - Forces that Shape CPV

Consumer CPV	Business CPV
Demographics	Firmographics
Lifestyle	Corporate culture
Usage	Usage

opinions. Corporate culture represents matters such as organizational structure, growth orientation, entrepreneurial inclination, etc. A typical high-tech growth company will likely value supplier innovation, for example, as a more important benefit on their CPV balance scale than would a more conservative, mature company.

Usage behaviors are common to both the consumer and business-to-business sectors in Best's model. These are such factors as how much of a product they use, when they use it, or how often they think about buying it. For example, every large steel mill uses more electricity than does any large insurance company. Two very different companies such as these will construct different CPV models, with different benefit and cost attributes on the balance scale, for the same electric utility supplier.

As discussed above, demographics often play a major role in *identifying* market segments. It is important to remember, however, that the objective of that identification is to group the markets according to how they are likely to perceive CPV. Sometimes demographics work for that purpose, but sometimes they do not and going beyond demographics to identify group CPV perceptions is usually very productive. It would make sense if minivan manufacturers, for example, don't actually seek out 35-year-olds as much as they do those families who are currently buying baby diapers.

THE MARKET SEGMENTATION PROCESS

Effectively identifying relevant market segments is not as easy as it first appears to be. What makes it difficult is that market segments must be based on customer perception of CPV and, as we have discussed already, CPV exists only in the minds of the customers. Getting inside those minds is the hard part.

There are seven steps in the market segmentation process, as shown in Figure 5.2.[12]

Figure 5.2 - Steps in Segmenting Markets
_____

1. **Determine CPV-based segments**
    Group customers into segments based on similar definitions of CPV.
2. **Decide upon segment identifiers**
    For each CPV-based segment, determine which demographics & firmographics, lifestyle & culture factors, and use behaviors make the segments distinct and actionable.
3. **Evaluate segments for attractiveness**
    Determine the overall attractiveness of each segment based on company-specific criteria.
4. **Select segments for targeting**
    Determine which segments will be pursued with a unique segment strategy.
5. **Develop segment positioning strategy**
    For each segment, create a CPV-based "value proposition" and unique marketing mix strategy.
6. **Test segment strategy**
    Present the unique marketing mix strategy to target customers to determine effectiveness and possible improvements.
7. **Implement segment strategy**
    Refine the marketing mix strategy and roll it out.
_____

1. Determine CPV-based Segments

The first step is to identify the various needs of the overall target market. There is no way to do this other than to conduct high-quality, primary market research. Managers may think they know what customers want but, to some degree or another, they are often wrong about it. In the absence of good market research data, the information managers use is often subject to error, filtering, bias, and incorrect inferences. In addition, customers' needs are continually changing. CPV is, as we have discussed, a moving target that requires vigilance and perseverance to be accurately understood.

Several research techniques exist that help one understand CPV for market segmentation purposes. Observing prospective customers' behavior in real-life settings can provide key insights into understanding their perceptions of CPV. For example, a supplier to the nursing home industry hired researchers to observe how their existing product was being used. They determined from this work that there were some nursing homes where the training of the resident caregivers was inadequate and the products were being used improperly. This was not true in all cases, however, as workers in other homes were well trained and knew how to use the products properly. The importance of supplier-provided training and field support on the CPV balance scale of these customers, therefore, varied greatly between these two types of nursing homes. That was a key finding in deciding how training would be provided in conjunction with other product offerings.

Research experiments can be constructed to help managers discover the relative importance of the benefits and costs of CPV. For example, alternative versions of potential product offerings can be presented and reactions to the alternatives analyzed. This approach is commonly used to determine the importance of price in the CPV equation for consumer products. Other features of the offering can also be evaluated through carefully designed research experiments.

Most commonly, focus groups and surveys are used in the early stage of understanding CPV. Focus groups, or other exploratory research techniques such as in-depth interviews, are used to begin to identify CPV attributes and to learn about the scope and language to be used in succeeding descriptive research. That descriptive research work, usually involving surveys of some kind, is then used to clarify the issues and make more definitive conclusions about which attributes appear on the CPV balance scale and their relative importance on that scale.

Let's use as an example a small, private business college faced with the need to better understand the CPV of those who might enroll in its MBA program. From a survey of prospective students, it was determined that there were three basic sets of "needs" expressed:

> One group wanted the prestige of a nationally-known business school. They were less concerned about the curriculum of the institution they attended, but were willing to work hard to acquire the "correct" diploma.
>
> A second group was sincerely interested in being exposed to new information and hoped that their graduate school work would better prepare them for increasing management responsibilities on the job.
>
> A third group of prospective students only wanted to be able to say that they had an MBA. They wanted to minimize the effort it would take to earn the degree and did not care which school was on the diploma.

Clearly, the definitions of CPV for these three groups were very different. To attract these students, the school would have to address each group with a different marketing strategy. It was not clear at this point, however, how the school could identify which candidates fit into each of the three segments. We will pursue that in a moment.

2. Decide upon Segment Identifiers

In the course of the customer research in Step 1, it is important that as much information as possible be collected about the survey respondents. Such information is the basis of analysis for the researcher to determine how the various CPV-based segments can be readily identified in the marketplace. The easiest identification factors to use are often demographic – age, income, or address in consumer markets and industry, revenue, and number of employees in business markets. Such factors do not apply in every case, however, so all of the CPV influencers described in Figure 5.2 must be explored.

Take the case of particular financial investment products. While age is useful in categorizing certain financial investment needs, such as the need for capital appreciation for younger people and secure income sources for those who are retired, age does not help much when attempting to understand the risk orientation of stock market investors. We know that some people have been attracted to the flurry of Initial Public Offerings of new Internet-based companies. We also know that other people are averse to the risk these unproven stocks might carry with them.

The question becomes, for the CPV-based market segmenter, how to identify which potential investors will most likely fall into each of these categories. Age doesn't help. And neither do other commonly-used demographic data, such as income, marital status, family size, or geographical location. But some indicator is required, because without it there would be no way to identify the target market.

In fact, several criteria describe effective segment identifiers:

REPRESENTATIVE
MEASURABLE
ACCESSIBLE
ACTIONABLE

Representative

Segment identifiers must correlate well with distinguishable differences in CPV. Every company can be identified by an NAICS (formerly SIC) code. But NAICS codes fail to assist in identification when dealing with cross-industry offerings such as data communications services because they fail to accurately reflect the prospects' CPV in such areas.

Measurable

Segment identifiers must permit the identification and measurement of the related market segment. Left-handed people have unique needs in connection with certain physical activities, such as writing, eating, or playing golf. But serving that market segment has proven difficult because very little data are available for identifying lefties. There is a market segment, but it is difficult to identify its members.

Accessible

Segment identifiers must facilitate communication with and access to the targeted market segment. An electric utility company providing value-added services is most interested in those companies with critical continuous manufacturing processes that cannot afford to experience power outages. Knowing this is of minimal help, however, because there is no single place, such as a trade association or a cross-industry trade journal, to identify those companies.

Actionable

Segment identifiers must reflect customer needs that can be reasonably addressed by the company. Knowing only that women are more influential in the purchase of new automobiles than are men is not very useful because it is simply too large a market segment on which to develop effective marketing strategies. Similarly, a small manufacturer of mechanical fasteners might find that there are 20 different types of buyers for their products. That is too many for the company to address with separate marketing strategies.

Finding effective segment identifiers is somewhat of a fishing expedition. As much of the potential identifier information as possible is gathered during the CPV-based research effort so the analyst can search for correlations that will permit the identification of the segments. Figures 5.3 and 5.4[13] list the most common segment identifiers used in consumer markets and business markets, respectively.

Returning to our business school example, the school marketer requires indicators to help her distinguish between the three CPV-based segments previously identified: "prestige buyers," "knowledge buyers," and "diploma buyers." In the course of her market research, the school marketer collected the data shown in Figure 5.5. From these data, she was able to make the following analysis.

Figure 5.3 - Typical Segment Identifiers for Consumer Markets

Geographic

World region - which continent or part of the world?
Country region - which part of the country?
Market size - what is the population of the market?
Density - is it urban, suburban, or rural?
Climate - what's the prevailing weather?

Demographic

Age - what age group is targeted?
Gender - is the target primarily male or female?
Family size - how many in the household?
Household life cycle - is the target primarily single, married, with children, etc.?
Income - home much does the household spend?
Occupation - how do they make a living?
Education - what is the highest level of school completed?
Religion - what religion is practiced?
Race, nationality - what is the market's primary ethnic background?

Psychographic

Social class - what are relative spending patterns?
Lifestyle - what do they enjoy doing?
Personality - how do others see them behave?

Behavioral

Occasions - what events do they celebrate?
Benefits - what general benefits do they value the most?
User status - how experienced are they in using the offering?
Usage rate - how often do they use the offering?
Loyalty inclination - are they inclined to repeat purchases?
Readiness stage - how close are they to purchasing?
Attitude toward product - how important are the benefits of the offering to them?

Figure 5.4 - Typical Segment Identifiers for Business Markets

Demographic

    Industry - what industries define the target customers?

    Company size - how much revenue, number of employees, number of locations, etc.?

    Location - where do the companies operate?

Operating Variables

    Technology - what are the underlying technologies used by these companies?

    Frequency of use - how often are the offerings used?

    Customer capabilities - what is the level of expertise?

Purchasing Approaches

    Purchasing function organization - is the purchasing function centralized?

    Power structure - which function (engineering, marketing, finance) dominates purchasing decisions?

    Existing purchasing relationships - are these companies already our customers?

    General purchasing policies - do they use RFPs, competitive bids, sole sourcing, etc.?

    Purchasing criteria - what do they consider when evaluating alternative offerings?

Situational Factors

    Urgency - do they need immediate service or support?

    Specificity - do they need a specific offering or select from a range?

    Size of order - what are their typical order sizes?

Personal Characteristics

    Buyer-Seller similarities - are the values and business styles of the target customers similar to ours?

    Attitudes toward risk - what is their business risk orientation?

    Loyalty - what is their inclination to reward suppliers with repeat business?

Figure 5.5 - Example of Segment Data for a Business School

	Prestige	Knowledge	Diploma
Age	22-28	25-35	25-40
Employment	Student or underemployed	Employed or underemployed	Unemployed or underemployed
Employer	Large	Small or large	Small or large
Gender	M or F	M or F	M or F
Income >$40k	5%	60%	15%
Local alma mater	25%	80%	35%
Own residence	5%	50%	20%
Married	12%	65%	30%

The Prestige buyer is generally younger and more often still in undergraduate school. If employed, he is more likely working at a larger company. He probably is single and lives in an apartment. The Knowledge buyer, on the other hand, is a little more mature, probably married, and living in his first home. Perhaps related to his age, he is more affluent than the Prestige buyer. The Diploma buyer might be older than the other categories but is currently earning less and is not satisfied with his current job. He is more likely to have done his undergraduate work outside of the local area than is the Knowledge buyer. Gender is not a distinguishing factor between the three buyer types, and any of them might be working at a large, local company.

Although these indicators don't make identification of members of each of the three CPV types as easy as the marketer would probably wish for, a picture of each of the balance scales is beginning to emerge from these data. Now the market segmentation process can move on to the next step.

3. Evaluate Segments for Attractiveness

Having developed the beginning of a picture of each of the potential market segments, the next step is to evaluate each individual segment in regard to its potential to the business. This is done by gathering information about four characteristics of the market:

MARKET SIZE
PROJECTED MARKET SIZE
ACCESSIBILITY
COMPETITION

Market Size

To be of interest, the market segment must be of substantial size relative to the company evaluating it. Violation of this criterion has been referred to as the "bunny burger" fallacy. The legend is that a wannabe fast-food company desiring to distinguish itself from the established hamburger chains would do so by offering a burger made of meat from bunny rabbits. Few people would probably be interested in such a product, but the hope was that the company could dominate the small target market that would. Fortunately, no evidence of anyone ever actually adopting such a strategy has surfaced.

Projected Market Size

It is also necessary to evaluate the expected future size of the market segment to evaluate its attractiveness. Many software developers do this when they evaluate the attractiveness of targeting the market segment of Macintosh computer users. Although there are estimated to be more than 22 million current users of the Macintosh platform today, some people in the personal computer industry do not believe that number is likely to grow in proportion to those using Microsoft products on their PCs. Faced with limited resources, some software developers are focusing, instead, on the expected growth market.

Accessibility

A market segment is only attractive to a company if it can be readily addressed. Many entrepreneurs thought that the emergence of capitalism in the old Soviet Union created great opportunities and new markets. Most of them found, however, that the "old ways" of government intervention, poor market communication, and inadequate transportation for the populace were significant barriers to realizing the apparent potential of these markets. In some parts of the world, government regulation of numerous industries remains a real barrier to market accessibility.

Competition

Of course, the current suppliers in a market segment must be investigated to understand the likelihood of a successful entry by a new player. Enterprise Rent-A-Car found the own-car-replacement segment to be a much more attractive market in view of the dominance of the other rental car companies at the airports. Had it not, it would probably have been limited to off-site locations at the airports because the established rental car companies had already staked their claims to counter space and nearby parking.

The manner in which these criteria are applied to potential target market segment analysis varies from company to company. Some use an elaborate scoring system, weighting each factor and multiplying that weight by an assigned attractiveness score. This approach results in a single index number of "attractiveness" for each segment, which makes comparisons quite easy. Others, however, perform the evaluation on a more subjective basis. That's not inappropriate because the judgments necessary in evaluating segment attractiveness are inherently subjective.

4. Select Segments for Targeting

A more important consideration must be applied to each of the potential target market segments – the matter of "fit" with the company's own capabilities. Certainly, most companies would prefer to "lead with their strengths" and "avoid their weaknesses" to the extent the available target markets will permit them to do so.

Back to our business college example. The marketer evaluated the three potential market segments, the "prestige" buyer, the "knowledge" buyer, and the "diploma" buyer, for attractiveness. She believed that the size and growth prospects for the first two of the three segments were about equal – the MBA was showing few signs of diminishing in stature among young college graduates and many young graduates resided in the geographic area served by her school. She did speculate that the "diploma" buyer might be most receptive to "distance learning" programs conducted via the Internet, which would make that segment the largest of all by removing the traditional geographic boundaries of classroom teaching. She believed that accessibility was not a problem for any of the segments because her school was fully accredited and was, therefore, entitled to and capable of promoting its services to all candidates.

Competition was clearly different for each of the three potential segments. The pecking order of the "prestige" schools was clearly established and reinforced each year by various publications and surveys stating which schools were most highly regarded. The makeup of the graduate school faculties at each of the schools determined how effective their traditional classroom sessions were. And "distance learning" was a concept in an emerging stage, wide open for anyone with the resources to create the new capabilities it demanded.

The marketer then considered her own school's capabilities in connection with each of the three potential segments. Clearly, it was not currently one of the "prestige" schools most people would identify. It could probably attain such status, but it would require significant investment in its teaching resources and a national marketing campaign, both of which would take money and time to accomplish. She decided to eliminate the "prestige" buyer from consideration in developing her marketing plan.

This school was currently quite competent in its traditional education programs, so it was clear that the "knowledge buyer" should continue to be addressed. The growth potential for the "diploma buyer" was difficult to ignore, however. Her school had a good Information Technology orientation so it could probably develop the capability to be a significant player in the distance learning business. She decided that, with the approval of the school's administration and strategic leadership, she would make the "diploma buyer" her first priority and the "education buyer" her second. She would have to come up with a more flattering title, however, for her new, favorite target market segment.

5. Develop Segment Positioning Strategy

Every marketer understands the importance of a positioning strategy. Some academics refer to it as a USP – a Unique Selling Proposition. There is not much new to be added here about positioning strategies, except for one very important point that so many sophisticated managers sometimes forget:

> Each targeted market segment requires a *unique* positioning strategy.

Ultimately, a positioning strategy consists of the "4 Ps" of marketing strategy, namely product, promotion, pricing, and placement. The starting place for the positioning strategy is a summarized "value proposition." A value proposition describes the fundamental values that are to be delivered to address a specific market segment's CPV.

For our business school example, a value proposition for the "diploma buyer" segment might be:

> We provide a convenient method for busy people to obtain the MBA degree with a minimum of disruption to their lifestyle in the shortest possible time.

For the second priority segment, the "education buyer," the value proposition might be:

> We provide a quality educational program for successful managers to learn practical business skills from experienced faculty members and highly qualified classmates.

The significance of these two statements is, of course, the different actions that must be taken by the school to fulfill each of them. It can be readily seen that those actions will be very different, based on the value propositions of these two different segments. That is the significance of establishing a positioning strategy for each target market segment. Any manager who does not have a segment-specific value proposition for each of her target market segments is unprepared to implement any marketing strategy at all.

6. Test Segment Strategy

It has been a long time since we have mentioned the need to be talking to customers. It was only in Step 1 that market research was conducted to understand CPV and collect enough demographic and other data necessary for identifying the resulting CPV-based segments. In subsequent steps, segments were analyzed, evaluated for attractiveness, and prioritized for the company, and a positioning strategy was developed for each segment. Now it is time to go back out into the marketplace to verify our conclusions and test our decisions.

Professor Best suggests a technique known as "storyboarding" to test the company's value proposition against prospective customers' CPV. In this method, various value proposition statements are presented to a panel of customers who are asked to indicate their preferences. The links between segment characteristics and preferences for the various value propositions are then analyzed to see how close the company came to optimum solutions. Whether this method is used, or some other direct test with customers and prospects, it is essential that such a test be conducted.

7. Implement Segment Strategy

Is it necessary to say, "Now, go do it?" Yes, it is. As discussed in Chapter 3, most marketing failure is in the implementation steps. Many marketers know how to talk about segmentation (and the other issues addressed in this book) but have great difficulty in making anything different happen in their company as a result.

Segment-specific marketing strategies require segment-specific activities. An instruction manual for a household product must be printed in larger type if it is targeted at an elderly market segment. The promotional catalog for industrial fasteners must be printed on heavier weight paper if it is intended to withstand the shop-floor abuse of a heavy manufacturing market segment. The health-food products of a pharmaceutical manufacturer must be made available through food distributors if that is where the grocery store market segment expects to find them. These are not simply theoretical concepts we are talking about here. This is segment-specific marketing, requiring the delivery of segment-specific benefits that have readily-perceptible value to the customers in each of those segments.

THE IMPORTANCE OF SEGMENTATION

Why worry about market segmentation? Why not just "go for it" and see how much of the world's business can be captured before the competition notices? The answer is because customers are demanding more than any one business can deliver. By identifying, prioritizing, and targeting specific parts of large markets, limited resources can be deployed to deliver greater CPV to those individual parts.

Some years ago, customers were more understanding of suppliers' needs and limitations. When Henry Ford told them that they could have their Model T in any color "as long as it was black," they understood that to demand a white one would have been fruitless. It was too difficult for Ford to make them in other colors, and no one else would do it for them either. So, customers accepted what was easiest for their suppliers to do because that's all they could get. But, that's no longer the case.

Today, customers want their *own* needs met, and they can usually find someone who will do that. Customers are in charge and they are demanding that suppliers listen to them and respond with solutions on their terms. The challenge to meet customer demands is overwhelming for virtually any business organization. The only viable approach is to narrow one's focus to identifiable market segments where the company can best compete.

SUMMARY

The process of targeting market segments is really one of prioritization. Whether she does it consciously or unconsciously, every manager is regularly prioritizing target markets to deploy limited resources. Doing it well requires a thorough understanding of the CPV of each part of the total market and the ability to separate and identify those parts into well-defined market segments.

Market segmentation can be pursued to various degrees along a continuum from mass marketing (where no segments are established), to segment marketing (where large portions of the total market are identified), to niche marketing (involving smaller divisions of the market), and finally to individual marketing (dealing with one customer at a time). The currently popular term "one-to-one marketing" refers to something larger than individual marketing because it involves using manufacturing or delivery flexibility to customize solutions for individuals in a market segment.

Market segments should be defined based on the differing perceptions of CPV by portions of the total market. This is not the same as identifying market segments by demographic criteria such as age, income, or NAICS code. Such demographic information, as well as factors such as psychographic, behavioral, operating, and other characteristics, are used to *identify* market segments to access them. The underlying defining characteristic of market segments is similar CPV.

Market segmentation consists of seven steps: (1) grouping customers by CPV, (2) determining identifying characteristics for each subgroup, (3) evaluating the inherent attractiveness of each segment, (4) prioritizing the segments for the individual company, (5) developing segment-specific positioning strategies, (6) testing those strategies with customers, and (7) implementing the strategies.

The effort required to work through all of these steps is a necessity for successfully competing today. The shift of power to customers has resulted in overwhelming demands for unique and specific solutions to each of their needs. No company can successfully address all of those demands. Rather, today's best competitors carefully listen to their customers, group them into segments according to their similar CPV, and implement segment-specific strategies to deliver superior customer value.

REFERENCES

[1] Brian O'Reilly, "The Rent-A-Car jocks who made Enterprise #1," *Fortune*, October 28, 1996, pg. 125(3).

[2] www.enterprise.com/car_rental/fewer than/facts.html, 12/30/99.

[3] *St. Louis Post-Dispatch*, January 25, 1998.

[4] www.enterprise.com/car_rental/fewer than/inTheNews/19991014a.htm, 12/30/99.

[5] For additional resources on market segmentation, see Art Weinstein, *Market Segmentation: Using Demographics, Psychographics, and Other Niche Marketing Techniques to Predict and Model Customer Behavior*, (Chicago, Probus Publishing, 1993); Michael J. Croft, *Market Segmentation: A Step-by-Step Guide to Profitable New Business*, (New York, Thomson Business Press, 1994); Michael Treacy and Frederik D. Wiersema, *The Discipline of Market Leaders: Choose Your Customers, Narrow Your Focus, Dominate Your Market*, (Reading, Addison-Wesley, 1996).

[6] See David A. Aaker, *Strategic Market Management,* (New York, John Wiley & Sons, 1998).

[7] See Alan S. Cleland, *The Market Value Process: Bridging Customer and Shareholder Value,* (San Francisco, Jossey-Bass, 1996), Chapter 3.

[8] "Sex. Reefer? And auto insurance," *Fortune*, August 7, 1995.

[9] www1.progressive.com/progressive, December 31, 1999.

[10] Don Peppers and Martha Rogers, "In Vendors They Trust," *Sales & Marketing Management*, November, 1999, pg. 30.

[11] Roger J. Best, *Market-Based Management*, (Upper Saddle River, Prentice-Hall, 1997), pg. 119.

[12] Adapted from Best.

[13] Adapted from Philip Kotler and Gary Armstrong, *Principles of Marketing: Eighth Edition*, (Upper Saddle River, Prentice-Hall, 1999).

CHAPTER 6

CPV and Product Innovation

Most products are not as simple as they first appear – especially from the customer's point of view.

Schneider National is the world's largest long-haul truck-load freight carrier, with more than 40,000 trucks on the road. On first impression, the offering looks straightforward: Schneider will carry from Point A to Point B whatever freight can fit into one of their bright orange trailers. In fact, most of its business is in the "van" category (the big box trailers), rather than in flatbeds or other specialized equipment such as tankers. Therefore, as one executive said a few years back, "When you back our trucks up to the loading dock and look into the empty trailer, they look pretty much like all the others." That sounds an awful lot like the dreaded "commodity" business, where the offerings of all the competitors are the same and the only thing left to compete on is price.

Don Schneider, the second generation owner and operator of this nearly $3 billion business, is a whole lot smarter than that. The words "customer solutions" roll off his tongue regularly when he gives his frequent speeches explaining his success. And he has pioneered a long list of product innovations to deliver those solutions during the years. The life cycle of those innovations is very short, because intense competition drives others to quickly copy what he has done. But, he knows that is the nature of his industry and deals with it by *continuing to evolve his product offering to meet increasing customer needs.*

Schneider's "core benefit" is moving freight from one place to another. Beyond that, however, Schneider's offering has come to include important elements of enhanced product attributes, support services, packaging, and branding. Product attributes include physical issues, such as providing the right trailer for each load. Heavy loads reach maximum weight limits in less space, so the 45-foot trailers are best for those. Lighter loads, however, fill up the standard trailer before weight limits are encountered, so the 53-foot trailers are better. Other product attributes reach into the service realm, such as assuring availability of units when and where they are needed, dedicated teams of dispatchers assigned to large customers to facilitate placing orders, driver training programs to ensure their courtesy and cooperation at the loading docks, and even service guarantees, backed up by real monetary incentives, for meeting narrow time-windows for pickup and delivery schedules.

Support services revolve largely around information management capabilities. Nearly ten years ago, Don Schneider shook up the transportation industry when he installed a computerized tracking unit in each of his trucks.[1] The idea of providing real-time information to customers about their individual loads was unique at that time and provided a significant competitive advantage for his offering until the other carriers caught up with the technology. Even as such tracking systems have become common throughout the transportation industry, Schneider continues to upgrade his. Recently, the company announced the installation of an upgraded system that will help track the status of the trailers in addition to the tractors.[2]

Packaging and branding go hand-in-hand at Schneider. People outside of the industry may not be aware of this private company, until the color scheme is mentioned. From that point on, it becomes impossible to drive a mile on any

Interstate highway without noticing the bright orange trucks. Customers acknowledge the "Big Orange On-Time Machine" as the industry leader, a company that "everybody" uses to move long-haul freight. (Some people at Schneider even claim all the orange cones found out on the highway as "Schneider eggs" left behind by their trucks, but that's not official.)

There's much more to this complex business, of course. But even these few examples describe a trucking business that differs from anything that could be considered a "commodity." Don Schneider figured that out a long time ago and built an exciting industry leader out of what might be considered a traditional, mundane business.

HOW CUSTOMERS VIEW PRODUCTS

Most managers are familiar, by now, with Theodore Levitt's admonition to avoid "marketing myopia."[3] He pointed out that customers don't buy drill bits – they buy ways to make holes. The distinction is fundamentally important – customers seek solutions to their needs. And, they choose between alternative solutions on the basis of Customer Perceived Value (CPV). The challenge in product development, therefore, is to (1) determine those customers' needs, (2) understand how customers evaluate CPV in connection with solutions to those needs and, then, (3) develop an offering that delivers the greatest CPV.

So what? Doesn't everybody know this by now? The answer to this simple question is a curious one. According to product development guru Robert Cooper, most managers *do* know what it takes to successfully develop product offerings. "Surely after myriad studies into new product performance, almost every product developer should be able to list the 10 or 15 critical success factors that make the difference between winning and losing. [The *Journal of Product Innovation Management*] and others have published many articles during the years ... so many that anyone introduced to new product management since 1980 should be as familiar with the critical success factors as a school child is with the ABCs. And the first among those requirements is to listen to the customer to determine his needs."

Nevertheless, points out Cooper, "We still make the same mistakes. Recent studies reveal that the art of product development has not improved all that much – that the "voice of the customer" is still missing, that solid up-front homework is not done, that many products enter the development phase lacking clear definition, and so on."[4] In other words, we know that we should start by understanding customer needs and CPV, but we are not very good at actually doing it.

As a beginning to a solution for this problem, it may be helpful to define what we include in the term Product Innovation.

WHAT IS PRODUCT INNOVATION?

We prefer the term product innovation to "new product development" because not everything that needs to be done to a company's offerings will be "new." Every time a field sales representative agrees to a customer's request that the product be shipped a week earlier than normal or that the standard invoice will be manually processed to add additional detailed information to it, a product innovation decision is being made. Most publications that address topics under the heading of new product development will not extend to such minute levels of product decisions, but we believe it is valuable to do so. Because customers have no such arbitrary cutoff level for what they ask of suppliers to deliver CPV, some requests will certainly lead to the development of entirely new product offerings. Others will simply require a field sales representative to deliver something extra on any given workday.

Most scholars envision six levels of product innovation.[5] They are shown, weighted by their frequency of occurrence, in Figure 6.1.

New to the World

These are the product innovations that make the headlines. Examples of consumer products falling into this category have been well publicized, including the first personal computer, GPS systems, and new communications services such as interactive cable. Similarly, the business-to-business marketplace is seeing "new to the world" innovations at an increasing rate, particularly in the information management and communication fields. The rewards for a successful new to the world offering can be spectacular. However, according to one study, only 10 percent of all new products fall into this category.

Figure 6.1 - Levels of Product Innovation

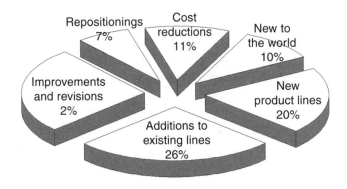

New Product Lines

These are "new to the company" offerings of products that already exist in the marketplace. Almost 20 percent of new products fall into this category. When IBM entered the market with a PDA (personal digital assistant) based on Microsoft's CE software, it was second to the already dominant PalmPilot offered by 3-Com. What is significant about this classification is that, in addition to requiring nearly all of the investment of a "new to the world" product, the new entrant carries with it the added advantages and disadvantages of an already established market.

Additions to Existing Product Lines

Also known as "product line extensions," these are products that are new, but related to the existing offerings of the company. Lexus' development of a Sports Utility Vehicle was an addition to existing product lines. It was an entirely new product, but one with which the company has both experience in producing related offerings and an established market. This is the largest category of new product developments, representing just under 26 percent of the total.

Improvements and Revisions to Existing Product Lines

The near-annual new car models are one of the most visible examples of this kind of product innovation. In the industrial sector, every adjustment or "tweak" to a current product in an effort to better meet the specific needs of a particular customer or customer set could be considered an "improvement or revision to existing product lines." The customized invoice for that special customer, as described above, is another example of this kind of product innovation. This category is equal in size to the previous one, representing slightly less than 26 percent of all new product developments.

Repositionings

Repositionings are existing products that are moved to new applications or markets. These are found frequently in the pharmaceutical business when a proven drug is determined to be effective for another purpose, such as the use of aspirin for preventing and treating heart disease. Arm & Hammer's repositioning of baking soda from strictly a cooking ingredient to an air freshener is renowned. It is estimated that only about 7 percent of new product offerings belong in this category.

Cost Reductions

These innovations are considered to be new products because they require new methods, production, or specifications for the supplier but aren't always recognized as anything new by customers. They usually generate a more efficient solution to a customer need than that which is currently available. A metal coatings company in Ohio, for example, combined a zinc coating capability with a sheet steel painting process into one plant to eliminate the transportation costs normally incurred by customers in moving the steel from one steel processor to another. Cost reduction innovations such as this represent less than 11 percent of all new product developments.

The value of laying out this scheme for classifying the extent of product innovation is to provide managers a framework for evaluating their own product innovation plans. It would seem that the level of risk and reward associated with each of these levels would form a continuum, "new to the world" being the highest risk and reward to "cost reduction" being the least. However, this may not be the case. Dr. Cooper cites his own research,[6] which suggests that the lowest levels of innovation (improvements and revisions to existing products, repositionings, and cost reductions) show a success rate much the same as the highest levels of innovation as well as financial returns far exceeding the higher innovation strategies. The highest levels of innovation (new to the world and new product lines) are close behind with impressive success and financial return rates. He indicates the least productive innovations, both in terms of success rate and average financial return, are those in the middle (additions to existing product lines). Apparently, the best approach is to either be very innovative or not very innovative at all.

There is another point to be drawn from these data, however. The lack of clear evidence that the most innovative approach is likely to be the most successful causes us to look for a different indicator. That indicator, as the reader might expect by now, is CPV. This is not a trivial point in view of the amount of attention currently being paid to "innovation" as the basis for building competitive advantage. The ability to recognize and adapt rapidly to change is a requirement of modern business and certainly product innovation has resulted in some very dramatic success stories in the most recent decade. But, just as with several other important business concepts such as shareholder value, employee involvement, and continuous quality improvement, innovation should not be mistaken as the ultimate performance objective. The only objective worthy of standing above the others (not *instead* of them, but prioritized *ahead* of them) is the ability to deliver superior CPV.

PRODUCT DEVELOPMENT PROCESSES

Most discussions on how to develop new or better product offerings dwell on the importance of establishing *processes* for that purpose. Robert Cooper, referenced previously, is thought by many to be the "father" of the stage-gate product development process – a series of create-review-create-review activities where increasingly specific activities take place toward the creation of the new product offerings. Figure 6.2 shows a typical stage-gate product development process. After each creation activity (the "stage") a formal review activity takes place (the "gate") at which a go/no-go decision is made. If the product concept fails to meet the preestablished criteria at any such gate, the concept is either dropped from further development or returned for rework to an earlier stage in the process.

Lucent Technologies has developed a stage-gate product development process it uses in many areas of its software development efforts. It involves activities from idea generation to supporting the eventual installed base of software customers and consists of 10 defined stages and 8 gates. Lucent credits the process with improving senior executives' awareness of product development activities, improving communication throughout the organization, and establishing a basis for continual revision and improvement of the process.[7]

The idea of a stage-gate product development process was based on two fundamental principles: First, an established process (of any kind) represents agreement within the organization on what resources will be dedicated to the effort. It acknowledges how those resources will be used, encourages communication across organizational functions about the work, and provides a basis for the organization to learn from experience and, thereby, improve the process over time. All of this is positive. Second, the stage-gate process helps the organization to manage risk by limiting the resources expended on product concepts at early stages (before they have met preestablished evaluation criteria) when the risk is relatively high. This concept has recently come under greater scrutiny by many managers. The concern has emerged that the stage-gate process approach overemphasizes risk reduction at the expense of cycle-time. In other words, the sequential nature of the stage-gate process takes so long that it may not be worth the additional control over risk that it provides.

Figure 6.2 - Example of a Stage-Gate Process

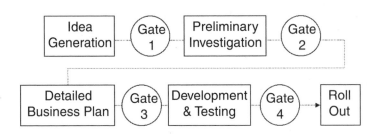

Solutions currently emerging for any shortcomings in the original stage-gate development process all seem to revolve around conducting more of the creation activities in parallel, instead of sequentially. This approach requires moving some activities earlier in the process, before evaluation "gates" that previously would have been required before work began. This may result in more wasted work, advocates say, but it certainly reduces the elapsed time to producing a new product ready for the marketplace. And that is worth the cost.

For example, Hewlett Packard develops much of its computer software using an approach called "Evolutionary Product Development."[8] Referred to as "Evo" for short, the program's philosophy is to design, develop, integrate, and test the software code in very small pieces with many iterations spaced only brief periods of time apart. Frequent customer feedback is used to modify and improve the software even during the development stages. Sometimes a single piece of software will be delivered to customers and returned for revisions up to six times in a single year.

There are instances, of course, where companies are not using any established process at all to control their product development efforts. This is usually for the same reason that process management has been slow to be adopted in every other area of the company: because the term "process" is erroneously thought of by managers as something that must be slow, cumbersome, and bureaucratic. As discussed in Chapter 3, however, this is an unfortunate misunderstanding. In fact, a "process" is already in effect everywhere results are being produced. That is, activities *are* being performed in some sequence, usually across functional lines, whether or not those activities have been identified by management and documented as such. So, a new product development process actually exists in every company that has produced a product innovation of any level. Most people who think they don't have a new product development process in their company actually have one – it is simply not being managed.

Choosing whether that process is a strict sequential one (which emphasizes control of financial risk) or a more parallel one (which focuses on reducing cycle time) depends upon a particular company's unique situation. In most cases, the answer probably lies somewhere in the middle of the two extremes. The design of the new product development process is an important management responsibility, overshadowed only by one other principle: understanding and incorporating CPV into that process.

PRODUCT DEVELOPMENT STAGES

All of the activities in any new product development process can be recategorized into one of three, more general, stages:

> IDEA GENERATION
> CONCEPT DEVELOPMENT
> PRODUCT REALIZATION

These are useful categories for identifying the real work that needs to be done in understanding CPV throughout the product development process.

Idea Generation

To get started with product development, of course, the manager needs a product *idea*. Ideas can come from sources both internal and external to the company and both of these kinds of sources should be aggressively pursued.

Internal to the Company

Many product ideas originate from somewhere within the company itself. These can come from anywhere, from top management, marketing and sales, as well as R&D, engineering, customer service, product delivery, and warranty support. Usually, the challenge within a company is to develop a process that captures and nurtures the numerous ideas that could emanate from all of these sources.

Sources of new product ideas from within the company are those that result from some kind of interaction with customers and those that come purely from internal circumstances. The largest number result from employees performing their customary work and identifying an unmet customer need in the process. The objective is to encourage this kind of thinking among employees and to capture the ideas so that they can be properly evaluated for feasibility.

The other kind, those that occur from some serendipitous set of events inside of the company, can be equally valuable. Internally generated ideas, without significant customer interaction involved, often come from functional areas such as R&D or engineering, but can appear from anywhere in the organization. The hair restoration product, Rogaine, was a result of such circumstances. The primary ingredient of Rogaine, called Minoxidil, was being tested as a high blood pressure medicine. Subjects of this drug testing complained of a side-effect that hair had begun to grow on not only their heads but also their backs, arms, and cheeks. The manufacturer, Upjohn, pursued this effect and the new product was conceived. 3M's famous Post-It notes were also the consequence of a failed product in one configuration resulting in a product idea for another area.

At the idea generation stage, harvesting ideas from internal sources unrelated to customer interaction is an important activity that must be encouraged. Those ideas, however, must be evaluated for CPV at an early stage to avoid wasted investment in a product idea that has little value to the customer. A modern version of a strip of flypaper that was developed in the engineering lab of a large household products company seemed like a good idea when it was in the lab. Scientists had discovered a chemical that would both attract and kill household flies, so they packaged it into an attractive plastic container for use in the kitchen. This technological breakthrough was not accepted by consumers, however, who were not enamored with the idea of collecting dead flies in their kitchen. The product was a failure and soon was withdrawn from the market.

External to the Company

Studies have shown that the best new product ideas come from the marketplace.[9] This is especially true in industrial product innovations. "Best" in these cases means the ultimate success rate of the product ideas, so it only makes sense that those ideas that come from the customer are usually best received by those customers.

Customers Don't Know What They Want

It is at this juncture that the argument that customers are not a good source of product ideas must be addressed. Some managers say that customers really don't know what they want and cite the Sony Walkman and the first Apple Computer as examples of that. In fact, Sony's Akio Morita has often been quoted as saying, "The public does not know what is possible to do, but we do. So instead of doing a lot of market research, we refine our thinking on a product and its use and try to create a market for it." But one should be wary of Morita's use of the term "market research." Perhaps Sony did very little "polling" of customers at the idea generation stage of the Sony Walkman, but it is clear that the product idea came from a very insightful understanding of customer needs. Perhaps Morita already carried that understanding with him, but good marketing research is usually critical to the idea generation stage. We also suspect that the understanding Morita leveraged to such great success in the development of the Walkman was originally gained through a great deal of experience in the marketplace. Apparently he just doesn't equate that experience with the term "market research."

We like the metaphor that Vihay Mahajan and Jerry Wind used of a physician and a patient.[10] A physician does not expect a patient to decide what medicine should be prescribed. The patient certainly needs to be examined by the doctor, however, to determine his condition and needs. No responsible physician would suggest a treatment without doing so. From the examination of the patient, then, the doctor is expected to decide what is the best approach to solving the problem. Similarly, managers should not expect customers to suggest what products should be developed. It is imperative, however, that the supplier understands the needs of the customer before attempting to meet those needs by way of defining a product offering. So, the starting place for product development is with the customer. Sometimes the manager will be lucky and the customer will suggest product ideas directly. More often, however, the customer will be describing his needs. That is all that can really be expected.

How to Understand Customers

At the idea generation stage, then, there are three ways to gain information directly from customers:[11]

BE A CUSTOMER
WATCH CUSTOMERS
ASK CUSTOMERS

Be a Customer. This is a technique that many managers already use to better understand their own employees and operations in the hope of improving their performance. Managers will often "take over" for frontline employees by working a shift in the plant, or answering phones in the call center, or clerking on the sales floor. Usually, those managers come away from the experience with much greater appreciation for the challenges their employees face and with some ideas on how those employees could improve the way they work. The same approach should be used to uncover customer needs in the product development idea generation stage.

Managers occasionally should be "customers," purchasing the product through the channels that most customers normally encounter. They should try using the product just as a customer does. They should try getting the same follow-up service a customer might require. And, equally important, they should try doing all of these things with the competition's product and see what the differences are. It is unlikely an insightful manager could come away from such experiences without generating some ideas about new or improved solutions to customer needs and ways to deliver increased CPV.

Watch a Customer. The next best thing to "being a customer" – and sometimes more practical – is "watching customers." Of course we mean watching customers with the discipline and expertise required to better understand CPV.

S.C. Johnson Wax, a leading manufacturer of household products, almost always begins the idea generation process by sending researchers out across the country to visit homemakers in their own homes. These researchers spend entire days with these consumers, simply following them around the house and watching as they perform common chores. For example, when researchers recognized what a problem consumers were having with ladders, pails, and hoses when trying to wash the outside of their second-floor windows, the idea of a no-rinse, streak-free, spray on window cleaner was born.

The same value in watching customers can be gained in an industrial setting. When a leading manufacturer of paperboard products spent some time in the plants of its customers, watching them use the very products it had shipped to them, it realized that these customers were laminating several pieces of its paperboard together as a part of their manufacturing process to gain the product strength and consistency they sought. From this experience, the idea for a premium priced prelaminated board was developed.

Ask a Customer. There is simply no reason not to ask customers, and competitors' customers, for new product ideas. No reason, that is, as long as the questions asked of customers are of the type that they can answer. That usually means asking them about their needs (the patient's symptoms) rather than asking them directly about products (the remedies to be prescribed by the doctor).

American Electric Power (AEP), one of the country's largest electric utility companies, began looking for new product ideas in the face of deregulation. Customers, understandably, had a difficult time thinking of the company as anything but a provider of electricity. Nevertheless, AEP went to those customers and asked about their needs in the broader area of energy use and management. They found, in the case of large retail chains, that these customers took the provision of the electric current itself for granted. The problem they were still grappling with, however, was how to manage the consumption of that electricity at multiple remote locations where they had no technical personnel located. From this discovered need came the idea for AEP's Datapult service, an Internet-based metering and monitoring system designed to manage energy consumption at multiple locations. Within two years, the business had grown to include a wide range of information services, including Datapult Information Source, Datapult Billing Services, Datapult Monitoring, Datapult Central, Datapult Analysis, and Datapult Notification. The company that was only recently a traditional electric generation utility is now a major player in the information management industry because it asked customers what they needed.[12]

The most effective research methods for understanding CPV are *exploratory* in nature. That means that the interactions will be less structured and driven more by customer interests than those of the manager. The data collected will be more *qualitative* than quantitative in form. And the questioning will incorporate a great deal of *laddering*, whereby the researchers will keep asking probing questions, each question based on the answer to the previous one, to get to the bottom of actual customer needs.

Often, the best customers to talk to about product innovation ideas are not "representative" customers but, rather, "lead users." Lead users are the early adopters of current offerings and among the most sophisticated of current customers. They are most thoughtful about how and why they select new offerings and are able to articulate the connection between those offerings and the needs they are seeking to address. In industrial markets, lead users often include executives of trade associations, industry "experts," and the most successful managers among the current customer set.

Idea generation research takes considerable skill and experience, which is why there is so much poor exploratory research being done and why this kind of work has sometimes failed to produce its intended results. Done properly, however, it is *the best* source of successful new product ideas.

Concept Development

The difference between a product *idea* and a product *concept* is one of specificity. Regardless of the product development process used by the company, product concept development involves continually adding more details and substance to the idea to push it forward from someone's brainchild to a commercialized offering.

Nowhere is the need for rapid product concept development more apparent than in the world of the Internet. Netscape developed its web browser, Navigator, from an idea to a commercialized product in the full glare of customer view. Version 2.0 was made available in January 1996, and feedback from that release was used immediately in the development of Version 3.0, which appeared on February 14, just six weeks after the previous one. Additional versions were introduced on February 22 and, again, in early March. The purpose of this approach was to identify the specific product features valued by most users and to incorporate those features into a final product.[13]

Goals of Product Concept Testing

As the product concept is developed, the manager's ability to interact with the customer and gain useful feedback grows. At these stages, the manager is able to ask the customer for information about specific proposed solutions to his needs rather than trying simply to engage in a freewheeling dialogue. The research, in other words, moves from being purely *exploratory* to being more *descriptive* in nature.

In fact, at these stages of the process, multiple goals are established for the information obtained from customers.

Screening

Throughout the entire product development process, the need to make incremental go/no-go decisions remains. As previously discussed, this is the very nature of the process – to continually evaluate whether additional resources should be invested in the product's development. This is the primary objective of customer research conducted throughout the product conceptualization stages.

It is important to remember, however, that the manager is attempting to avoid *both* kinds of mistakes. First, of course, is the error of investing in a product that will not be successful in the marketplace. Equally important, however, is the error of killing a product concept that might have been successful. Many people believe, in this age of short product cycles and pressure from the customer to innovate, that the second type of error is the more serious.

Improvement

Another objective of gaining customer feedback during the product concept development process is to contribute to the product specifications in a way that actually improves its chances for successful commercialization. As the product concept becomes more and more concrete, specific reactions about CPV can be gathered from customers and incorporated into the design.

Bose, manufacturer of electronic sound equipment, was developing a high-end ceiling-mounted speaker for commercial offices. For acoustical reasons, the product design included a fabric cover. When the product concept was presented for customer feedback, however, objections to the fabric cover surfaced. Installers pointed out that paint darkened when applied to a cloth surface, so painting it to blend in with the ceiling color was difficult. In addition, architects and builders doubted that the fabric cover would meet fire retardant regulations in spite of company reassurances. In the final product specifications, the acoustic advantages of the cloth covering were outweighed by the customers' preference for a customary metal grill, and the product was well received.[14]

The challenge for customer research at this stage is to gather customer improvement suggestions as early as possible in the development process. Improvements can be incorporated into the product design much less expensively and much more effectively if their need is recognized at an early stage.

Estimating Market Size

As the development process unfolds and the product concept becomes concrete, the company's projections of marketplace acceptance can be improved. Such projections are being made throughout the product development process, even from the very beginning when the idea is subjected to the very first screening process. These become more credible, however, as the evolving product concept moves closer to reality and customers are able to give more specific feedback.

Issues in Product Concept Testing

There is no form of marketing research quite like product concept testing in the sense that it involves the attempt to gain product-specific feedback about a product that does not yet exist. This challenge diminishes, of course, as the development process continues and the product develops into something that can actually be experienced by the customer. By definition, however, product concept testing ends when the product exists. Therefore, there are some unique issues to consider in the product concept testing stage.

Definition of the Concept

The most critical issue in product concept testing research is the development of the concept statement. At the early stages, this statement is usually only a narrative description of what is intended to constitute the offering (Figure 6.3). Later, it becomes sketches (where appropriate) and prototypes. Throughout this evolution however, careful attention is necessary to what is included in the concept statement and how those elements are presented to the customer.

Figure 6.3 - A Sample Product Concept Statement

A New Video Rental Service - This service is provided from kiosks in shopping malls and from drive-up booths in mall parking lots, similar to some film processing companies. Only the top 100 videos will be stocked at any time, with the inventory updated monthly to stay current. Rental fee will be $2 for a 1-night rental. Extra days will cost $3. Customers will sign-up as "members" and receive a plastic card with a magnetic strip to speed the rental process. Waiting time, therefore, will be minimal. Members will also receive a list of current titles each month. There will be sufficient kiosks and booths in targeted neighborhoods so members can find one no more than a 5-minute drive from home.

When circumstances warrant it, more sophisticated depictions of the product concept may be worthwhile. For example, when Hewlett Packard was considering a new PC pointing device consisting of two rolling cylinders mounted perpendicularly to one another, the company produced a video that demonstrated a mock-up of the device and a simulated computer screen to show how the device would work. Although HP had no prototype or product to show, this "concept statement" very effectively helped gather prospective customer feedback about the potential new offering.

Definition of the Market

Like all of the other issues involved in the middle of a product development process, the description of the target market is still very much a hypothesis. Research must be designed to test that hypothesis for the same two types of possible errors: Whether the product will be accepted by the intended target market or not, and whether it would be accepted by other markets.

Some years ago, a major international packaging firm developed a new aerosol container. Made of plastic rather than metal, it looked better, felt better in the hand, didn't rust, and was cleaner. To move into production, however, the company had to decide among alternative markets for the product innovation. High-volume, low-value markets such as personal care products required one set of product specifications, testing procedures, and production equipment. Low-volume, high-value applications such as medical products required a different set of decisions about those things. The company could have pursued either, or both, of these potential markets depending on availability of resources and its strategic objectives.[15]

Product Attributes

For the first time since customer needs led to a new product idea, specific product attributes begin to be defined during the product concept testing stage. This means that feedback from customers about those specific attributes can begin to be collected. This is critical in order for the research results to be useful for management. To the extent it becomes increasingly possible as the product concept is developed, information about both attribute importance and attribute performance expectations should be obtained.

Ford and General Motors missed on the original minivan because they thought that the front-wheel drive configuration would not provide sufficient towing capability. Chrysler, on the other hand, conducted in-depth market research that convinced it that heavy duty towing was not an important attribute for this new product. "The people we're selling it to don't tow. A very small percentage of Americans on a regular basis tow more than a Class 1 trailer; we can tow a Class 1 trailer." So, they introduced the "van that handles like a car" and dominated the minivan market for many years.[16]

The product concept development phases of the product development process present unique challenges and opportunities for incorporating customer feedback into the design of new offerings. Because the design of new offerings presents once-in-a-product-life-time opportunities to deliver CPV, it makes sense to address these challenges and to invest in these opportunities.

Product Realization

Product realization describes the activities involved in moving out of the product development phases and into full production and delivery of the new offering. For this very reason, customer feedback at this late stage of the product development process is obtained and used very differently than at earlier stages. In fact, at this stage the customer research looks very much like Customer Satisfaction research (see Chapter 10). This is because it is essentially too late to make significant changes to the product features without incurring extraordinary costs and seriously disrupting a planned roll-out schedule, so the product is very close to having to be considered a finished product. Customer feedback is still valuable at this stage, but more for the purpose of fine-tuning features, managing after-sale support, or inputting the information into an additional new product development effort.

Generally, final product testing is conducted in any of three ways:

Trade Shows

Sometimes, companies elect to introduce new products during events at which their industry and their customers are conveniently gathered in one place. The advantages of this approach are its relatively low cost and, if the trade show occurs when the information is needed by the company, the speed with which feedback can be received. The disadvantages include the limited sample to which the product is being exposed (this sample would, in fact, be classified as a "convenience sample" by statisticians and the research results would be very suspect) and the public nature of the test (both competitors and key customers would be seeing the new offering).

Industrial products sold through distributor and manufacturer rep organizations are often introduced at trade shows held primarily for this very purpose. Because many of these products are produced "to order" for customers, additional refinements are still practical in response to feedback received on the floor of an industry trade show.

Beta Testing

In this type of early product introduction, a limited number of customers are selected to use the new product and asked to provide feedback to the company about their experience with it. The distinction of this type of market test is that the customers involved are informed that the product is unproven and that they are participating in pre-commercialization testing. The advantages of this approach are the reduced risk of damage to a brand or company image in the event of disappointment with the new product and the straightforward nature of the communication that can take place between the company and the participating customer users. The only disadvantage in conducting a beta test is the time and cost involved. In most cases, those investments are well worthwhile.

A manufacturer of heavy industrial equipment developed a new tree harvesting machine. With huge, sharp knife blades, this machine stripped the branches, cut the trunk into uniform pieces, and loaded those pieces onto a conveyor. It worked well during the company's testing, and it was a great success the first time a customer tried it in a beta test situation. The second customer test, however, was conducted in a rain storm. The machine sank hopelessly into the soft floor of the forest. Major design changes to the machine's traction system were required, but those changes involved much less expense and embarrassment than would have been incurred with a large product recall after a complete market introduction.[17]

Experiments

The term "experiments" includes a wide range of research efforts, alike in that they all are controlled tests consisting of defined subjects (customers exposed to the new offering), variables (features of the offering, its promotion, and its delivery), and control groups (customers exposed to variations in the variables or nothing at all). Traditional "market testing" refers to an experimental roll-out of a new product offering. Such market testing is more often conducted in consumer arenas than industrial, because the target market for industrial offerings usually consists of fewer individuals and, therefore, control groups are more difficult to establish.

With consumer products, the test marketing experiment is usually conducted to verify sales projections or evaluate different product launch strategies. A manufacturer of a new instant breakfast drink, for example, initially introduced its new product in four cities. In two of those markets the product was positioned as a "great-tasting breakfast drink." In the other two, it was promoted as a "convenient, easy-to-prepare breakfast drink." Sales results in the test markets were used to select which positioning would be used in the national product rollout.[18]

Some companies are electing to eliminate test marketing because they believe that the time involved to conduct such experiments is not justified by the usefulness of the information gained.[19]

THE IMPORTANCE OF PRODUCT INNOVATION

The very purpose of every new product development process, whether formal or informal, elaborate or simple, planned or spontaneous, is to define how a company can best deliver CPV. Because CPV exists only in accordance with the perceptions of customers, it seems apparent that every product innovation effort should include gathering and incorporating customer input. Still, many managers fail to take advantage of these opportunities.

In a recent study of new product and service professionals at companies introducing nearly 11,000 new products during the past five years, the respondents identified the major reason new product/service ideas failed.[20] Nearly half of the respondents identified "lack of understanding of market needs" as the major problem. The next major problem, "lack of internal support," was named by only 13 percent. In other words, improving the understanding of CPV, even by a small amount, would have tremendous impact on the success rate and, therefore, the profitability of new product development.

SUMMARY

Numerous studies have demonstrated that the effective use of customer input in the new product development process contributes significantly to the probability for commercial success of the new product. Many managers, however, do not want to spend the time or money to do customer research. Often, the emphasis on shortening the development cycle time takes precedence.

Nevertheless, continual *product innovation* has become a requirement of most businesses. The term product innovation encompasses all forms of new product development from "new to the world" discoveries to simple "cost reductions" on existing offerings.

All companies create new products through some kind of *product development process*, although some of those processes are undefined and even may not be recognized as a process. Stage-gate processes emphasize reduction of financial risk, while processes with more parallel activities emphasize reduction of development cycle time. The proper selection from among the numerous types of product development processes varies greatly from company to company and depends heavily on the unique circumstances of each company. The underlying commonality among them is that every product development process attempts to determine *how* the company will deliver CPV.

Although the specifics of different product development processes vary greatly, they could all be reduced to three major stages: idea generation, concept development, and product realization. There are numerous and differing opportunities within each of those stages to gather and incorporate valuable customer input.

Compelling evidence exists that the use of customer input in the product development process increases the probability of success for that product. If managers better understood this Return On Investment, they would likely be much more eager to seek out and use marketplace information about CPV.

REFERENCES

[1] "Computers give trucker an edge," *The New York Times*, May 25, 1991, pg. 17.

[2] "Orbcomm is truckin'," *PC Week*, May 31, 1999, pg. 76.

[3] Theodore Levitt, "Marketing Myopia," *Harvard Business Review*, July-August 1960, pg. 45.

[4] Robert G. Cooper, "The Invisible Success Factors in Product Innovation," *Journal of Product Innovation Management*, March 1999. pg. 115-133.

[5] Robert G. Cooper, *Winning at New Products: Accelerating the Process from Idea to Launch*, (Reading, Addison-Wesley Publishing, 1993). For additional resources on product innovation, also see Thomas D. Kuczmarski, *Managing New Products: The Power of Innovation*, (Englewood Cliffs, Prentice-Hall, 1988) and Michael E. McGrath, Michael T. Anthony, and Amram R. Shapiro, *Product Development: Success Through Product and Cycle-Time Excellence*, (Boston, Butterworth-Heinemann, 1992).

[6] Cooper, *Winning at New Products*, pg. 14.

[7] Bill Ausura and Nancy Barone, Lucent Technologies, "Leading Product Management," presented at the International PDMA Conference, Marco Island, Florida, October 20, 1999.

[8] Bill Crandall, Hewlett Packard, "Evolutionary Product Development," presented at the International PDMA Conference, Marco Island, Florida, October 20, 1999.

[9] *The Source of Innovation*, (New York, Oxford University Press, 1988).

[10] Vijay Mahajan and Jerry Wind, "Rx for Marketing Research," *Marketing Research*, Fall 1999, pg. 7.

[11] Adapted from Abbie Griffin, "Obtaining Customer Needs for Product Development," Milton D. Rosenau, Jr., editor, *The PDMA Handbook of New Product Development*, (New York, John Wiley & Sons, 1996).

[12] www.aepes.com/datapult/, January 14, 2000.

[13] Marco Iansiti and Alan MacCormack, "Developing Products on Internet Time," *Harvard Business Review*, September-October 1997, pg. 108.

[14] Dan Dimancescu & Kemp Dwenger, *World-Class New Product Development: Benchmarking Best Practices of Agile Manufacturers,* (New York, AMACOM, 1996).

[15] Cooper, *Winning at New Products*, pg. 239.

[16] Jeffrey D. Swaddling and Mark W. Zobel, "Beating the Odds: Using Exploratory Research to Create Highly-Valued New Products," *Marketing Management*, Winter/Spring 1996, Vol. 4, No. 4, pg. 21-33.

[17] Cooper, *Winning at New Products*, pg. 217.

[18] Cooper, *Winning at New Products*, pg. 221.

[19] Cooper, *Winning at New Products*, pg. 223

[20] Kuczmarski & Associates, Inc., *Winning New Product and Service Practices for the 1990s,* Chicago, 1999.

CHAPTER 7

CPV and Pricing

E.I. du Pont de Nemours & Company will celebrate its bicentennial very soon. The company was founded in 1802 and incorporated in the U.S. in 1915. Today, it operates in 65 countries with almost 97,000 employees. It calls itself "a science company, delivering science-based solutions that make a difference in people's lives in food and nutrition, health care, apparel, home and construction, electronics, and transportation." In 2000, it was among the 50 largest U.S. companies in the Fortune 500. This huge, venerable organization, though, still needs to understand individual markets and how their products bring value to those markets to set its prices. They need to understand CPV. There's no other way.

Many years ago, DuPont developed a new, polyethylene resin to be used by other firms in the manufacture of flexible pipe.[1] The resin was called Alathon 25, and it was superior to then-existing alternative products because it was significantly more durable. Pipe made from Alathon 25 was proven to install with less breakage and have greater endurance, whether buried or used above ground, compared to pipes made with alternative resins. Specifically, Alathon 25 pipe was rated to have a failure rate of no more than 3 percent, compared to alternate products with failure rates of 7 to 8 percent. That was a huge performance advantage, but what was it worth in terms of price?

Like most manufacturers in the industrial sector, to set the price of its manufactured product DuPont had to worry about the CPV of its offerings at both the level of the end user and that of the other members of the value chain. For Alathon 25, the end user was the farmer who used the finished pipe to irrigate his fields and the value chain partner was the pipe extruder who used DuPont's product to make the pipe. DuPont's analysis started with the end user.

DuPont started with a "reference price" – the price of the current pipe typically being used by farmers for this application. At that time, it found that price to be $6.50 per hundred feet. It then examined the incremental "value in use" that farmers would gain from using Alathon 25 pipe. Because they would have to buy 4 to 5 percent less pipe as a result of breakage, DuPont found that farmers would save around $4 per hundred feet of pipe. This amount was based on the price of the pipe not purchased, the savings in installation labor, and an estimate of reduced crop failure because of irrigation problems. Based on this value in use analysis, farmers should have been willing to pay almost $10.50 per hundred feet of Alathon 25 irrigation pipe.

Pipe extruders bought raw material from DuPont or others and put a little more than 16 pounds of it into each hundred feet of pipe they sold to farmers. For every such hundred feet of pipe, the added $4.00 in end user value the new material produced meant the extruders should be willing to pay almost $.25 more per pound of Alathon 25. (Existing resins for this kind of pipe cost extruders less than $.28 per pound.) There were some "down sides" of the new resin for extruders. Less breakage of the pipe in the field meant less sales for the extruders. That, plus the risk of using a raw material available from only one supplier and the increased selling costs connected with introducing a new, higher priced product, caused DuPont to take a little more than $.10 off its premium price estimate. It could justify a price premium of less than $.15 per pound over competitive resins currently *available, therefore, or less than $.43 per pound.*

Of course, DuPont understood that "value in use" analysis is just one of the many factors involved in effectively setting prices. Customer perceptions depend upon how well users understand and trust projections of "value in use." Ultimately, it is CPV – not "value in use" – that drives buying behavior.

CPV can be nudged toward "value in use," however, by an effective educational and selling strategy. DuPont altered its approach to include such a strategy. After having progressively cut its price on Alathon 25 for many years in unsuccessful attempts to get this new product to "take off," this time it raised its price from $.355 to $.380 and saw sales double in the ensuing year.

Price has always been a fundamental part of the company's marketing mix: Product, promotion, place, and *price*. Still, many companies have treated decisions about price as something entirely separate. Pricing decisions are often removed from the hands of the marketers who are making all of the other marketing mix decisions and given, instead, to a separate staff or to the finance function. It's as if all of the other variables of the company's strategy are decided upon and then, almost as an afterthought, the offering needs to be priced. If the principles of Customer Perceived Value (CPV) are considered, however, this would not be the way pricing decisions are made.[2]

Careful readers may have noticed that we don't separate *price* from the other costs the customer evaluates in determining CPV. Price, from the customer's view, is just one of the negative elements that must be put on the right-hand side of the CPV balance scale (see Figure 7.1), along with the other acquisition costs (shipping, administration, installation, etc.), operating costs, insurance, taxes, training, and process modifications. Of course, price is the most obvious of the customer's costs, and some, less sophisticated, buyers tend to overemphasize the relative importance of price. But even when dealing with those customers, it is important for the company to remember that pricing is just one of the strategic variables employed to generate revenue.[3]

Figure 7.1 - CPV Balance Scale

INPUTS TO PRICING

So, how does the pricing process begin? As with most important decisions, the process is one of gathering information and then analyzing it. The information required for pricing decisions comes from three places:

THE CUSTOMER

THE COMPETITION

THE COMPANY ITSELF

Customer Pricing Information

It would seem obvious that – because the marketer's objective is to get the prospective customer to take action (purchase an offering) – the most important information about how to price the offering would come from understanding the customer's positioning of price on his CPV balance scale. Often the customer is not consulted at all, however. Some companies are reluctant to go to the customer for this kind of information, because they believe that it will not be accurate or useful. They are concerned that, if asked about price, the customer will only enter into the negotiation process and will hide his true feelings about how much he would be willing to pay. "The customer isn't going to actually tell you what their top price would be," they would say. These companies also have concerns about leaking information prematurely about their pricing intentions to both customers and competitors.

None of these concerns, however, reduces the need to gain a customer's perspective about the role of price in Customer Perceived Value. To counter the difficulties, several different approaches must be used to gain this understanding.

Economic Value

The most objective approach to understanding customer perspectives about price is the determination of economic value or, as some call it, value-in-use. With this approach, the economic costs and benefits received by the customer from the offering, as compared to some *other* offering, are calculated and added or subtracted from the price of that substitute offering. The result is the calculated *economic value.*

A manufacturer of landing gear mechanisms for large truck trailers calculated the economic value of its new-and-improved versions to use as a selling tool. Landing gear is the legs at the front end of a semi-truck trailer that support the trailer in a horizontal position when it is disconnected from a truck tractor. When needed, it is cranked down into a vertical position by a hand-operated crank. The landing gear is moved back up under the trailer floor when the trailer is connected to the tractor.

The starting point for an economic value calculation is the price of the currently used offering or an alternative being considered for purchase – this is the *reference price.* For the landing gear, this was the company's previous model mechanism, or any competitor's current offering. (This calculation was computerized by the company and allowed the reference price to be anything the analyst selected.) The cost savings, or increases, that the new offering provided were then added or subtracted from the reference price to determine the economic value. A simplified example of this calculation is shown in Figure 7.2.

Figure 7.2 - Sample Calculation of Economic Value
(without consideration for Present Value calculations)

Price of alternative model		$6,500
Savings with new model:		
Increased road time-revenue per day	$2.00	
Reduced idling fuel costs per day	.20	
Reduced idle driver pay per day	.80	
Reduced workers' comp premiums per day	.10	
Total savings per day	$3.10	
Avg. # work days/life of component	1,000	
Total savings per component		$3,100
Economic value of new model		$9,600
Suggested price of new model		$8,500

In this example of truck trailer landing gear, the principal improvement in the newly designed model was the speed with which the gear
could be positioned given the same amount of effort by the driver.
This meant that less time was spent by the driver manipulating landing gear and the truck and trailer were idle for less time. All of the
savings from this reduced downtime (wages and fuel) and the gains
in revenue created (more miles per day) were added to the old price
to demonstrate what the new mechanism is worth to the customer in
economic terms.

This is useful information, and helps the manager to infer how
the customer should perceive the value of his offering. It is nothing
more than that, however. This information represents reality, not perception – and, as we know, customer perception is the only thing that
matters in defining CPV.

Price Sensitivity

Another aspect of understanding the role of price in CPV is to understand the importance to the customer of the price attribute on his

CPV balance scale. Nagle identified five factors that influence the sensitivity of buyers to price differences among their buying alternatives. They are:[4]

UNIQUE VALUE OR PRICE-QUALITY EFFECT

SUBSTITUTE AWARENESS OR COMPARISON EFFECT

TOTAL EXPENDITURE OR END-BENEFIT EFFECT

SUNK INVESTMENT EFFECT

INVENTORY EFFECT

Evaluating these factors helps the manager anticipate how customers will probably react to a pricing decision.

Unique Value or Price-Quality Effect

Buyers are less sensitive to prices when their alternatives seem very different from one another in other aspects of perceived value. In other words, the more elements of benefits or non-price costs that are "in play" on the CPV balance scale, the less important price becomes to the overall evaluation. This is the fundamental principle of competing on CPV.

This factor is also a variation on the "commodity trap" concept discussed in Chapter 4. With a commodity, there are no distinguishing features to be placed on the CPV balance scale *other than* price, so commodities are forced to compete on price alone. Adding differentiators to the balance scale usually reduces the importance of pricing differences.

When customers perceive more value in the benefits and non-price costs of an offering, they generally expect to pay more for it. A copy machine, for example, that produces more copies per minute, can print on both sides of the paper, and collates multiple copies of documents would be expected to cost more than one that has fewer options. Unless brand name is perceived as being a significant benefit or is associated with other performance features, however, customers would probably be very sensitive to a price difference between a Canon machine with the same performance specifications as a Xerox machine.

Substitute Awareness or Comparison Effect

When customers have fewer perceived alternatives, they are forced to be less sensitive to price. They may perceive fewer alternatives either because they are unaware of them, or because it is difficult to make comparisons of the value of these alternatives.

So-called "tourist traps" are obvious examples of these effects. Prices are usually much higher near large, downtown hotels, and customers tolerate them because they are unaware of alternatives that might be just down the street and around the corner. Or they tolerate the higher prices because it would be inconvenient to find a taxi to travel to other locations that offer alternative benefits and costs.

Industry is not immune to difficulties in determining price sensitivity. For purchases in which it is difficult to compare CPV attributes, buyers are often less concerned about possible price differences. With expensive services that are nearly impossible to evaluate until after they are incurred, such as consulting services, many companies restrict their choices to a few "preferred vendors" even though less expensive alternatives are probably readily available.

The Internet has rapidly reduced the importance of the Substitute Availability or Comparison Effect. With increased information available about offerings in nearly every area, buyers are less often faced with the inability to identify or evaluate alternatives. This has caused the consumer to be more sensitive to the price of the latest technological advances in computers, for example, because locating and comparing alternatives are much easier than they used to be.

Total Expenditure or End-Benefit Effect

Buyers are usually less sensitive to prices if the expenditure is a small part of their total income or if it is a small part of their total costs. This is a reflection of customers experiencing a "shopping cost" of performing the CPV evaluation itself. If comparing benefit and cost attributes on the balance scale becomes more trouble than it is worth because the purchase is a relatively small one, there is less interest in knowing whether there are price differences among the alternatives.

One pharmaceutical company found that the price of some of its nutritional products was scrutinized more closely in nursing homes than it was in hospitals. Its analysis indicated that because hospitals are in the business of treating acutely ill patients, their purchases of nutritional supplement products was a smaller percentage of their overall expenditures than that of nursing homes. In the nursing homes, nutrition was more often the primary concern surrounding patient care and the purchase of dietary supplement products accounted for a greater proportion of total expenditures. Nursing homes were very sensitive to differences in the pricing of these products.

The same effect often holds true in consumer markets. Many new car buyers include sophisticated sound equipment in their purchases, spending many times more on their car radio than they would ever consider spending for a radio in their home. Although they might spend more time listening to music in their cars, the justification for spending so much on a sound system is often that the additional $500 was less significant when included in the overall $30,000 price of the new car.

Sunk Investment Effect

When purchases are connected to a substantial previous investment, buyers are usually less price sensitive. The interesting aspect of this price sensitivity effect is that it is generally a short-term phenomenon. Sunk investments are generally of a long-term nature and when that long-term time frame is reached they are no longer significant, increasing price sensitivity toward the related purchase.

Fuel is one of the most significant costs of commercial airlines. In the short run, however, they show little sensitivity to fluctuations in the price of aviation fuel. They do not buy less when prices go up because their investment in their fleet requires that they keep buying the fuel to keep the airplanes producing revenue. The airlines' long-term projections of the cost of aviation fuel do significantly impact long-term decisions, such as equipment purchases, schedules, etc. If fuel prices are projected to be relatively high in the long term, the airlines will find ways to reduce their consumption and buy less.

Inventory Effect

Buyers are less sensitive to prices of goods that cannot be stockpiled or inventoried. In other words, if the buyer cannot easily adjust the timing of his purchases, he will be unable to be as price sensitive as he might otherwise be. This effect is usually very short term.

How the Inventory Effect impacts the buying decision is largely dependent on the buyer's expectations of future prices. Sensitivity is reduced in inflationary times when a buyer expects prices to rise and he is unable to purchase the offering and store it for future use. Sensitivity increases, however, when prices are not expected to rise.

The significance of these price sensitivity effects is that they can be used to evaluate the customer's likely response to pricing decisions. An astute manager can, for example, determine whether or not customers can stockpile their offering and whether customers expect that prices will rise in the future, remain steady, or fall. Similar analyses can be performed for each of the effects described here. The results are valuable information for managers to make more informed decisions about how customers might perceive the price element of CPV.

Listening to the Customer

In addition to understanding economic value and customer price sensitivity, additional information is available about customer perceptions of the price element of CPV by asking about or observing purchase behavior directly. This must be expertly done, however, to avoid the problems of customer gamesmanship.

Tracking Customer Behavior

Often, much information about how customers perceive prices is available from internally available records of their previous behavior. The challenge is to find and use this kind of information effectively.

The grocery industry is most advanced in the use of historical transaction information obtained from its relatively sophisticated system of check-out scanners and data mining. Subtle price adjustments can be made on any number of individual SKUs, and the impact on customer buying behavior can be readily determined. This approach is more practical and relatively easy to do in high-volume retail sales situations where generalizations may legitimately be made.

Experiments

Research experiments can sometimes be conducted to evaluate customers' perceptions of prices. This is also a technique that has greater applicability in the consumer products world, where volumes are high and customer sets can be readily separated into test and control groups. Pricing experiments in the grocery industry are a very close cousin to tracking customer behavior as described. The only differences in a full-fledged research experiment are the proactive manipulation of individual prices and the establishment of a control group to which the price changes can be compared. Often, pricing experiments are conducted in the product testing phase of the new product development process (Chapter 6).

Surveys

Here we are referring to any type of research survey including brief interviews (conducted face-to-face or on the telephone), questionnaires distributed via the mail, or electronically delivered instruments.

When approaching customers directly to probe into pricing issues, direct questions such as "How much would you pay for this?" are usually not very useful. Respondents are usually either unable or unwilling to answer such questions accurately.

What *can* be done, however, is to develop questions that require respondents to make choices between alternatives connected with prices. These are called *choice decisions* and much can be learned from them based on careful design and analysis.

Suppose a hotel chain wants to determine what value customers place on the availability of suites and recreational facilities. The researcher begins by specifying the possible offerings. Figure 7.3 shows the eight possible offerings when testing room size and the availability of recreational facilities at two price points.

Figure 7.3 - Customer Choices for Conjoint Analysis

Choice	Room	Rec. Facilities	Price
1	Suite	Available	$150
2	Suite	Not available	$150
3	Regular	Available	$150
4	Regular	Not available	$150
5	Suite	Available	$95
6	Suite	Not available	$95
7	Regular	Available	$95
8	Suite	Not available	$95

The next task is to have customers indicate their preferred choice when each of the offerings are paired (e.g., choices 1 vs. 2, 1 vs. 3, 2 vs. 3, etc.). Preferences are determined for all of the possible pairings. Conjoint analysis would be then employed to determine the relative importance customers place on room size versus recreational facility availability relative to price.

The value of marketing research for supporting pricing decisions is often minimized because it is not practical to walk up to a customer and ask directly, "How much is this product worth to you?" There is much to be learned, however, from asking customers *about* pricing. Just as customers should not be expected to directly identify all new product opportunities, neither should customers be expected to set prices. But, that does not reduce the importance of learning everything possible about customers' needs in the case of product development and customers' pricing perceptions for pricing decisions. After all, because the objective is to understand and manage CPV, understanding customer perceptions of pricing alternatives is a fundamental requirement in the pricing process.

Competitive Pricing Information

Competitors who offer substitute products compete on every element of the CPV balance scale. Understanding which benefits and costs are considered by customers when evaluating competitive offerings is a fundamental requirement of every strategic plan. Price, however, often stands out above all the other attributes because price is usually the most easily controlled and quickly changed of all the CPV attributes. In fact, managers need to understand three aspects of their competitors' pricing strategy:

> PRICES
>
> COSTS
>
> STRATEGIC REACTIONS

Competitors' Prices

Most managers believe they know the price of their competitors' offerings, but many actually don't. The only competitive price that is relevant is the one perceived by the customer, and that's not always what it first appears to be.

The pricing of industrial goods is often so complex that it is difficult to clearly determine what the "bottom line" price of an offering is. The common use of practices such as off-invoice discounts, surcharges for services, and periodic rebates or volume rewards may effectively make apple-to-apple comparisons to competitors' prices very difficult.

Sometimes such practices are so obscure that even customers don't understand how they affect the ultimate price they are paying. In such a case, the manager must become clear about the significance of the competitor's strategy. If the adjustment is an add-on to which the customer is oblivious, that could be smart pricing. If it is a discount that the customer doesn't appreciate, however, that could be "leaving profit on the table." A smart manager will learn from these practices by understanding how CPV is perceived by the customer and what impact that has on his buying decision.

Competitors' Costs

Learning how competitors make their money can be a great help to strategic planning and to developing a competitive pricing strategy. If the competitor is a rational entity, cost structures can result in limits to his strategic alternatives.

Understanding competitors' cost structures may not be as difficult as it first appears. The extensive disclosure requirements for public companies means that this kind of information is relatively easy to obtain. The limitation here is that the details of costs and profitability are not always provided for smaller business units of a company, and that business unit might be the actual competitor of interest. In such cases, further investigation may be necessary.

Sometimes cost information from competitors is difficult to obtain and must be inferred from public appearances. The more the manager knows about the competition, however, the better her inferences can be.

Competitors' Anticipated Reactions

If learning about competitors' prices and costs isn't difficult enough, it is also necessary to evaluate competitors' anticipated responses to pricing decisions. Because it is relatively easy to adjust prices in response to competitive actions, the time frame in this aspect of competitive behavior is very short, and the manager must anticipate what competitors will do in response to its pricing, all the while making the decisions.

Obviously, anticipating competitors' pricing reactions is a guessing game – even the competitors have not yet decided what they will do. But, based on the premise that history often repeats itself, it is possible to anticipate what competitors might do by reviewing what they have done in the past. Nagle describes the following four categories of pricing behavior and what signals their occurrence.

Cooperative

Cooperative pricing behavior is characterized by the apparent desire to maintain the status quo in the marketplace. This competitor has, in the past, changed prices in proportion to other firms to maintain the differences that have always existed. He has also, at times, adjusted his output when industry demand has changed to maintain equivalent market share.

The competitor that adopts a cooperative pricing strategy is often one of a few large players in an industry. Industry capacity is not disproportional to market demand, and large competitors are not plagued with excess production capacity. The cost structure in the industry is probably very similar from one firm to the next.

Adaptive

This competitor is even more of a price "follower" than the cooperative competitor. He adjusts prices in accordance with industry leaders but will take any opportunity to increase his market share by selling more aggressively when demand increases and backing off selling efforts when demand prices decline. The assumption of this competitor is that his pricing actions don't influence the industry.

The adaptive pricer is usually a smaller player in an industry that is dominated by others.

Opportunistic

The opportunistic pricing competitor is always attempting to increase his market share by taking advantage of pricing changes. He will be the first to cut prices, but slower to follow price increases of others. If others cut prices first, the opportunistic pricer will try to recover his position by quickly cutting his prices in response.

The successful opportunistic pricer enjoys lower unit costs than others in the industry or has significant excess production capacity available. He may be a newer entrant in the industry trying to gain market share. This competitor tries to negotiate price cuts to gain business without competitors or other customers learning about it.

Predatory

Although clear-cut predatory pricing is illegal in the United States, it probably occurs in some situations. With this approach, the competitor makes large price cuts to attempt to drive others out of the business. Usually focusing on one competitor at a time, his objective is to cause the competitor to incur such significant financial losses that it cannot continue to compete.

The predatory pricer is driven by the desire to drive a competitor out of business, either because its pricing has damaged the pricer in the past or because the pricer will benefit in some other way by eliminating the competition (and is not likely to be detected doing it). The predatory pricer must have more financial resources than its targeted competitor or lower costs or some other financial basis to survive a bloody price war.

The wise manager will gather all the information she can about her competitors and consider this information when making pricing decisions. She must do this, of course, within the constraints of trade laws. Primarily, these laws prohibit collusion between competitors, which includes any direct communication between them concerning pricing. During a price war in the airline industry a few years ago, American Airlines' CEO Robert Crandall was secretly recorded by Federal agents suggesting to Braniff's president that they both raise fares by 20 percent. Braniff declined the offer and in doing so probably saved Crandall from conviction for illegal price fixing.[5]

Company Pricing Information

The third source of information for input into the pricing decision, in addition to that from customers and competitors, is the information available from within the company itself. Primarily, we are referring here to cost information. Although established prices should *not* be based solely on the seller's cost structure, costs are one important element in determining an appropriate price.

Figure 7.4 shows the relationship between cost, CPV, and price.[6] Cost provides the floor below which a company would not sell the product. The difference between the unit cost of an offering and its price is called, of course, the margin. CPV forms the ceiling for the price, because above that level it is accepted that no customer will decide to buy the offering. Depending on the pricing objectives of the company and competitive pricing actions, the price must lie somewhere between the company's cost and its customers' CPV.

Figure 7.4 - Relationship of Cost, CPV, and Price

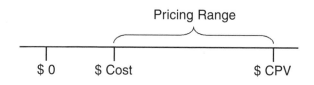

By now, it should be obvious that the quantified value of the CPV is a subjective estimate of a very complex thought process on the part of the customer. It is impossible to precisely determine such a value because it does not even exist with any precision in the mind of the customer. Nevertheless, for pricing purposes, an estimate of the customer's upper limit is probably a desirable objective.

There is no such problem when developing the cost figure, which provides the floor for the pricing decision. We are finding now that some accounting techniques can be improved upon and must be used with great care, but the fact remains that most companies are capable of determining the unit cost of their offering if they choose to invest the required effort.

The problem with product costing is that not even the accountants agree on a *single* answer to the question of what a product costs. This difficulty results from two accounting principles: *fixed costs* and *relevant costs*. The problem revolves around which of these various costs should be considered in each calculation. See Figure 7.5 for an illustration of these concepts.

Figure 7.5 - Alternative Costing Methods

	Fully-Allocated Costs	Variable Costs	Direct Costs
Direct labor	$4.00	$3.00	$3.00
Direct material	2.00	2.00	2.00
Sales commissions	.50	.50	.50
Manufacturing overhead	1.50	1.50	
Selling costs	1.00	1.00	
Corporate G&A	2.50		
Total product cost	$11.50	$8.00	$5.50

The *fully-allocated cost* calculation includes every possible cost associated with the product, including a portion of the fixed costs (the equipment, in this case) and all indirect costs, including overhead and administration. This approach to the calculation satisfies those who are most comfortable with the philosophy that "somebody has to pay for these things." If the anticipated volume of product is produced at the anticipated cost and sold at the anticipated price, the resulting profit will be exactly as expected.

The two problems with the fully-allocated cost calculation are: (1) fixed costs are allocated on the basis of projected volumes (not actually likely to occur), and (2) costs that would exist whether or not this product is sold are included in the calculated costs. Either or both of these circumstances can result in manufacturing and pricing decisions that are not in the best interests of the company.

The *variable cost* calculation eliminates the allocation of fixed costs to the product. This results in a cost estimate that remains accurate at all volume levels. If the management decision relates to a time frame shorter than the entire life of the long-term asset, then a variable cost calculation is more appropriate.

The problem with this approach, however, is that the cost of those long-term assets is not accounted for at all. If margins are very small (as computed based on the variable product cost), it is possible that the company would not recover the cost of the long-term assets employed and, therefore, incur an economic loss during the long term.

The *direct cost* calculation goes one step further than the variable cost calculation by removing even some of the variable costs from the arithmetic. The costs removed are those that are indirect and vary on some factor other than the volume of product sales. Administrative costs are a straightforward example of such costs because, even though they are variable and not long term in nature, incurring them is not directly related to producing the product itself. For instance, a plant superintendent would retain his job (perhaps in supervising the manufacture of some other product) even if none of the product being costed was produced.

Critics of the direct cost method argue that even more costs incurred by the company are being ignored in this approach. If this cost was used as the basis for the pricing "floor," they would say, the price might be set so low that it would result in the company "losing money on every sale."

Knowing which costs to include in the calculation of product costing lies in the time frame within which management decisions are being made. In the long term, all costs are variable, so the methods begin to approach the same answer. For any shorter time frames, however, some costs should be considered "sunk" and no longer relevant to the current decision being made. In other words, each of the methods shown in Figure 7.5 is correct, and each of them is wrong. It all depends on the nature of the decision being considered.

Management Judgment

Before leaving this overview of what is involved in making pricing decisions, another item should be mentioned. In addition to information gathered from the customer, the competition, and the company itself, a great deal of management judgment will be necessary to decide how to price an offering. There are so many projections, assumptions, and vagaries involved in pricing that much of the process remains more of an art than a science. Although we are firm believers that objective information gathered from sources in the marketplace can provide invaluable help in reducing uncertainties and improving the ability of managers to make the best decisions, all of that information must still be processed by and distilled into a final answer based on the judgment of the manager.

PRICING STRATEGIES

With the company's strategic objectives clarified and all available information inputs tapped, the manager must select a pricing approach to position the all-important pricing attribute on the customer's CPV balance scale. There exist just a few alternative pricing approaches:

> COST-BASED PRICING
> COMPETITOR-BASED PRICING
> CPV-BASED PRICING

Cost-Based Pricing

Setting prices based on the supplier's costs is the simplest and perhaps most widely used approach to pricing. Although it ignores both CPV and competitors' strategies, it is favored by many managers because cost data are readily available and using these data seems to provide a sense of order that is comforting. In some industries, cost-based pricing has evolved to the extent that it is considered to reflect, to some degree, customer and competitor expectations.

Markup Pricing

This is the most widely used approach to pricing based on costs. As shown in Figure 7.6, a unit cost is calculated for the offering and, to that, a predetermined markup is added. This is done throughout the marketing channel until, at the end-user level, the final price results.

Figure 7.6 - Example of Markup Pricing

Cost per unit	$8.00
Markup at 20%	1.60
Price	$9.60

Markup pricing is widely used in the construction industry, for example, where unit costs for every aspect of a construction project are well established. The task of the estimator in establishing the price of a large building, for example, is to identify all of the cost elements involved in the project and then simply add a profit markup. The practice has become so widely employed that the perceived economic value, as determined by the customer, is usually derived by the very same method.

Government agencies often require the cost-plus-markup approach to pricing its purchases. The intent, apparently, is to eliminate any possibility of overcharging by a vendor by requiring it to base its profits on the costs it incurs. Unfortunately, this logic does not support its purpose. As described at the beginning of this chapter, once a contractor has been awarded a contract on this basis, concerns about delivering the greatest value at the minimum cost no longer exist. In many cases, the more the contractor spends, the more profit he makes.

Cost-plus-markup prices are not necessarily favorable to sellers, either. Basing prices on costs means prices are not related to Customer Perceived Value, and, therefore, sellers cannot compete for business on the basis of the superior value they might be able to deliver. In other words, cost-plus-markup contracts tend to favor low-cost, low-CPV providers over others.

Target Profit Pricing

This pricing method is a subtle variation of the price-plus-markup approach. In target profit pricing, costs to the supplier of the offering are determined and the price is set at the level required to provide the seller with a predetermined profit. Figure 7.7 shows a simplified target profit pricing example.

Figure 7.7 - Example of a Target Profit Price Calculation

Capital invested in offering	$1,000,000
Targeted ROI	20%
Required profit	$200,000
Expected units to be sold	100,000
Required profit per unit	$2
Cost per unit	$8
Price	$10

This pricing method is widely used for reasons similar to those discussed for the price-plus-markup approach. Because target profit pricing is based on costs, the calculations are relatively easy and concrete. The automobile industry, for example, has for many years priced many of its vehicles based on attaining a 15 to 20 percent return on its investment.[7] Some very famous exceptions to this practice have occurred, however. Iacocca's market-oriented pricing of the first Mustangs in the 1960s is an example of one such exception.

The primary danger of target pricing to the seller is that the results are completely dependent upon an accurate projection of the volume to be sold. Only if that projected volume is realized will the targeted profit actually be attained. In all other cases, the pricing method will fail to meet its objective.

Competitor-Based Pricing

Pricing methods that move a step closer to those based on CPV are those based on competitors' prices. These are most often used by companies with smaller market shares that apparently believe their competitors are in a better position to evaluate market demand and customer perceptions.

Going Rate Pricing

Going rate pricing is, simply, a price *follower* strategy. With this approach, the company sets its price at, or slightly above or below, the point at which it believes the other companies with similar offerings will price their offerings. Gasoline retailers can often be seen practicing going-rate pricing by watching their competitors' price sign from across the street.

The underlying logic of "going rate pricing" is that the industry, as a whole, may be more capable of evaluating the market conditions that affect prices than can the individual firm. The disadvantage, of course, is that the company using it is electing not to use price to its advantage as an element of the marketing mix. This is probably why most users of the going rate pricing approach are the smaller participants in their respective industries.

Sealed Bid Pricing

Companies that participate in competitive bidding processes are practicing sealed-bid pricing. In such situations, the objective is to bid less than the other bidders but high enough to provide an acceptable profit to the firm. Many government agencies practice such competitive bidding processes.

The sophisticated sealed-bid pricer is playing a game of probabilities. Based on experience with the process, the bidder must estimate the likelihood of his bid being accepted at various discounting levels. The lower the bid price, the more likely the firm is to win the business but the lower the resulting profit to the firm will be. These factors can be combined, arithmetically, to calculate the *expected profit* related to each bid.

The disadvantage of this pricing approach to the buyer is that it is not helpful in trying to maximize CPV. Factors such as short-term capacity constraints or the level of current business with other companies will drive the pricing of each potential supplier. In other words, the *best* supplier may become unavailable if it has enough other business when the next bidding process occurs.

CPV-Based Pricing

Sometimes special circumstances or necessity require companies to price based on internal cost considerations or how their competitors price. In most cases, however, price should be determined based on its expected impact on the prospective customer (Figure 7.8). After all, the objective of the supplier is to influence the behavior of the customer to the greatest extent possible, and pricing is one of the most obvious ways to create that influence.[8]

Figure 7.8 - CPV-Based Pricing Strategies

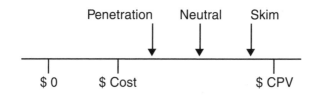

Setting price is such a complex and subjective matter that it's impossible to provide specific instructions on how to reach a final decision. Under the heading of CPV-based pricing, however, there are only three general directions to go:

> SKIM PRICING
> PENETRATION PRICING
> NEUTRAL PRICING

Skim Pricing

The company attempts to charge the maximum acceptable price to a relatively small portion of its potential market in the price skimming approach. The objective is to maximize profitability by charging a higher price even at the expense of selling a lower volume. Skim pricing is targeted at those customers who place greater weight on the benefits on the left side of the CPV balance scale and, therefore, will accept a higher price on the right side.

Airport restaurants and retail outlets have long practiced price skimming by charging more for products and services of equivalent value to that which is available at off-airport locations. Their objective has been to capitalize on the increased value of convenience to airport travelers to support the acceptance of these higher prices. In doing so, these retailers have chosen to forgo the market of non-travelers that otherwise might be attracted to dine or shop at these airport stores, thereby maximizing profits.

Often, price skimming cannot be maintained indefinitely because of competition. This results in the need to adjust the price downward throughout the life cycle of a product from when it is most unique in its introductory phase to when it becomes less distinctive in its more mature stages. This is because the number and weight of distinctive benefits on the CPV balance scale are declining and, therefore, the negative weight of a high price must be reduced in response.

Intel Corporation uses a skim pricing approach to the sale of its computer chips. When first introduced, prices are set very high, sometimes as much as $1,000 per chip. This limits the market for the new chip to those few who value most highly the incremental computing power provided by the chip or, simply, the importance of owning the "newest and the best." As that narrow market segment becomes saturated with the product, and competitors threaten to duplicate the technology, Intel drops its prices. By developing a continuous stream of innovative chips, the company is able to maintain a portfolio of products that cover all segments of the market, while skimming the highest possible price within each segment.

Penetration Pricing

The objective of penetration pricing is to sell the greatest possible volume to maximize profits. The pricing is lower, nearer the supplier's actual costs, to make the price attribute on the CPV balance scale have less of a negative impact on the customer's evaluation and tip the scale significantly toward the perceived benefits. This pricing approach is most successful in situations where increased sales volume results in cost savings to the supplier. In other words, when the fixed costs of the offering are relatively high, increased volume becomes more important and penetration pricing may be appropriate.

Several discount airlines have attempted to enter markets by adopting a penetration pricing approach. Because *most* of an airlines' operating costs are fixed per flight operated, filling the seats on each plane is a critical objective. Because the airline industry generally avoids competing on the basis of distinctive *benefits* on the left side of the CPV balance scale – preferring to allow customers to choose primarily only from schedule differences – the pricing attribute on the right side of the balance scale becomes one of the most influential in shaping customer behavior. People's Express was quite successful by lowering prices and filling up their seats. Unfortunately, they were unable to attain actual cost levels below any of the major airlines and could not sustain their penetration pricing approach for very long. Without profits, of course, the company eventually failed.

Neutral Pricing

The compromise is to seek a "happy medium" between the two more aggressive pricing approaches (skimming and penetration) and to seek price levels as close as possible to what customers would expect, based on their evaluation of the other benefits and costs on their CPV balance scale. This technique can be referred to as *neutral* customer-based pricing. Companies that emphasize competing on attributes on the CPV balance scale *other* than price are most often using a neutral customer-based pricing approach.

Clearly, as indicated in Figure 7.8, the selection between a skimming, penetrating, or neutral pricing approach is not a discrete one – they are simply points along the continuum between the company's costs and the customer's CPV. They serve only to highlight the differences between the approaches and provide some basis for rationally considering alternative pricing strategies.

The other issue this discussion draws out, we hope, is that the effectiveness of a pricing strategy will always be impacted by how the customer perceives the value of the offering. Price is just one element on the CPV balance scale and will be evaluated by the customer relative to the benefits and other costs he perceives. That is why it is critical for the manager to understand CPV to the greatest extent possible to make wise pricing decisions.

SUMMARY

Price is only one of the attributes that customers place on their CPV balance scales. Pricing decisions must be made in that context.

The manager will always require input from three sources for making effective pricing decisions. Understanding the customers' perception of the value of the offering, as well as the customers' sensitivity to price, is the most important issue. Understanding customer sensitivity to price is largely a matter of understanding the attributes, and their weights, that customers place on their CPV balance scales. Second, the manager needs to gain an understanding of competitors' prices, costs, and probable reactions to pricing decisions. Finally, the manager needs input about his own company's cost structure and capabilities.

With all of this information, managers can select from a range of possible pricing approaches, some based primarily on internal costs, others on competitors' prices, and the best on customer perceptions. Pricing decisions are usually subjective and difficult. Much of that subjectivity, however, and the uncertainty that accompanies these decisions can be offset by gaining a superior understanding of the benefits and costs that exist on the customers' CPV balance scale.

REFERENCES

[1] This example is primarily from E. Raymond Corey, "E.I. du Pont de Nemours & Co.," *Industrial Marketing: Cases and Concepts, 2nd Edition*, (Englewood Cliffs,

Prentice-Hall, 1976), pg. 179-187.

[2] For additional resources on pricing, see Thomas T. Nagle, *The Strategy and Tactics of Pricing*, (Englewood Cliffs, Prentice-Hall, 1995); Roger J. Best, *Market-Based Management: Strategies for Growing Customer Value and Profitability*, (Upper Saddle River, Prentice-Hall, 1997), Chapter 8; Robert J. Dolan, "How Do You Know When the Price Is Right?" *Harvard Business Review*, September-October 1995.

[3] See Leonard L. Berry and Manjit S. Yadav, "Capture and Communicate Value in the Pricing of Services," *Sloan Management Review*, Summer 1996, pg. 41.

[4] Adapted from Nagle, Chapter 3.

[5] Philip Kotler and Gary Armstrong, *Principles of Marketing: Eighth Edition*, (Upper Saddle River, Prentice-Hall, 1999), pg. 344.

[6] Adapted from James C. Anderson and James A. Narus, *Business Market Management: Understanding, Creating, and Delivering Value,* (Upper Saddle River, Prentice-Hall, 1998), pg. 188.

[7] Kotler and Armstrong, pg. 315.

[8] See Aimee L. Stern, "The Pricing Quandary: How to Raise 'em When the Buyer is Boss," *Across the Board,* May 1997, pg. 16-22.

CHAPTER 8

CPV and Channels

As in most mature industries, marketing channels in the U.S. automotive industry have evolved over many years. At the beginning, it was a 3-level system with the manufacturers selling to distributor/wholesalers who subcontracted to dealers to sell to end-user customers. By the 1920s, the manufacturers decided that they could push more cars if they had a more direct, controlling relationship with their dealers, so the distributor/wholesalers were eliminated. Dealers franchised directly by the manufacturers were granted the privilege of selling cars at retail and, in return, guaranteed by the manufacturers that their competition would be limited (a limited number of dealers were authorized and all consumer sales were required to go through one of those dealers). The matter of who bore the risk of inventory ownership was never completely clear, however, and was a cause of friction between the manufacturers and dealers for many years. For the most part, however, the franchised dealer system worked very well for both of those parties for about 70 years.[1]

But it didn't work very well for customers. Prodded by pressure from the manufacturers to move more product, most auto dealers learned to sell very aggressively. Americans were enamored with the annual new releases of streamlined cars and came to accept the unpleasant experience of buying a car. "Americans have traditionally bought cars by visiting cigar-smoking men in checked sports coats" and then, driving away in the new vehicle, "looking to make sure he still had his shirt on his back."[2] No customer ever said he liked the process, but given the few, if any, alternatives he tolerated this cost because the benefits on the other side of the CPV balance scale were sufficient.

Today, additional alternatives are becoming available to customers, resulting in a revolution in the structure of marketing channels for automobiles. The Internet, of course, is at the heart of these changes, and the various players are still jockeying for the most prominent roles.

The early new entrants into automobile marketing are mostly web-based start-ups. The largest, Autobytel.com, was launched in 1995 and quickly recruited more than 3,000 traditional auto dealerships across the country to join its network. Recently, Autobytel.com boasted that it is generating more than $1 million in car sales per hour!

But, how does Autobytel.com fit into the marketing channel for cars? This company and its competitors simply represent an additional layer between the manufacturer and the end customer. Because of long-standing franchise agreements, all new cars are sold by traditional dealers. Autobytel.com only refers customers to the dealers. It doesn't even promise a lower price than customers could obtain without its intervention. The company's claim to a role in the marketing channel is based solely on eliminating the unpleasantness of the customer-dealer interaction. Based on the success of Autobytel.com, however, that seems to be quite enough.

Auto manufacturers themselves, meanwhile, continue to struggle with what the next marketing channel should look like. Ford Motor Co. is conducting experiments with CarPoint.com, Carclub.com, and Priceline.com to determine what to do. General Motors is operating BuyPower, a site that allows prospects to explore a vast inventory of cars. In all cases, however, shoppers still must go to a dealer to pick up and pay for their new cars. Some industry leaders say the traditional dealer will always be a channel member, but others are still looking for a way to provide all the benefits of a showroom in another, more user friendly, way.

And it is the customer that is causing all of this commotion.

Marketing channels literally add an additional dimension to the marketing mix. Unlike the variables of product (Chapter 6), price (Chapter 7), and promotion (Chapter 9), the "place" element of the Four Ps usually requires the cooperation of more than one business entity. Especially true in the consumer sector, but often in the industrial sector as well, most manufacturers enlist the help of other companies to deliver their offering to the end customer. Middlemen and retailers, of course, exist *only* to serve as members of a marketing channel. Because there are multiple members of a marketing channel, channel decisions are often complex.[3]

The management of marketing channels is one of the best opportunities for companies to gain a competitive advantage. That is because the other three Ps have been the primary focus of competition and efforts to squeeze more Customer Perceived Value (CPV) out of them have often been exercised before. Some also say that marketing channels are more difficult for competitors to duplicate because (a) their construction is longer term in nature, (b) they require the establishment of structure between organizations, and (c) they are based on the development of relationships and people.[4] In addition to being more complex, channel decisions may represent one of the more promising areas for differentiation and competitive advantage.

PURPOSES OF MARKETING CHANNELS

Marketing channels can be used to add CPV for the end-user customer in many ways. Understanding those ways is important for designing the best system.

Facilitating Access of Customers and Suppliers

Middlemen and retailers enable customers to identify and evaluate offerings from various suppliers, and help deliver suppliers' offerings and promotional messages to their target markets. These functions primarily involve *communication* functions, such as sales calls, store displays, price quotes, order placement, etc.

Industrial manufacturers' representatives illustrate these functions well because they are the *only* functions that this type of middlemen usually perform. In the consumer sector, both the retailer and upstream middlemen such as distributors make contributions by facilitating communication between the customer and manufacturers.

Providing Logistics Services

Handling the product on its way from the manufacturer to the end customer is the traditional role of middlemen, consisting of breaking bulk, providing assortments, warehousing, inventory management, and delivery. In some cases, middlemen will take title to the product when they handle it, thereby taking on some of the financial risk for inventory as it moves through the channel.

Third-party logistics companies primarily provide these kinds of services. Some third-party logistics companies provide a full line of services, while others specialize in particular aspects such as warehousing or transportation.

Adding Value Directly to the Offering

While the first two channel functions, facilitating communication and providing logistics services, certainly add value to the offering, this third function involves the direct modification or enhancement of the product itself. Sometimes this entails physically modifying a product, such as assembling, fabricating, or finishing. In other cases, expertise is added to the offering through consulting, integrating, or systems design. In addition, supporting services such as in post-sale service and support may be added to the offering.

Many companies participate in the marketing channel by specializing in one or more of these value adding functions. The steel coating and lamination industry, for example, is a $9 billion industry that takes finished steel forms from steel manufacturers and changes their shape or performance and then passes it along to wholesalers or end users.

Figure 8.1 is a list of specific activities that often occur within marketing channels. These activities, as well as the categories of ways in which market channel members can contribute to CPV, lie at the heart of the decisions about channel make-up that each member of the marketing channel must address.

Figure 8.1 - Middlemen Functions

Selling and promoting	Management services
Buying and assortment building	Packaging
Bulk breaking	Assembling
Warehousing	Fabricating
Transportation	Finishing
Financing	Customer services
Risk-bearing	Integrating
Market information	Delivering

TYPES OF MARKETING CHANNELS

The traditional manufacturer-distributor-retailer channel, with each member operating relatively autonomously of the others in the channel, is an oversimplified description of the possibilities available for increasing the CPV delivered to end customers by multiple companies combining forces. Kotler and Armstrong call the new channel structures *systems* because they are actively managed as a coordinated unit.[5]

Vertical Marketing Systems

Vertical marketing systems (VMS) are channels that consist of the traditional players (producer, middlemen, retailer) but are actively managed in a coordinated fashion to better produce the desired CPV. They may take on several different forms.

Corporate VMS

In this structure, all (or most) of the traditional functions, from producer to retailer, are owned by a single corporate entity. This approach provides the company with the greatest possible control over all aspects of delivering CPV to end-user customers. On the other hand, it carries with it the greatest possible financial requirements and risk, as well as the requirement for the greatest variety of management expertise.

Wal-Mart's recent entry into the manufacture of laundry detergent marks another example of the retail giant's development of a corporate VMS. It manufactures or contracts for the soap and packaging of the product. It operates one of the world's most sophisticated logistics companies, which transports the product through its own warehouses on its own trucks. Finally, it sells the product from its own retail store shelves. With this approach, Wal-Mart is leaving no part of the functions of the marketing channel to chance or to anyone else's decision-making process.

Contractual VMS

These channels are based on comprehensive contractual relationships between otherwise independent companies. If it is working well, customers often cannot discern the difference between a corporate VMS and a contractual VMS. The purpose of a contractual VMS is to reduce the variability inherent in looser channel structures, without the financial requirements of one company owning all of the channel functions. The Independent Grocers Alliance (IGA), Ace Hardware, and Sentry Hardware are examples of contractual VMS.

An intense form of contractual VMS is the franchise system – the fastest growing of all forms of retailing in recent years, accounting for almost 40 percent of all retail sales in the U.S.[6] In the most common form of contractual VMS, manufacturers or producers enter into franchise agreements with retailers, as in the case of the auto manufacturers, Century 21 Realtors, and McDonald's restaurants. Other forms of the franchise system can occur within the marketing channel, however, such as the agreements that Coca-Cola has with its bottlers and Coors Beer has with its beverage distributors.

Cooperative VMS

These vertical marketing systems exist because one member of the channel is powerful enough to assume the role of channel leader. The leader, under this circumstance, may be any member of the channel from manufacturer to retailer. Manufacturers with strong brands, such as Procter & Gamble, can sometimes become very influential with middlemen and retailers. Situations in which middlemen are able to take the leadership role in marketing channels are relatively rare, but can occur. Such is the case of importers of specialty products, for example liquors and wine. Retailers are becoming the more frequent leaders of cooperative vertical marketing systems as the access to end-user customers becomes ever more important to the entire channel. Wal-Mart, Home Deport, and Toys "R" Us are examples of this current trend in retailing.

Horizontal Marketing Systems

What Kotler and Armstrong call horizontal marketing systems are simply nontraditional combinations of channel members formed to better perform one or more of the traditional channel roles of producer, middleman, or retailer.

The gradual blending of grocery superstores (such as Kroger and Safeway) and variety discounters (such as Wal-Mart and Kmart) is one example of new horizontal marketing systems. The offerings of both of these types of traditional retailers has grown dramatically during the last decade to the point that Kroger is now selling small appliances and yard tools while Wal-Mart SuperCenters are offering full-line grocery departments. In addition, nontraditional offerings such as banking services, event ticketing, and travel services are finding that these retail outlets are serving their marketing channel needs very well.

Hybrid Marketing Systems

A hybrid marketing system is Kotler and Armstrong's terminology for companies that utilize multiple marketing channels for the same offering. In almost every such case, the intent is to reach different segments of the end-user market by using a marketing channel that best meets the needs of each segment.

Sometimes the distinction between industrial market segments is based on the size of the customer to the supplier. Large customers are called *national accounts* and managed by a small cadre of consultative selling specialists called national account managers. Smaller customers, on the other hand, might be served through a direct sales force or another channel member, for instance, a distributor.

In the consumer sector, most large retailers are trying to determine how they will operate both their traditional bricks-and-mortar retail stores as well as their e-commerce outlets on the Internet. In these cases, the objective is usually to serve different needs of an otherwise single segment of customers. The e-commerce offering provides easy access, wide selection, and delivery right to the consumer's door. The bricks-and-mortar store provides selling assistance and the ability to "touch and feel" the product before purchasing it.

The primary advantage of a hybrid marketing system is that more market segments can be targeted with a variety of different ways to deliver CPV. The disadvantage is the complexity of the system, which results in greater financial requirements, more management challenges, and the potential for customer confusion.

IMPORTANCE OF MARKETING CHANNEL DECISIONS

As is true in each of the other marketing mix decisions, the make-up of marketing channels should be based on CPV. Stating this is more significant than it might first appear. How customers perceive the output of a marketing channel may cause managers to design and manage channels in ways that they might otherwise not have done.

The lubricating product known as WD-40 is found in 75 percent of all U.S. households, despite its being made by a relatively small company that offers no other products. Giants such as 3M, DuPont, and GE have tried to displace WD-40 from its leadership position in this niche market without success. The company's success is based largely on its ability to develop and manage an incredible marketing channel consisting of nearly every form of retail outlet imaginable. WD-40 is everywhere. The company ensures that it maintains this availability to the consumer by actively managing its outlets with special deals, point-of-sale displays, and promotional campaigns.

Gucci, on the other hand, learned the hard way that too many retail outlets was to its disadvantage. For a long time, this Italian company paid little attention to its marketing channels – it just kept making and shipping its products to whomever placed an order. By the late 1980s, Gucci products could be found in thousands of retailers, including some low-end outlets where this luxury product would not usually be expected to appear. This contradicted Gucci's luxury image – an important part of its CPV. When Gucci management realized what was happening, it restructured its marketing channels to include less than 500 retailers in total, each one selected to be consistent with the desired upscale image. In one year after these changes, profits were up by 45 percent![7]

INFORMATION REQUIREMENTS FOR CHANNEL DESIGN

Because of the added dimension involved in marketing channels – more than one player being involved – the development of an effective marketing channel results from several different companies agreeing on the best way to deliver CPV to end-user customers. To some degree, therefore, each member of the marketing channel should have input into the decision on how the channel will be constituted. It is most convenient, however, to view the design of the channel from the viewpoint of the manufacturer or producer, because that is where the offering originates.

The first step in the channel design process is to analyze the situation from every possible aspect. That means gathering information about these four elements:

CUSTOMERS
THE PRODUCT
THE COMPANY
CHANNEL MEMBERS

Customers

The end-user customer is, of course, the most important source of information about marketing channel requirements. Because the objective is to maximize the contribution of the marketing channel to total CPV, it is necessary to thoroughly understand what the customer places on his CPV balance scale that can be impacted by the marketing channel. Kotler suggests that there are five categories of such things.[8]

Lot Size

How many units of the offering is the customer likely to purchase at one time? Large companies purchasing personal computers a hundred at a time have different channel requirements than does the individual household that buys one computer every two or three years.

Waiting Time

How long does the customer expect to wait for delivery after the order is placed? Customers would likely wait a few days to get the exact new car they want but need the repair part necessary to get the old junker back on the road right away. Channel requirements for new cars are different, therefore, than car repair parts.

Spatial Convenience

How far does the customer expect to travel to receive the offering? Most of the SOHO (small office, home office) market travels to a Staples, Office Depot, or OfficeMax to pick up office supplies. Large companies, however, expect supplies to be delivered to their loading docks, so companies provide delivery service for larger orders.

Product Variety

How much variety does the customer expect to evaluate at one time and location? Independent insurance agents offer clients the appearance that they will compare policies from different insurance companies to best meet their needs. Company affiliated agents sell only their own company's products. The decision about which agent structure to use is an important channel decision for insurance companies, hopefully based on the expectations of their target market.

Attributes of the Offering

The manager must understand each of the benefits and costs that the customer places on his CPV balance scale to determine what the marketing channel's role in connection with those attributes should be. Kotler calls this criterion *service backup* and includes under this caption credit, delivery, installation, and repairs services. It is actually somewhat broader than that, however. Every CPV attribute should be examined to determine which channel member is best equipped to contribute that aspect of the Value to the offering.

Most raw beef, for example, is delivered to grocery stores by the "side." At the store, that side of beef is carved into individual portions and packaged in plastic wrap. This is done this way, presumably, because the grocery store is more capable of efficiently packaging individual portions of meat than is the packing house that slaughtered and cleaned the beef. Where brand identity is a part of the value equation, however, such as with Perdue chicken, the individual packaging (which carries the brand identity) moves up the marketing channel to the brand owner. The distributor of Perdue chicken products, therefore, delivers it to the grocery stores already in individualized packages.

Sometimes which channel member contributes an element of CPV is as simple as who can do it more cheaply. This is the basis of much *outsourcing* in the field of logistics. Modern public warehouses, for example, are rapidly expanding their traditional break bulk-and-ship function to include other services such as import/export services, packaging, carrier management, display building, labeling, transportation management, and light assembly. If, by specializing in such activities, the warehouseman can do it for less cost than can the manufacturer, then CPV is increased (maximum benefits, minimal costs) by assigning the function to the warehouse operator.

The Product

Rosenbloom points out several aspects of the offering itself that must be considered in designing marketing channels.[9] Those aspects with the most impact are reviewed here.

Unit Value

Usually, the lower the value of the product, the longer the marketing channel must be. This is to spread the costs of distribution over all of the many products that most middlemen handle, thereby allowing each unit to incur less cost. Few grocery items, for example, are sold directly by their producers to consumers because such a distribution system would be very costly.

Degree of Standardization

Usually, the more standardized a product, the greater the contribution of middlemen. For example, industrial fasteners are generally sold through wholesaler/distributors, because the manufacturer produces a 3/4 inch bolt in large quantity runs. Distributors who break bulk to individual orders and offer a variety of nuts and bolts add significant value to the individual bolt. Large, custom-made machinery, however, is often purchased by the user directly from the manufacturer – because in this case there is less opportunity for a middleman to add value.

Degree of Technical Sophistication

It is generally difficult for middlemen to add CPV to the most technical products because of the specialized knowledge required during the sale as well as for service and support. Therefore, the most technical products are often sold directly by manufacturers or through a relatively short marketing channel. Where the market size permits, however, middlemen may address the specialization required and join the marketing channel. This is the case where large personal computer retailers have entered the market for after-the-sale service and support of that equipment.

The Company

The capabilities of the manufacturer itself must be understood to properly design a marketing channel and evaluate which channel member is most capable of making each contribution to CPV.

Size

The economic impact that a company has on the marketing channel is one source of channel *power*. (Channel power is the ability to make decisions on behalf of the other members of that channel.) We'll examine the other sources of channel power later in this chapter, but for now it is sufficient to point out that a larger player is more likely to be able to influence the other channel members and, therefore, impact the structure of the channel. In other words, a small manufacturer probably has a greater need for the assistance of middlemen to move his product to the customer than does a large manufacturer.

Financial Strategy

One of the primary purposes of a marketing channel is to share the investment requirements and associated risk cumulatively involved in delivering CPV. Therefore, the greater the financial resources of the company, the less need there is for the help of other channel members. This financial requirement is relative, of course. General Motors budgeted $2 billion to buy out only 1,500 of its 8,500 franchisees, suggesting that these middlemen are extremely valuable to GM.[10] Even this industrial giant could not practically substitute its own financial resources for those provided by its marketing channel.

Management Expertise

After the age of the conglomerates in the 1960s and 1970s came the age of *focus* in the 1980s and 1990s. Many business experts advise that the marketing channel should be used to deploy the most specialized expertise possible to the cause of delivering the greatest CPV. Manufacturers should manufacture, they say, and hire transportation experts to move the product, warehouse experts to store the product, and sales experts to promote the product. Nike is an extreme example of this practice, having built a company with nearly $9 billion in annual sales without any manufacturing facilities of its own. Everything at Nike, except for product design and marketing activities, is outsourced, because Nike management believes that design and marketing is where their expertise lies.

Strategy Requirements for Control and Flexibility

The longer the marketing channel, the less control and flexibility retained by the manufacturer. Where control and flexibility is important, therefore, the channel must be designed to accommodate it. The huge trucking firm, Schneider National, for example, maintains a large direct sales force because it is unwilling to delegate this work to a transportation broker. By selling its services directly, it facilitates the delivery of value-added logistics services (control) and allows the company to better deal with the seasonal fluctuations in demand that occur each year in the trucking business (flexibility).

Channel Members

Information about potential channel members must be collected to select the best alternative among them. Some information is collected from end customers, based on their all-important perceptions of channel members with whom they have direct interaction, some is gathered from the remainder of the marketplace, and some must be obtained by direct communication with the potential channel member. Here are a few of the issues that should be clarified about potential channel members before the channel design decision is finalized.

Capabilities

The selection of a middleman or retailer is really a matter of deciding if someone else can do the job better than the company can do it itself. Therefore, the object here is to identify the types and capabilities of potential channel partners so that those capabilities can be matched up with the proposed channel strategy.

Michael Dell, the founder and CEO of direct-seller Dell Computer, insists that he embarked on the direct-selling strategy because the attributes of Customer Perceived Value on which he wanted to distinguish his company (technical consulting, customization, and rapid delivery) were simply unavailable from the traditional marketing channels for personal computers.[11]

Compatibility

Marketing channel members visible to the end customer must make sense to that customer if they are going to be able to contribute to the delivery of CPV. For example, when Compaq Computer designed its marketing channel for its industrial markets, it chose to forgo the traditional business-to-business approach of a direct sales force and rely, instead, on the ability of giant consumer retailers such as CompUSA to also serve these industrial markets. The success of this strategy was dependent on (1) the ability of CompUSA to develop the capabilities necessary to serve this different market and (2) the acceptance of those industrial buyers of CompUSA as a legitimate source for their needs. In this case, the decision was apparently a good one because, while Dell and Gateway gain a lot of publicity for their direct sales efforts, Compaq remains the largest seller of computer systems in the world.

Channel Member Strategy

Every successful marketing channel is, in a sense, a *partnership* dedicated to deliver the greatest possible CPV to the end-user customer. Such a partnership requires the cooperation and commitment of each member to that cause. This can happen only if the members' goals and strategies are congruent.

For example, it is Wal-Mart's strategy to offer high-volume, competitively priced consumer products that don't require much point-of-sale support. The inventor of a new, high-tech product requiring introduction to the narrow consumer market segment of "early adopters" would probably find Wal-Mart's lack of interest in his product frustrating. What is at issue in this case, however, is a mismatch of strategies. The inventor would do better to develop marketing channels with middlemen whose strategies are more compatible, such as special interest magazine, mail order, and specialty products retailers such as Sharper Image.

POWER WITHIN MARKETING CHANNELS

We touched briefly on the issue of *power* in the marketing channel when we described hybrid cooperative marketing systems earlier in this chapter. We now need to address how channel members gain power and what the results of wielding that power can be.

Sources of Channel Power

We define power as the ability of a channel member to influence or control other channel members in the performance of their respective roles. This power can be formally assigned to one of the channel members by agreement among the parties, or it can be informally assumed and executed by one of the members. In either case, the power is based on one of several sources.[12]

Legitimate Power

This is the term used when members of a channel decide, based on their own values and reasoning, that another channel member is entitled to be the leader. In a vertical marketing system where the channel roles are performed by companies owned or legally related to one another, the parent company will likely enjoy legitimate power over the other members. A variation on this is when complex legal agreements are struck between channel members, such as a franchise agreement, wherein the agreement itself defines the channel leader, granting that entity legitimate power.

Historically, the largest economic entity in the marketing channel usually gained legitimate power granted by the smaller channel members. The automobile manufacturers, for example, were able to design and manage their dealership network much as they wanted, because of dealer-granted legitimate power. As proximity to customers has become a much more important factor, however, and all channel members recognize this phenomenon, even auto dealers are less likely to grant legitimate power to the manufacturers.

Referent Power

Referent power is the marketing channel's equivalent of "branding." Some members of marketing channels gain power because they are desired members of the channel. Channel members see this kind of leader as someone with whom they want to do business, so they are willing to give that member some degree of power over them as an inducement to participate in the channel.

Producers of luxury or exclusive products are those most likely to gain referent power. Manufacturers of such products often purposely limit their accessibility (by limiting the number of downstream channel members they allow to handle the product) to develop and maintain a sense of exclusivity. Rolex watches, for example, are sold only through a small network of specialty jewelry stores, as opposed to Timex watch's wide distribution system, which includes most variety retail stores. Small retailers aspiring to that same image of exclusivity, then, are often willing to grant referent channel power to Rolex, to make sure they are themselves a member of that watch maker's channel.

Expert Power

This kind of channel power is based on the member demonstrating expertise in an area important to the success of the channel, thus earning the right to make decisions affecting other channel members. Pioneer Seed Co., for example, rapidly gained market share when it began to share its significant knowledge about crop yield management with its distributors and farmers. Wholesalers in the pharmaceutical, automotive parts, and hardware parts industries, such as Cardinal Health, NAPA, and Cotter, maintain the channel leadership they enjoy by providing consulting services in management, merchandising, and human resources management to the small retailers to which they sell.

The problem with expert power is that it is lost when the expertise is fully transferred to the other party. Franchise agreements (a source of legitimate power) came about because the expert power brought to those relationships by such companies as McDonald's and Dunkin' Donuts was not protectable except by a written, legal agreement. Nevertheless, while it lasts, expert power enables companies to take a leadership role in marketing channels by demonstrating that they know more than the other channel members.

Reward Power

Outside of formal agreements that convey legitimate power to one channel member, reward power is probably the source of most channel leadership today. Reward power is granted by channel members because there is "something in it for them" to cooperate. In other words, the leader makes the other channel members a deal that is attractive enough to ensure their participation in the channel according to the leader's terms. Rewards, in this category can include profit margins, promotional allowances, volume discounts, and exclusive territories. Reward power is a negotiated power, so its extent and endurance are dependent on the nature of the deal.

The American automobile industry has demonstrated a cyclical use of reward power in dealings with its primary suppliers. In the 1980s, auto manufacturers began to use reward power more heavily when they realized they needed the expertise their suppliers could contribute toward improving the quality and reducing the costs of automobiles. Only then did they begin offering longer-term contracts (two to three years) to their best suppliers to ensure their participation with them. Recently, they have started to withdraw those kinds of rewards and revert to their previous "arm's length" approach to supplier relationships. It remains to be seen whether the suppliers will tolerate this approach or diversify away from the auto makers as they did in the 1970s.[13]

Coercive Power

Coercive power represents the "other side" of reward power. Rather than rewarding desired behavior, the wielder of coercive power attempts to *punish* undesirable behavior by withholding rewards, withholding product, or reducing purchases.

Jose Ignacio Lopez became infamous at General Motors for his use of coercive power over suppliers. He was promoted by new CEO Jack Smith from a purchasing position in Europe to take over the entire function at corporate headquarters in 1992. If someone wanted to do business with GM, Lopez and his staff would subject him to countless rounds of bidding and then demand even greater price concessions. If he resisted, Lopez would require an investigation into the supplier's own cost structure to find cost cutting measures that could be dictated by GM. Lopez was very successful in cutting overall costs at GM, but few suppliers expressed sympathy when Lopez jumped to Volkswagen and was subsequently indicted under trade secrets laws.

Although it is convenient to discuss the sources of marketing channel power one at a time as we have done, most channel relationships are less precise than this and each of the channel members has areas in which it may be the leader. Although more and more power is moving toward the customer and the retail outlet, middlemen still often exert power in the channel regarding matters of logistics and manufacturers regarding issues of product features. And all channel members use a combination of the sources of power we've discussed here to maintain their position in the channel.

FOCUSING ON CUSTOMER PERCEIVED VALUE

Ultimately, the fact remains that the purpose of a successful marketing chain is to deliver the greatest possible CPV. To do that, the needs of the end-user customer must rise above any conflicting needs of the marketing channel members, and that is a level of understanding difficult for many companies to attain.

Many middlemen in various industries are finding that their traditional role of break bulk-and-ship is not as valued by other channel members as it used to be. As retailers consolidate and increase in size, they are sometimes just as adept at the break bulk-and-ship function as middlemen can be. These large retailers are taking on this job themselves and cutting the middleman (and his share of the profits) out of the channel altogether. This phenomenon is called *disintermediation* and it is occurring in many different industries.

Middlemen affected by this trend must realize that it is a natural process driven by the ongoing need to increase CPV. Anytime that costs can be removed from the marketing channel without reducing customer-perceived benefits of equal value there exists the ability to increase CPV. Rather than decrying the reduction in perceived value of their traditional break bulk-and-ship function, these middlemen must step up to finding other ways to contribute CPV to the marketing channel or face risk of extinction.

To the extent that channel members recognize the "end game" of driving CPV, then, real *power* in the marketing channel comes from the ability to contribute to CPV. The member that can contribute an important part of CPV better than any other member will remain a valued and powerful member of the channel.

Most consumers probably don't know (or care) who the original supplier was of the power supply in their personal computers. For that and other reasons, computer power supplies are nearly a commodity product, and producers struggle to maintain share of their respective markets by competing primarily on price. They have little power in their marketing channel.

Intel Corporation manufactures a related device, the computer chip that manages the logic performed in the personal computer. Readers probably already know this, because Intel has successfully gone beyond just the manufacturing of these electronic devices to create additional CPV. Intel has spent millions of dollars in consumer advertising to build a *brand* that is valued by end-user customers. That brand is so powerful that the computer manufacturers, including giants such as IBM and Compaq, now must allow Intel's famous "Intel Inside" logo to appear prominently on their product packaging. Intel contributes to CPV by reducing the apparent risk to consumers of a difficult, technical purchasing decision. In the process of doing that, Intel has gained unprecedented power in the marketing channel for personal computers.

Using Research to Increase Channel Power

As we discussed at the outset, not all companies have discovered that Customer Perceived Value is the only thing that matters. To the extent this is true today, it is a relatively new phenomenon. The intensity of competition and the amount of information available to customers is greater than it used to be. Many companies that became large and successful with a product focus have yet to realize that things are different now. They are finding it more difficult than expected to convert to a customer focus.

Owning information is the key to attaining channel power. The ability to understand and communicate the principles of CPV to other channel members may be a form of *expert power* that proves to be more useful and valuable for the purpose of designing and managing marketing channels than any other.

Channel Member Research

Channel members, of course, each operate on their own CPV Management Cycle (see Chapter 3). That is, their actions are ultimately a result of their *perceptions* of what is best for them to do. Given their distinctive positions and roles in the marketing channel, differences in perceptions are common. The only way to cut through these differences is to conduct effective market research.

Rosenbloom tells the story of an industrial sealants manufacturer who was frustrated with its wholesale distributors' selling efforts on its behalf. The distributors' sales representatives were not properly using the manufacturer's product samples. From its perspective, the manufacturer believed that the package of samples provided was first-rate. Finally, it conducted research on these distributors and found that the samples package was difficult for the representatives to carry. It had been designed to fit into a briefcase, and these salespeople didn't carry briefcases! The manufacturer was able to make minor adjustments to the samples package and solve the problem.[14]

Most problems in channel management aren't that simple, of course. Members of a marketing channel need to understand the entire CPV balance scale of each of the other members of that channel. What do those members perceive to be benefits they contribute to CPV? What, in their view, are the benefits contributed by others in the channel? What is the relative importance (weighting) of each of those benefits, in the channel member's view? How do those members perceive that different channel members would impact the CPV ultimately delivered to the channel's end-user customer?

All of these questions can be answered with good marketing research. Too few companies realize, however, that sometimes channel members should be the subject of that research.

End Customer Research

One of our primary arguments in this book is that customer research can be more valuable than many managers expect if it is done properly. With regard to marketing channels, customer research is, in fact, too important to be left only to the channel member that happens to be closest to the customer. That channel member may not be conducting research, may be doing it poorly, or may be using it only to gain information useful to his specific role in the channel. Although shortsighted, it is not an uncommon approach.

Understanding end-user CPV on a firsthand basis can be helpful for other channel members to improve their own performance within the channel, and ownership of that information can be a source of channel power as well. Often, input directly from the customer can be a very powerful element in a debate about almost any management decision. Middlemen that are being disintermediated are better off if they understand that their problem is finding new ways to create CPV. Manufacturers with powerful brands will want to wield that power in the channel and customer input that validates the brand's power is invaluable in doing so.

A large electric utility company in the Midwest found that many of its major industrial customers had little understanding of what their customers valued about their offerings. These customers were predominantly old-line industrial products companies that were still primarily product-focused. In its search to find new ways to add CPV for these large customers in the face of deregulation, the utility offered to conduct end-user customer research for them. The results of that research, to be shared by both the utility and its customers, would be used to identify ways that the customer companies could become more customer focused. Although most of those opportunities had little to do with the generation of electricity, the utility company improved its relationships with these industrial customers (delivered greater CPV!) by gathering and sharing marketing research information from end-user customers.

Resolving Channel Conflicts

As marketing channels get more complex, *channel conflict* is more of a problem, often occurring when members of a channel focus on different objectives and, therefore, act in ways that are inconsistent with one another. Channel conflict can be categorized according to the relationship of the conflicting members in the channel.

Vertical Channel Conflicts

Vertical channel conflicts occur between different levels in a marketing channel. For example, when automobile dealers complain that the manufacturers are "dumping" too much inventory on them by requiring them to take more closeout models than they can sell in a reasonable time, it is a case of vertical channel conflict. Disagreements concerning the appropriate level of sales support that industrial distributors will provide for a manufacturer's line of products are another example.

Horizontal Channel Conflicts

Horizontal channel conflicts are those disputes that occur between similar members of a marketing channel. Franchisees that have conflicts with one another, such as Pizza Hut franchisees who complain about others dragging down the franchise image, are examples of horizontal channel conflicts. Sometimes horizontal conflicts are the result of vertical channel conflicts, such as when automobile dealers think that the manufacturers have granted too many dealer franchises, which results in too much cutthroat competition among the dealers.

Multichannel Conflicts

Multichannel conflicts occur when manufacturers establish more than one marketing channel and those channels encounter one another competing for the same customer. These conflicts can occur within the same company, such as when disputes arise between a field sales force and a national accounts team about how to serve a particular large customer. Another source of multichannel conflict has emerged in the form of e-commerce. Many consumer products that traditionally were sold at bricks-and-mortar retail outlets have now been made available via the Internet. Those two channels are engaged in heated battles to determine which can find the way to deliver superior CPV to win the right to survive.

There is a large body of literature devoted to managing and resolving channel conflicts. Its primary message, however, is that the cause and solution to such conflicts revolves around a system of goals and rewards for each channel member. Just like customers, channel members are usually driven by "what's in it for me." That's entirely appropriate, because that's how our system works so well.

And, there is a good solution readily available for all kinds of channel conflict. That solution is to recognize the end-user customer as the final arbiter of decisions about the marketing channel. Effective marketing channel members realize that the purpose of channels is to attract and retain customers. The best combination of skills and resources that can be assembled from respective channel members to increase end-customer CPV is the shape that every marketing channel should take. When the focus of all channel members becomes understanding how customers stack up the benefits and costs on their CPV balance scale, channel conflicts fade away.

SUMMARY

Managing marketing channels is complex because, by definition, more than one company is usually involved in a channel. Nevertheless, or perhaps because of that complexity, marketing channels represent exceptional opportunities for companies to increase CPV and, therefore, competitive advantage.

Marketing channels have three fundamental purposes: facilitating access of customers and suppliers to each other, providing logistics services, and adding value directly to the offering – representing the areas within which the channels can increase CPV.

As companies attempt to deliver more and more CPV by better managing marketing channels, those channels are receiving more scrutiny and management attention. Those that are being managed in an effective, coordinated manner are being called, by some, "marketing systems." Marketing systems come in three forms. Vertical marketing systems look like the traditional channels consisting of producers, middlemen, and retailers. These channels may exist within one company, may be based on contractual relationships between several companies, or exist based on more informal cooperation between the companies. Horizontal marketing systems are those where channel members are expanding their reach to serve more members and carry more variations of product. Hybrid marketing systems refer to the use of multiple marketing channels by a single producer for the same product.

Deciding what channels to use and how to manage those channels can be two of the most important strategic decisions a manager must make. Information to help in making those decisions involves an understanding of customers, the product, the supplying company, and other channel members. There are many things to know in each of those areas, all of which can help management to make better marketing channel decisions.

The right to make and implement decisions about marketing channels is based on relative "power" in the channel. Marketing channel power is granted to channel leaders based on legitimate power, referent power, expert power, reward power, and/or coercive power. Perhaps the greatest power of all, however, is superior knowledge of the specifics of CPV.

Good research is a fundamental requirement for gaining an understanding of CPV. Such research should be targeted at not only the end-user customer, but also the various members of the marketing channel themselves. The information gathered from such research is invaluable in designing marketing channels, acquiring and maintaining a leadership role in the channel, and resolving the inevitable conflicts that will occur among channel members.

REFERENCES

[1] See Alfred P. Sloan, Jr., *My Years With General Motors*, (Garden City, Doubleday, 1963), pg. 279-301.

[2] Alex Taylor III, "Who'll be the Amazon.com of the $1 trillion car biz? The Internet meets the auto market," *Fortune*, April 26, 1999, pg. 465.

[3] In addition to Rosenbloom and Stern, referenced below, other resources on channels include James C. Anderson and James A. Narus, *Business Market Manage-*

ment: Understanding, Creating, and Delivering Value, (Upper Saddle River, Prentice-Hall, 1998), Chapters 7 and 9; Roger J. Best, *Market-Based Management: Strategies for Growing Customer Value and Profitability,* (Upper Saddle River, Prentice-Hall, 1997), Chapter 9.

[4] Bert Rosenbloom, *Marketing Channels: A Management View*, (Orlando, Dryden Press, 1999), pg. 5.

[5] Philip Kotler and Gary Armstrong, *Principles of Marketing: Eighth Edition,* (Upper Saddle River, Prentice-Hall, 1999), pg. 357.

[6] Louis W. Stern and Adel I. El-Ansary, *Marketing Channels: Fourth Edition,* (Englewood Cliffs, Prentice-Hall, 1992), pg. 251.

[7] Rosenbloom, Chapter 5.

[8] Philip Kotler, *Marketing Management: The Millennium Edition,* (Upper Saddle River, Prentice-Hall, 2000), pg. 494.

[9] Rosenbloom, Chapter 6.

[10] Alex Taylor III, "How to buy a car on the Internet," *Fortune*, March 4, 1996, pg. 164.

[11] Rosenbloom, pg. 189.

[12] Stern and El-Ansary, pg. 273.

[13] Stern and El-Ansary, pg. 279.

[14] Rosenbloom, Chapter 9.

CPV and Marketing Communications

Starbucks sells a cup of coffee for $1.40, when coffee sells for $.50 at the store next door. How it can get away with that is a story of excellence in developing and leveraging a brand. Although some stock analysts are periodically critical of the company's performance, Starbucks Coffee Company continues to manage one of the great brand names in the world, often mentioned in the same category as Coca-Cola and Tide.

What is this Starbucks brand? According to the company itself, "Your Starbucks experience is so much more than just coffee. It's the conversation you have with a friend, a moment of solitude at the end of the day, a quick stop on the way to the movies. And in the tradition of the coffeehouse, it's also the chance to immerse yourself in eclectic and enduring music while you sip your favorite coffee."[1] Specifically, "the store, its ambiance and finally the coffee are the main touchpoints to connect with the consumer."[2]

The company's origin was one coffee shop in Seattle's Pike Place Market, first opened in 1971. Howard Schultz, the genius behind the development of the Starbucks brand, was hired by the coffee shop in 1982 as its director of retail operations and marketing. Within a couple of years of joining the company, Schultz convinced the owners of the original location to open a second site and, soon thereafter, Schultz bought the company from them. In 1987, he opened the first stores outside Seattle, in Chicago, and in Vancouver, B.C.

From the start, Schultz was "thinking outside the bean." With only one store, he was selling coffee beans to local grocery stores. By 1990, he had a contract with a national airline to serve Starbucks coffee on board, in 1991 he was operating a kiosk in the Sea-Tac International Airport, and in 1993 he began opening locations within Barnes & Noble bookstores. And that was just the beginning. Today, Starbucks has more than 2,200 retail outlets and strategic partnerships with a long list of distributors. More importantly, Starbucks has built such a brand identity that some people call every serving of coffee they consume a "cup of Starbucks."

The company lays out its strategy right on its very public website: "The Company's objective is to establish Starbucks as the most recognized and respected brand in the world."[3] And, of course, Starbucks' brand was built on much more than the coffee. It comes from the way in which the pieces of the customer's experience are put together. It includes the locations, and the music, and the ambience. It results in a unique experience that is the primary basis of the company's market valuation of more than $7 billion – more than seven times the value of the actual net assets of the company.

Today, loyal customers can buy not only coffee, but also compact discs, premium tea products, ice cream, malt beer, bottled iced coffee, and a magazine. To the dismay of skeptics, Schultz has recently announced his intention to also sell furniture through a to-be-developed website.

What makes Howard Schultz think people will buy furniture from him? It's all in the brand. A successful brand, like Starbucks, turns into a customer-perceived benefit on the left side of the customer's CPV balance scale. Because that benefit exists well beyond the other physical attributes of the specific product, it serves very nicely in the same place on the customer's balance scale for other offerings. And Howard Schultz appears eager to test just how far away from the original product offering that brand will stand up to the test.

WHAT ARE MARKETING COMMUNICATIONS?

Some people refer to the subject of this chapter as just plain "marketing" – the visible activities involved in connecting with prospects and customers to convince them to buy something. We prefer the term "marketing communications," however, because that preserves the one-word term for the broader subject of making strategy, managing the marketing mix, and maintaining a customer focus throughout the company. Marketing communications is about just one of the four Ps making up the marketing mix – Promotion.[4]

However, the breadth and complexity of marketing communications should not be understated. In many ways, it overlaps some of the other elements of the marketing mix, in that there are marketing communications issues to be addressed in the development of the offering itself (Product), the price positioning (Price), and how the product reaches the customer (Place). The reason these issues all tend to meld together is because the objective is singular: Influence the definition of Customer Perceived Value (CPV) by the target marketplace. For example, whether we call the color selection in the packaging of a consumer product a Product issue or a matter of Promotion has little consequence in the actions to be taken or the end result impacting customer perceptions. For our purposes, therefore, we will focus on the aspects of that fourth P, Promotion, as we discuss marketing communications in this chapter.

Purposes of Marketing Communications

Marketing communications serves two different purposes: First, prospects must be made aware of the benefits and costs of the offering to be able to mentally create their own CPV balance scale. The objective is to do this as truthfully as possible, while at the same time favoring the company's offering over others. Second, the interactions connected with communicating with prospects should, of themselves, create value for the prospect to the greatest extent possible. Every customer interaction is a "value opportunity," including the marketing communication interaction itself.

Types of Marketing Communications

To provide an "inventory" of marketing communication practices, it is convenient to think about these six categories:

ADVERTISING
PUBLICITY
SALES PROMOTION
DIRECT MARKETING
PERSONAL SELLING
RESELLER SUPPORT

Advertising

Advertising occurs in many forms – television, radio, magazines, newspapers, billboards, and Internet websites. The distinction of advertising from other forms of promotion is that it is public, one-directional, and should be targeted at a market segment rather than individuals. It can be very expensive or quite inexpensive, depending on the medium and scope of the campaign. Millions of dollars are spent trying to measure the effectiveness of advertising, but that remains a significant challenge, especially in the industrial sector.

The Super Bowl of advertising is the Super Bowl itself. On one Sunday in the middle of winter, companies of all sizes and shapes commit huge sums to communicate their message to an audience estimated at almost 88 million people. Recently, companies as diverse as General Motors, Andersen Consulting, and small dot-com companies have paid more than $2 million for each 30-second spot on Super Bowl Sunday.

A newer phenomenon in advertising is the "banner ad" available for purchase on popular Internet websites. These advertisements are small messages that appear on the user's screen and are related to whatever activity or topic the user is then engaged in on the host website. They usually permit the user to click on the ad and be immediately transferred to the advertiser's own website where some kind of offer is presented. Although the Internet community is still trying to determine how this advertising approach will work and how effective it can be, at this writing banner advertising represents a $2 billion per year industry. Yahoo!, the leading Internet website, delivers almost 80 million "eyeballs" to its advertisers, who pay less than $10 for every 1,000 times the advertisement is displayed.[5]

Publicity

Publicity carries the same characteristics as advertising in that it is public, one-directional, and is usually targeted at a market segment rather than individual prospects. It differs primarily by how the message is communicated. Publicity is intended to be a more credible message than can be conveyed via advertising because it appears to be "sponsored" or initiated by a credible, third-party source. It is also complementary to advertising in that it may reach some prospects who would be missed by traditional advertising methods.

An interesting example of a promotional technique that may bridge the gap between advertising and publicity is the placement of physical products or symbols in otherwise unrelated contexts. An entire industry exists, for example, for the placement of such artifacts on the sets of television and movie production studios. Product placement agencies negotiate with production companies to manipulate scripts and sets to insert identifiable products. In the movie *Home Alone*, there were no fewer than 42 mentions of 31 different name brand products. After the lead character in *E.T.* munched on Reese's Pieces, sales of that candy soared 66 percent.[6]

Sales Promotion

Coupons, contests, and premiums are forms of sales promotion campaigns. The purpose of these methods, as compared to advertising and publicity, is to generate some kind of immediate action from the prospect. Accordingly, effective sales promotion campaigns can often be more targeted at individual prospects than the other forms of marketing communications already mentioned.

Sales promotion, of course, occurs in the industrial sector as readily as it does in consumer businesses. Closeouts, product bundling, and limited-time offers are all forms of sales promotion.

Direct Marketing

This form of marketing communication is usually more specifically targeted at individual prospects than the broadcast methods of advertising and publicity. Direct marketing includes direct mail, telemarketing, and e-mail campaigns. Because it is more targeted than the public forms of marketing communications, direct marketing can be customized to be more personal and, therefore, more specifically appealing to the prospect. In its interactive forms, such as telemarketing and e-mail, it can begin to respond to prospect feedback and, therefore, deliver an even more customized message.

The aversion of Internet users to "spam" (unsolicited promotional messages) is a major force shaping the direction of direct marketing on the Internet. Nevertheless, the power of the Internet to reach many prospects effectively and inexpensively is sure to overcome the problems created by "spamming." Lacking high quality lists of e-mail addresses, the Hertz Corporation recently mailed a communication to its premium-level customers offering 5,000 "free" airline travel miles simply for providing the company with their e-mail addresses. Useful lists of e-mail addresses will soon be commercially available.

Personal Selling

Despite the availability of incredible new electronic media consisting of all forms of telecommunications technology, personal selling remains the most effective form of marketing communications in many settings. It is, of course, the ultimately interactive form of communication, allowing useful dialogue to occur between buyer and seller. It also enables, perhaps more than any other form, the development of a *relationship* that is important to the final stages of the buying decision making process.

The only disadvantage of personal selling, in most situations, is its relatively high cost. A recent survey indicated that the average cost of an industrial sales call is approximately $165, with calls in some industries reaching as high as $250.[7] This is why personal selling is usually utilized later in the selling process and in connection with higher-value, lower-volume offerings – which occurs more often in the industrial sector than in consumer businesses.

Reseller Support

In addition to all of the forms of marketing communication identified here that are directed at the end-user prospect, communication with other members of the marketing channel is important wherever those members can impact CPV. The objective of reseller support is the same as for marketing communications to prospects, namely to (a) communicate the benefits and costs of the offering and (b) contribute directly to CPV via the communication itself.

Types of reseller support are as varied as the imagination allows. In addition to direct selling to resellers, advertising and co-op promotions, for example, providing displays and selling aids to these middlemen clearly contributes to the two objectives of marketing communications. Trade show displays are a common form of supporting resellers. And, where appropriate, training programs and technical support provided to resellers can sometimes be a more efficient form of marketing communications than many others.

DESIGNING MARKETING COMMUNICATIONS

How marketing communications can be designed to convey and deliver the greatest possible CPV is dependent on three factors:[8]

> TYPE OF PRODUCT AND MARKET
> BUYER READINESS
> PRODUCT LIFE CYCLE

Type of Product and Market

The relative "volume vs. value" nature of the offering will dictate some aspects of a marketing communications strategy. That is, high volume-low value offerings, such as most consumer products, usually indicate more "push"-type communications, such as advertising and publicity. High-value, low-volume offerings, such as many industrial products, are usually supported by more "pull"-type marketing communications, such as direct marketing and personal selling. There are exceptions to these rules-of-thumb, however.

Starbucks Coffee Company, the subject of our chapter opening story, is a rare example of a high volume-low value offering ($1.40 for the cup of coffee and the music is free!) that has attained tremendous market share without spending a single dollar on traditional consumer advertising. Andersen Consulting, on the other hand, which sells individual consulting projects costing hundreds of thousands, or millions, of dollars, advertises heavily on broadcast television, in national publications, and even on billboards in major airports. Andersen Consulting's brand advertising campaign announced in late 1998 represented an investment of $44 million, and that amount was recently increased to $59 million.

Buyer Readiness

The effectiveness of alternative marketing communications will depend heavily on what message the prospect is most ready to hear. Generally, prospects must pass through a series of response states to finally take the action of buying:[9]

1. AWARENESS
2. COMPREHENSION
3. INTEREST
4. INTENTION
5. ACTION

Roger Best suggests that these states are hierarchical, implying that the prospect must go through them sequentially. This creates the familiar situation of the "numbers game." Some prospects will never become aware of the offering. Of those that do, only a percentage of them will move to the next level of readiness, the comprehension state. Additional prospects fall away while moving to the interest state, and so on. The objective of marketing communications is, of course, to move the greatest number of prospects from one stage to the next. This process is a good example of why Kotler and Armstrong define the term "marketing communications" as "managing the customer buying process over time."[10]

The best selection of marketing communications changes as the prospect state of readiness changes. Advertising and public relations are generally most effective at the early stages of readiness, such as awareness and comprehension. This is probably why so many start-up e-businesses are spending inordinately large amounts of money on television advertising in connection with events such as the Super Bowl. Their objective is to create awareness of their new offerings among as many people as quickly as possible. Exposing their message to 88 million people on Super Bowl Sunday is probably a good way of accomplishing that goal, as long as the number of such ads doesn't confuse the audience.

Sales promotion and personal selling are marketing communication activities that usually have greater impact moving prospects in the later stages of readiness. Couponing and limited-time discounts are designed to prompt immediate action from prospects. In the industrial sector, limited-time offers and high-level sales calls are made for the same purpose. Most experienced managers agree, on the other hand, that personal selling for the purpose of creating awareness (known as "cold calling") is usually a very expensive and inefficient form of marketing communication.

Stage in Product Life Cycle

The choice of marketing communications methods should also vary based on the stage in the product life cycle. In most cases, the buyer readiness state will parallel the product life cycle because of greater awareness among prospects of the offering the longer it has been in the marketplace. In addition, however, the stage in the product life cycle impacts the choice of marketing communications because the message itself must be different at those different stages.

At an early stage in an offering's life cycle, for example, more "pull"-type marketing communications, such as direct marketing and personal selling, will probably be necessary to clearly deliver the message about the new CPV an offering delivers. "Push"-type communications are more appropriate when the product is into its growth, maturity, or decline phases, because the message to be conveyed is simpler. These requirements are the basis of a common problem in managing industrial sales forces because new products require more of their effort and "old" products are easier to sell. Finding ways to motivate the sales force to exert the extra effort for introducing new offerings (where their effort is needed the most) typically involves aligning measurement and reward systems accordingly.

OPPORTUNITIES FOR MARKETING COMMUNICATIONS

Although inventories of methods and supplier-oriented considerations for making decisions about marketing communications are useful, it remains that the only thing that ultimately matters is CPV. That's why all of the types of management decisions covered in this book tend to "run together" and result in significant overlaps. And that's why the realization that the objective, managing CPV, must be used as the ultimate organizer of management actions is so important.

In designing marketing communications, therefore, it's often helpful to take another kind of inventory – an inventory of all of the interactions that take place between the supplier and the prospect and customer. Each of those interactions represents an opportunity, perhaps an inevitability, for the customer to receive a message from the supplier. As discussed in Chapter 3, we refer to every one of these interactions as Value Opportunities.

Value Opportunities can best be thought of by tracing the development of a customer relationship from the selling process clear through the after-the-sale support stage (Figure 9.1). At every one of those steps, there are Value Opportunities and marketing communications to be managed.

Promotion

Obviously, every time a prospect drives along a highway and sees a

Figure 9.1 - Value Opportunities for Marketing Communications

Promotion
Selling
Order taking
Delivery
Support
Resolving problems
Payment
Relationship management
Community activities

billboard or scans the advertisements in a trade journal, marketing communications is taking place. This category of Value Opportunities involves any of the kinds of advertising, publicity, and direct marketing described earlier in this chapter. The Promotion-related customer interactions are those first thought of in connection with traditional marketing communications efforts.

Selling

To consider all of the Value Opportunities available, we separate "selling" from the other forms of promotional activity. The objectives of marketing communications in selling interactions are to reinforce the CPV proposition and trigger buying action on the part of the customer. This is usually accomplished by sales promotion and personal selling with supporting collateral materials.

The most aggressive approach to reinforcing the CPV proposition, perhaps, is to provide the customer an actual "accounting" of the value provided by an offering. This requires a thorough understanding of the customer's needs and all of the benefits and costs the customer places on his personally-prepared CPV balance scale. The supplier quantifies each of those elements on the balance scale in dollar terms, and computes a total value amount. Including the price on the cost side of the balance scale, as it should be, means that any positive amount computed for total value provides evidence that a positive buying decision should be reached by the prospect. The message communicated this way can be quite compelling.

As with all CPV evaluations, this calculation is usually made by comparing one offering with another, or some other alternative. For example, the truck parts manufacturer (described in Chapter 7) developed a presentation tool that demonstrated the cost savings from its product's faster cycle time of lowering its brand of landing gear into position beneath a trailer. That calculation included such elements as reduced driver downtime (salary and benefits), reduced idling fuel costs (dollars per gallon saved), and increased on-the-road truck time (dollars of additional revenue producing capacity). This presentation added up the few dollars gained on each repositioning of the truck's landing gear, which, for large fleet owners, multiplied into millions of dollars of annual costs savings. It made the purchase price of the new equipment look insignificant in comparison and certainly improved the way the customer stacked up the benefits and costs of this equipment on his CPV balance scale.

Order Taking

Opportunities to reinforce the CPV proposition and add value to the offering abound in the order taking Value Opportunities. If orders are taken directly (in the personal selling activity, for example), the opportunity for *consultative selling* presents itself. Such an approach can result in additional sales, both in terms of additional quantities and additional offerings, while providing the customer with additional information needed for her decision making process and ongoing service and support.

Amazon.com has led the way in using technology to turn the order taking interaction with the customer into a Value Opportunity, reinforcing the CPV proposition and adding value for the customer. When books are ordered from that company, it records the purchase and, the next time that customer views the website, recommendations for other books based on her past buying history are presented.

Delivery

Delivery of the offering – a service or physical product – presents another Value Opportunity and another place to consider marketing communications objectives. Besides printed promotional materials that can be delivered with the basic offering, the physical appearance of delivery personnel can also be an important message sent by the supplier and a source of added CPV for the customer. Here's how one company used that concept to its advantage.

Cintas Corporation likes to be known as "the uniform company." When it promotes its uniform rental programs to its customers, it points out that the uniforms are much more than just shirts, pants, and jackets. To the wearer, its uniforms offer "pride, confidence, teamwork, productivity, morale, identity, and safety." To the customer of the person in the uniform, the appearance conveys "professionalism and competence." Those are the kinds of things that go on a CPV balance scale. Cintas sold more than $1.7 billion of "professionalism and competence" in its fiscal year ended in May 1999.

Support

Demonstrating to customers how to use their offering and assuring them access to additional resources from the company is another opportunity to add to CPV. In many businesses, for example, it is appropriate to assign people exclusively to supporting the most important customer accounts.

One of the large public accounting firms always assigns two of its partners to each client account. One of those partners is responsible for seeing that the work gets done on time, within budget, and meets applicable professional quality standards. That's the "engagement partner." The second partner's assignment is to develop a relationship with client executives and to make sure those executives are always aware of how the firm could provide additional services. That's the "client partner," and her role is primarily one of managing marketing communications.

Resolving Problems

Some research has indicated that customer satisfaction actually increases after a supplier fails but then properly recovers from the failure. This certainly suggests that problem resolution is a Value Opportunity where the CPV proposition can be reinforced and additional value added to the balance scale. Research indicates the best way to do this is to offer the customer both a reasonable explanation for the failure and compensation for his disappointment.

A few years ago, Southwest Airlines offered $25 tickets in celebration of its 25th anniversary. More than 4.5 million customers purchased the tickets, a much greater response to the promotional campaign than Southwest was prepared to handle. As a result, many of their frequent fliers complained that they had been shut out of the promotion, unable to get through the company's jammed customer service telephone lines. Southwest appropriately responded by offering both an explanation (a "bigger, wilder celebration than we had ever planned") and compensation (free round-trip tickets for their 590,000 frequent fliers).[11] What started out as a service failure turned into a positive customer interaction that delivered even more CPV to those involved.

Payment

Collecting money from the customer may appear to be an awkward time to reinforce the company's message about CPV, but it actually can work quite well. As with all of the other Value Opportunities, requesting and receiving payment provides an opportunity to interact with the customer and it should therefore be managed as an opportunity to add CPV.

In addition to printed material that can be inserted in an envelope with an invoice, one professional services firm uses invoices to describe the services it has provided in the most recent period. The description of those services can be done in many ways, but this firm clearly uses it as an opportunity to add CPV. Also, additional services are listed on the invoice and "no charge" indicated in the amount column, once again driving home the message that great value has been delivered.

Relationship Management

Relationship management as a separate function from selling consists of those value-added activities intended to do the very things that marketing communications does: reinforce the CPV proposition and add value to the offering. Perhaps relationship management is as *pure* a marketing communications effort as any other.

We have found, for example, that conducting customer research properly can be a very positive interaction with a customer. In addition to better understanding the customer's wants and needs, the research itself is a message to the customer that she is important and that the supplier wants to learn how to deliver even greater CPV to her. "Done properly" means that marketing communication issues are considered in designing and executing the research.

Community Activities

These are often Value Opportunities that are not clearly recognized as such. The role that company executives take in the community, the charities the company supports, and the appearance of the company's physical facilities are examples of things that send a message about the nature of the company and its offerings. Their impact should be managed as issues concerning marketing communications.

"Green" companies such Ben & Jerry's and Orvis make significant contributions to charitable causes and let their customers know that they do. Orvis' stated policy is to donate 5 percent of pre-tax profits to nonprofit organizations involved in protecting fish and wildlife habitat. During the last five years, the company has donated more than $5 million to such causes. It is likely that many of Orvis' typical customers are sympathetic to these causes and, therefore, stack another "benefit" connected with this philanthropy up on the left side of their CPV balance scale when they evaluate the benefits and costs of Orvis products as compared to alternatives.

BRANDING

As examples of the diverse nature of activities that are a part of marketing communications stack up, we begin to paint a picture of an important concept known as brand management, or *branding*. Some authors define a "brand" simply as a name or graphic identity that ties an offering to its supplier. We believe the concept is much more complex than that, and offer this definition:

> **Brand** – *an intangible CPV benefit attribute that differentiates the offering of one supplier from another.*

The customer-perceived attribute is separate from all of the other benefits and costs on the customer's CPV balance scale and results from all the interactions and marketing communications that take place between a company and its marketplace.

Brands are developed in the business-to-business segment as well, of course, and needn't have the geographical reach or cross-cultural impact of a Coca-Cola to be extremely valuable to their owner.

Brand Associations

Brand associations are anything that prospects link with the offering to form an impression of the brand.[12] Links to the Taco Bell brand might be the tiled roof on their buildings, the low prices they charge for large quantities of food, or the "Chihuahua with an attitude" that used to appear in many of its advertisements. It might even be the location of the Taco Bell store near the shopping mall. Most important, however, is that brand associations are ultimately selected and defined by the customer. As with all of the benefit and cost attributes on the customer's CPV balance scale, they exist only in the mind of the customer.

Companies work hard to offer up possible brand associations in the hope that customers will come to value them. *Brand management* is the use of every opportunity to create a consistent and positive image that can be used by the customer as a brand association.

These include product attributes, customer benefits, projective associations, and positioning associations.

Product Attributes

Attributes of the product are often selected to serve as brand associations. The reliability of FedEx package delivery service is highlighted in their slogan, "When it absolutely, positively has to be there overnight." FedEx prides itself on its highly reliable overnight delivery system and it wants everyone to associate it with that reliability. The company needed to be very careful in the execution of its 2-day service, which involves many more subcontractors making local deliveries, to avoid diluting its powerful brand identity. Other examples of product attributes serving as brand associations include Volvo's "safety," Deere's "reliability," and McDonald's "fast service."

A particularly important attribute in the development of brand associations is price. Customers often infer various product qualities by simply comparing the price of the product with others they consider to be their alternatives. Clearly, a part of the McDonald's brand identity is low prices. That company would be hard pressed, for example, to extend into the fine dining category because of the strength of their current brand. Examples abound in the industrial sector as well, such as the role that price plays in the positioning of the large consulting firms. The joke that some people make – "he must be an expert because he's from out of town" – partially stems from the use of high price as a branding association in that industry.

Customer Benefits

As we come to understand the customer's use of his CPV balance scale, there is a difference between product attributes and customer benefits. Benefits are the personalized extension of the attributes as perceived by the customer. Where product attribute brand associations can be extended to personal benefits associations, the power of the brand becomes even greater.

Michelin tires are believed to have superior traction in all kinds of weather. That's the product attribute. When that superior traction results in keeping the customer's loved ones safe in the car, that's the customer benefit. The cute little babies floating around inside Michelin tires in their advertisements are intended to drive home that customer benefit. As a result, babies become a brand association for Michelin tires.

Consumer advertising isn't the only way brand associations are established, of course, although they usually become the examples to which most people can relate. A lawyer who acts brash and assertive in social situations may be perceived as able to effectively utilize more aggressive tactics in the courtroom (which some may see as a CPV benefit attribute). When pharmaceutical products are widely advertised, some physicians may be more comfortable prescribing their use because that is a "safer" decision than recommending some lesser known drug. Thus, the CPV benefit attribute to the prescribing physician is "less professional risk."

The problem with tangible attributes and benefits as brand associations is that they are actually measurable and, therefore, subject to competitive "one-upmanship." Accusations that Volvo's crash tests had been rigged went right to the heart of that company's brand identity and could have wiped out the product's market differentiation altogether. That is why some experts believe that intangible associations, while probably more difficult to develop are more effective and valuable in the long run.

GE's association with quality ("Quality Goes in Before the Name Goes On"), Wheaties with success ("The Breakfast of Champions"), and Prudential with stability ("Own a Piece of the Rock") are examples of successful intangible customer benefit associations.

Projective Associations

Sometimes brand associations extend further on the intangibility scale by projecting an image of something only remotely associated with the offering. These are called projective associations and they take several different forms.

Some brand associations are made with a particular use or application of the product. In the consumer world, Coors Beer associates its product with the outdoors, mountains, and hiking, while Miller seems to prefer associating theirs with dancing and late-night parties. Although probably used less in industrial settings, projective brand associations occur there as well, such as Transamerica's use of its distinctive headquarters building.

Brand associations are sometimes made with people that the customer would like to emulate. Examples of this approach include the slinky female models that speak for diet foods and the muscle-bound male athletes that represent all kinds of sports equipment. An extension of this technique is, of course, the celebrity spokesperson, for which Nike is most famous. Oddly, the fictitious celebrity spokesperson – such as the posthumous characterization of Colonel Sanders used by Pepsi's KFC unit – can be equally effective.

Those believing that brand associations occur only in the consumer world need only attend any major trade show to be proven wrong. Anonymous models are frequently a part of industrial displays to convey (apparently) sophistication and some kind of beauty. Celebrities also appear for expert testimonials or, perhaps, simply to convey a sense of quality and worldliness. We were recently entertained by a competent Elvis impersonator at a convention of librarians. The product's connection with Elvis remains a mystery, but we admit that we still remember the product's brand name.

Another form of projective association is connected with geography. Much like associations with types of people or celebrities, some brands are based on a relationship with a particular country or region of the world, such as the connection that automobiles have with Germany. Mercedes and especially BMW use their Germanic base to ask customers to project an impression of quality, speed, and styling. Volkswagen, on the other hand, downplays its country of origin preferring to convey an image of practicality and fun. Both approaches are legitimate and seemingly quite successful.

Positioning Associations

The final category of brand associations consists of positioning the offering relative to other products or competitors. The intent is to capitalize on something already familiar to the customer to convey an image of a new or different product.

The U.S. Postal Service has attempted for several years to gain a presence in the overnight package delivery business by comparing itself to the dominant players in that industry – FedEx and UPS. Unfortunately for the Service, it already has a strong brand identity as the slow, plodding carrier who walks the mail up to your front door, no matter what the weather. To be a serious contender in the industrial market, it needs to change that image to one of jet planes and fast-moving delivery vans. It is apparently attempting to do that by leveraging the strong image of FedEx's planes and UPS' brown trucks in its "Fly Like an Eagle" advertising campaign.

Brands as Customer Benefits

To earn their place onto the CPV balance scale, brands must be perceived by prospects and customers as benefit attributes (or, hopefully not, as cost attributes) relevant to their buying decision (Figure 9.2). They might do this for several reasons:

MANAGING INFORMATION
CONFIDENCE IN THE BUYING DECISION
INCREASED SATISFACTION IN USE

Managing Information

A brand can carry huge quantities of information about an offering, making it easy for the prospect to make a selection without incurring significant "searching costs." The benefit attribute placed on the CPV balance scale, in this case, would be something like, "I don't have to shop around if I buy this." Or, of course, the brand could have a negative impact and end up on the right side of the balance scale with the description, "Buy this one? No way!"

Industrial supplier relationships often rely heavily on the branding effect. Because of past experience, a supplier comes to be known as a reliable source of high quality products at a reasonable price. In

Figure 9.2 - Brand as a CPV Benefit

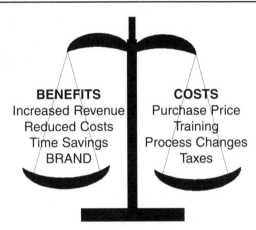

other words, the supplier has become "branded" as a good source. When the buyer needs a product that appears in this supplier's line, it is simply easier and less costly to place the order with that supplier than to go through an extensive process of preparing specifications, preparing a request for proposal, and carefully comparing the responses from multiple vendors. The *brand* provides enough information, in this case, for a careful buyer to select the current supplier.

Confidence in the Buying Decision

When a buyer engages in a careful search but finds too much or confusing information about alternatives, a brand can make the selection easier. The benefit on the left side of the CPV balance scale is something like, "All other things being equal, I have confidence in this brand." Or, in the worst case, it is on the right side and says, "Because I have to make a choice, I'll avoid this brand." In this case, the brand could be the attribute that literally tips the scale in situations where the buyer would have difficulty making a decision.

National accounting firms compete primarily on brand because the services they offer, auditing and tax advice, are largely generic. If a first-time buyer of services from a firm of this type had no personal acquaintances in the accounting profession, chances are high that she would make her initial telephone inquiry calls based on an overall image of the various firms. To make a decision between them would be very difficult unless she was able to distinguish between brands and place the one she was most comfortable with on her CPV balance scale.

Increased Satisfaction in Use

A brand is most powerful when it impacts the use of, or experience with, the offering itself. This phenomenon is easiest to see with brands that are designed to convey feelings of luxury or superiority. The benefit on the left side of the CPV balance scale, in this case, might be described as, "I'll feel good if I buy this one." Most people are familiar with this effect in connection with such consumer products as Tiffany jewelry, Coach leather products, and Smirnoff vodka. It's also the only reasonable explanation for the purchase of proprietary drugs instead of their generic equivalents.

The value a brand contributes to the experience of a product can also be found in industrial situations. Some years ago, IBM was successfully capitalizing on its brand in the market for mainframe computers. Although those products never carried the performance or cost advantages of equivalent computers from DEC or Tandem, they outsold competitors by relying on the benefit that the "Big Blue" brand delivered to IT executives. Everyone in that business agreed that "You could never be fired for buying an IBM." It was simply the safe thing to do.

An effective brand can end up on the CPV balance scale of prospects and customers. Making sure it appears on the left side, as one of the offering's benefits, is the challenge that every manager faces.

Brands as Assets of Suppliers

Creating an effective brand has, perhaps, even greater value to the supplier than to the customer. In fact, the identification of brand as an asset is thought to have originated with investment bankers who found many companies selling for much more than the value their financial assets would justify. In attempting to explain that phenomenon, they found themselves describing such things as "image in the marketplace" and "customer loyalty." Upon further analysis, they found several specific benefits accruing to the owners of effective brands, including the following.[13]

Efficiency and Effectiveness of Marketing Programs

Customers who carry an attribute on their CPV balance scale related to a positive brand image are easier to sell to than others. The balance scale is already tipped in the brand owner's favor, so less time and effort must be expended to add other items to the left side and remove negatives from the right side.

The value of this benefit to the supplier, however, is tempered by the reality that creating and maintaining the brand image itself is not inexpensive. It is estimated that Coca-Cola spends more than $115 million each year in advertising media purchases alone to defend and continue to build the world's most powerful brand. General Motors has reported that it spent $3 billion on advertising, including production costs and media purchases, in 1998.[14]

Enhanced Customer Retention

The flip side of the benefits of brand to customers (namely, management of information, confidence in the buying decision, and enhanced satisfaction in use of the product) represent perhaps the most important benefit to the supplier – brand loyalty. When customers place brand benefit on the left side of their CPV balance scales, they are less likely to shop around for competitive offerings and more likely to "cut some slack" for the supplier when things don't go well.

It is well established that retaining current customers is much more profitable than acquiring new ones.[15] Brand loyalty is one way to develop some inertia for current customers to cling to. The knowledge that a firm has this advantage can be reason enough for potential new entrants to think twice about the costs they will likely incur in offsetting the advantage of the incumbent's strong brand.

Improved Prices and Margins

Loyal customers influenced by a strong brand will sometimes pay more and almost always cost less to sell and service than other prospects and customers. That equates to improved margins for the owner of the brand.

Notice that this is still all about the CPV balance scale. If an effective brand is recognized by the customer and placed on the left side of the balance scale, it will support more negative weight on the right side from a less competitive price. It also lessens the need to provide additional benefits on the left side, such as sales promotions or other promotional activities.

Brand Extension Opportunities

Brand extensions are new product offerings that leverage the success of an existing brand. They provide the owner of a strong brand the opportunity for growth that others simply do not have.

Simple product line extensions can benefit from leveraging an existing, effective brand. New tools introduced under the Craftsman brand owned by Sears are more likely to achieve marketplace acceptance than the same products offered without that benefit. Andersen Consulting, now the largest management consulting firm in the world, originated as a specialty department of the accounting firm Arthur Andersen & Co. Although now separate entities, the instant credibility of the accounting firm's brand can be largely credited for the consulting firm's rapid growth.

Product diversification opportunities can also arise from leveraging an existing brand. The Orvis Company originally built its brand identity in the fishing equipment business, selling high quality fly fishing rods. That quality brand was leveraged to its advantage, so that today Orvis' name is on an extensive line of clothing, luggage, pet equipment, travel services, and even a special edition Ford sport utility vehicle.

Trade Leverage

As discussed in the previous chapter, the establishment of a position of influence and power in a marketing channel is dependent on the relative contributions of CPV. When a brand provides CPV, the owner of that brand gains influence with other channel members and stands to benefit more from its efforts.

Perhaps at this date, strength of brand is about the only power that P&G retains over the dominant big-box retailers such as Wal-Mart. As we've discussed previously, large retailers have used their proximity to, and influence with, the consumer to accumulate powerful bargaining positions with all of the companies farther up the marketing channel. Manufacturers are facing severe pressure to lower prices and, in some cases, are even being required to pay fees to the retailers to get their products onto the retailers' shelves. It is clear that the brands P&G brings to those channels, such as Tide, Crest, and Pampers, are the most important factors they bring to balance the retailer's power.

Rest assured that the same phenomenon exists in the industrial sector. For example, Owens Corning Fiberglas uses its "pink" brand of insulation to its advantage in both the residential and industrial building markets. While others make materials with equivalent or better installation and insulation specifications, many distributors, contractors, and retailers favor the pink product because of the power of that brand. In most markets, that brand power even supports a premium price for what is otherwise a generic building material.

Competitive Advantage

An effective brand provides the owner with customer-perceived reinforcement of the attributes that make it superior to its competitors. This increases entry costs for competitors and provides the brand owner extra time to respond to competitive attacks.

Was it the taste of Diet Rite Cola that did it in? Not likely. More likely, it was just too difficult for it to overcome the world's strongest brand in Coca-Cola. Can a small IT consulting firm in Cleveland, boasting the smartest programmers available, compete nose-to-nose with Andersen Consulting for the big software conversion project? Perhaps, but the smaller firm is certainly waging an uphill battle against the better known giant of the industry.

These examples are not about small versus large, because there are numerous examples of small companies overtaking the complacent larger ones in many different industries. Rather, they are about the strength of strong brands against those that lack a brand identity. A brand is a business asset requiring investment and development and returning increased growth and profitability. A strong brand is the ultimate result of effective marketing communications.

SUMMARY

We use the term marketing communications to refer to the fourth P of the marketing mix – Promotion. It should be understood, however, that the boundaries between marketing communications as promotion and other strategy and marketing mix issues is very fuzzy.

The objectives of marketing communications are two-fold: First, there is an educational aspect whereby the attributes representing benefits and costs on the customer's CPV balance scale are communicated. Additionally, there are opportunities for marketing communications to actually *add* benefits to the CPV balance scale, and those should be leveraged wherever possible.

Marketing communications utilizes many different tools, including advertising, publicity, sales promotion, direct marketing, personal selling, and reseller support. The development of a marketing communications strategy and the selection of the most appropriate tools largely depends on the type of product and market, buyer readiness, and the stage of the product in its life cycle. We suggest that a good way to develop a marketing communications strategy is to examine all of the Value Opportunities and determine where CPV can best be communicated or added.

Branding is the ultimate result of an effective marketing communications strategy. A brand is an intangible CPV benefit attribute that differentiates an offering from others. It results from a successful marketing communications program that establishes *associations* in the minds of prospects and customers between the offering and other things such as product attributes, customer benefits, projective associations, and positioning associations.

Brands can contribute value to the CPV balance scale by serving as aids to the customer in managing information, by increasing the prospect's confidence level in his buying decision, and by increasing the satisfaction gained from using the offering itself. Branding benefits to the owner of the brand are even more numerous and include adding efficiency and effectiveness to marketing programs, enhancing customer retention, supporting higher prices and margins, providing brand extension opportunities, adding leverage with market channel partners, and providing distinctive competitive advantage.

REFERENCES

[1] www.starbucks.com/books_and_music.asp?sid..., January 28, 2000.

[2] Michael Hartnett, "The Future of Brands," *Advertising Age*, November 8, 1999.

[3] www.starbucks.com/overview.asp?sid..., January 28, 2000.

[4] For additional resources on marketing communications, see Edward L. Nash, *Direct Marketing: Strategy, Planning, Execution*, (New York, McGraw-Hill, 2000); David Ogilvy, *Ogilvy on Advertising*, (New York, Random House, 1987); Sergio Zyman, *The End of Marketing As We Know It*, (New York, Harper Business, 1999).

[5] "To the Victors Belong the Ads," *Business Week*, October 4, 1999, pg. 39.

[6] Laurie Mazur, "Screenland's Dirty Little Secret," *E*, May-June 1996, pg. 38.

[7] "The Cost of Doing Business," *Sales and Marketing Management*, September 1999, pg. 56-57.

[8] See Philip Kotler and Gary Armstrong, *Principles of Marketing: Eighth Edition*, (Upper Saddle River, Prentice-Hall, 1999), pg. 434.

[9] Roger J. Best, *Market-Based Management: Strategies for Growing Customer Value and Profitability*, (Upper Saddle River, Prentice-Hall, 1997), pg. 243.

[10] Kotler and Armstrong, pg. 423.

[11] Kathleen Seiders and Leonard L. Berry, "Service fairness: what it is and why it matters," *The Academy of Management Executive*, May 1998, pg. 8-21.

[12] See David A. Aaker, *Managing Brand Equity: Capitalizing on the Value of a Brand Name*, (New York, Free Press, 1991), Chapter 5.

[13] See Aaker, Chapter 1.

[14] Matt Carmichael, "Coca-Cola's No-Brainer Still Reinforces Brand," *Advertising Age*, February 14, 2000, p. 56.

[15] See Frederick F. Reichheld, *The Loyalty Effect: The Hidden Force Behind Growth, Profits, and Lasting Value,* (Boston, HBS Press, 1996).

CHAPTER 10

CPV and Operations

The moral of this story is that even the biggest and the best can forget about the implementation phase sometimes. Nothing – making strategy, developing product offerings, segmenting markets, etc. – will make any difference if the implementation isn't there to deliver CPV to the customer.

Toys "R" Us was founded in 1948 when Charles Lazarus opened a baby furniture store in Washington, D.C. Priding himself on listening to his customers and trying to give them what they asked for, he opened his first toy supermarket in 1957. Now considered one of the original "category killers," Toys "R" Us is today an $11 billion business with nearly 1,500 stores located around the world.[1]

In April 27, 1999, Toys "R" Us launched its Internet-based service. It set up a subsidiary, Toysrus.com, in Silicon Valley, across the country from its own New Jersey headquarters. The new company raised more money from a venture capital firm, signed up Leo Burnett as its advertising agency, purchased a $30 million fulfillment center in Memphis, Tennessee, and set about to find its leader. By August, John Barbour, a Hasbro toy executive already living in Northern California, was brought on board as CEO. From the start, the goal was "to be the clear leader in the on-line retail market for toys and children's products by the fourth quarter 1999."[2]

As the premier retailer that it is, Toys "R" Us was mas-

terful at marketing communications and sales promotion. In addition to its retention of a world-class advertising agency, in November 1999, Toys "R" Us announced a partnership with Microsoft to appear as the "toy anchor merchant" on that company's prominent MSN eShop website. Accompanying this arrangement came Microsoft's support in the form of daily product specials, gift guides, gift finders, e-mail newsletters, and banner advertising.[3]

To make sure the new on-line store opened with a boom, in October 1999 Toys "R" Us announced its plan to offer free shipping for the entire holiday shopping season. Then, on November 7, it introduced a $10 off coupon for purchases of more than $25 on-line. That coupon was so well received that, within days, it was announced that the offer would be continued through December 1.

Everything was in place for a spectacular retail season except for one thing – the processes and infrastructure necessary to execute the strategy. Gap #3 and Gap #4 of the CPV Delivery Cycle were wide open, ready for the worst to happen. And it did.

As soon as the $10 off coupon hit the newspapers in early November, the infrastructure at Toys "R" Us was overwhelmed by customer responses. Although the company had quadrupled its computer capacity in advance, that wasn't nearly enough. It tripled that to try to stay alive. The computer system fell so far behind that the Memphis distribution center didn't even know that sales were booming.[4]

Phone lines were swamped with customers ordering or trying to find out the status of their orders. Vice President Joel Anderson was quoted as saying, "If we could have started all over again, I would have focused on the people side even more." The company tried to react, going from 20 order processing representatives to 600 in 60 days. As the orders finally arrived in Memphis, the company went from 150 warehouse workers to 1,200 in less than 90 days. But it was too late. On December 10, the company announced that it would take no more holiday orders. Worse, however, many of the orders received prior to the cutoff weren't delivered for Christmas. Representative of the many disgruntled customers, a class action lawsuit was filed against Toys "R" Us in Seattle for its failure to live up to its customer commitments.

Toys "R" Us certainly wasn't the only e-business to have difficulties dealing with its promotional success in the 1999 holiday shopping season. It was, however, one of the most prominent companies to fail so miserably with the blocking-and-tackling issues of servings its customers. One industry analyst pointed out that brick-and-mortar companies held core competencies in moving massive amounts of product to retail outlets efficiently but had yet to master shipping small orders to consumers in a price-effective manner. The strategy was probably great, but the implementation was a disaster.

David Packard, of Hewlett-Packard, once said, "Marketing is much too important to leave to the marketing department." If what he meant by "marketing" was delivering Customer Perceived Value (CPV), which we believe it was, then we certainly agree. Closing, in particular, the last two gaps of the CPV Delivery Cycle described in Chapter 3 requires the coordinated effort of the entire organization.

PRIORITIZING CPV IN OPERATIONS

The traditional functionally-oriented organization used by most businesses has its purposes. By collecting functional experts into groups, they are better able to communicate with each other and, especially, help in training their junior members. The problem, of course, comes when the different functional groups must coordinate and cooperate. Kotler describes the typical problems that arise when organizations attempt to manage across functional boundaries.[5]

Engineering

Traditionally, engineering and marketing have been asked to view the world quite differently. Being closest to the customer, marketing people have probably advocated meeting the customers' needs earlier and more vehemently than others. Engineering, on the other hand, has been charged with minimizing production costs. Their responsibility has been to design products and services, and the processes that produce and deliver them, with the greatest possible conformance to specifications at the lowest possible cost. Often, their approach to attaining those goals has been maximizing standardization in every way possible. As Frederick Taylor taught long ago, repetitive actions are more easily managed than those that vary.

A preference for standardizing outputs seems to fly in the face of delivering CPV. Every request for a customized response to an individual customer is an attack on the desire for standardization. It is no wonder that marketing people often believe that engineers are too rigid, and engineers believe that marketers keep changing their minds and are, therefore, not to be trusted.

But, as the power has moved to the customer and the objective of the organization *must* be to deliver greater CPV, a solution is needed to reconcile these viewpoints. That solution, in its ultimate form, is mass customization. This approach marries the desire of engineers to control the production processes and minimize costs while supporting the marketers with output that better meets individual customers' needs.

One form of mass customization is *unbundling*. Owens Corning's internal logistics function, for example, has unbundled all of its freight management services so that its "customers" can select the attributes of CPV that they value the most. The logistics engineers like those customers having access to any of their designed systems. And the marketers get positive feedback from customers that their individual needs are being met.[6]

R&D

The R&D and marketing functions sometimes view product development differently. R&D staff, to Marketing's way of seeing it, are usually scientists and technicians who get so involved in the technical aspects of products and services that they lose sight of what the purpose of the offering really was in the first place. Their focus is often on esoteric solutions that are elegant in their own right. Never mind the customer. A brilliant computer scientist we once worked with, when approached about a problem with a computer program that crashed every time the user hit the F1 key, suggested the solution was to tell the customer, "Don't hit the F1 key."

Marketing people, on the other hand, are sometimes viewed by R&D staff as too often "dumbing down" their specifications to meet only the simplest, most visible needs of the customer. Or, they are asking for offerings that have all "sizzle" and no "steak" – not caring enough about the product's true technical capabilities.

This simple conflict is why many companies have focused greater effort on assuring that their new product development processes are cross-functional and encourage a high level of involvement from all functions of the company from the very beginning. In addition, the heavy use of valid information from customers at all stages of the development process provides a basis for reconciling the disparate views of the various functions within the company. After all, the customer is the final arbiter of CPV.

A major telecommunications company completed a significant revamping of its products to include all the latest technological capabilities – bells and whistles, as they say. Still, customer response was lukewarm at best. From some belated customer research, it was found that customers didn't sense a need for more product features but would have appreciated better repair service. Marketing might have known this all along, but R&D wasn't listening to them. In this case, the entire product development effort was wasted because customers were not involved early enough in the process to eliminate any discrepancies between the viewpoints of R&D and Marketing.[7]

Manufacturing and Operations

The term "manufacturing" usually refers to the production function for a product and "operations" refers to delivering a service. The distinction is unimportant. What is important is the traditional difference in viewpoints between those that sell the offering and those that produce and deliver it.

Like engineering, manufacturing and operations are concerned with efficiency and conformance to specifications. Their daily concerns involve matters such as machine breakdowns, supply outages, and staffing shortages. The sales clerk that views a customer's question as an interruption of his effort to restock the shelves is a simple example of the traditional production viewpoint in a retail setting.

Marketers, on the other hand, are sometimes viewed by production people as those that make unreasonable demands on them and make promises to customers that are impossible for them to live up to. The marketing people, it seems to them, don't understand the economics or challenges of operating a production facility.

Once again, the solution to this potential conflict is to encourage everyone to focus on delivering the greatest possible CPV. The better everyone in the organization understands customers, particularly people in the manufacturing and operations functions, the less conflict will occur around goals and methods. Usually, this requires more than simply explaining customer needs to those in production functions. It requires firsthand access to research information and personal interactions with customers.

The customer call center for the credit card arm of giant retailer, The Limited, is located in a windowless building in central Ohio. Everyday, more than 400 employees file into this building, go straight to their cubicles, put on their headsets, and talk for almost eight hours with customers about billing and collection problems. Although these company representatives are well trained and highly motivated, after the first few dozen calls it is still too easy for those customers to become faceless voices whining about trivial matters. To help combat that, a female mannequin named Susie (actually, her name is frequently changed) sits in a chair near the employee entrance. She is dressed each day in a stylish outfit from The Limited's nearby warehouse. The employees each touch Susie on their way in and refer to her by name. Susie is a reminder that customers are real people, with real needs, and that they are the sole reason these people come to work each day. She clears up any confusion about what's important.

Administration

Many administrative people do not trust the marketers. Purchasing criticizes marketing's ability to forecast requirements. Financial people get nervous about Marketing's budget requests for large investments that are hard to measure, such as advertising, promotion, and the sales force. The accounting department does not understand why Marketing won't keep better records and turn their reports in on time. And the credit department wishes Marketers would quit trying to sell to everyone, including those who probably will not pay.

Marketing people, on the other hand, get frustrated that the "bean counters" in the back office don't give them better support. Purchasing people say "we can't do that" too often. The budgeting process is a time-consuming activity that attempts to be much more precise than it can possibly be about forecasting customer demand. The accounting people think it is more important that their forms get filled out than Marketing spending time with customers. And the credit department is full of uncaring people who would prefer the company would sell to only a small, select segment of the total market.

These problems exist, of course, because each of the functional groups have different goals and objectives. Too often, Marketing is supposed to sell, Finance is to allocate resources (with an eye to reducing costs), Accounting keeps track of the money, and Credit collects from the deadbeats. With such a fragmented view of the world, it is no wonder that conflicts arise.

The solution is to stop managing functional groups and begin managing business processes.

MANAGING BUSINESS PROCESSES

Although we have referred to *processes* in this book several times already, it is not too late to stop and define the term.

> **Processes** – *individual activities that, performed in sequence, produce some kind of output or result.*

This definition, then, encompasses many things not previously recognized as being a process. A family working together to make vacation plans is engaged in a process. Getting the oil in your car changed on a Saturday morning is a process. Identifying these, and the more complex work of a business organization, as processes is the first step toward managing them, and thereby, changing the results that come from them. The results we are looking for are, of course, delivering superior CPV.[8]

Five Core Business Processes

Adair and Murray define four "core business processes" that are a part of every business organization.[9] We add a fifth:

1. "DEVELOPING PRODUCTS" PROCESS
2. "GENERATING ORDERS" PROCESS
3. "FULFILLING ORDERS" PROCESS
4. "SUPPORTING CUSTOMERS" PROCESS
5. "MANAGING THE BUSINESS" PROCESS

These five are used as a starting place because together they encompass all the work that is performed in a company.

These core processes are, however, too general and too high-level to be of much practical use for management purposes. Fortunately, these processes lead a hierarchy whereby each consists of several more specific processes, as shown in Figure 10.1. Understanding this hierarchy and working down through it to find the process that specifically produces the result the manager needs to address is exactly how effective managers "trouble shoot" performance problems.

Notice that we refer to all processes in the present participle verb form – that is, verbs ending in "ing." This implies that action is inherent in every process to produce the results that come from it and is, therefore, more descriptive of the process itself rather than those results. Most managers, for example, will find it easier to locate the source of customer complaints about sales floor courtesy by addressing the "Greeting the customer" process rather than looking for something called "Courtesy to the customer."

Figure 10.1 - "Generating the Order" Process - Partial Hierarchy

Developing products
    Planning strategy
        Generating product ideas
        Developing product concepts
Generating Orders
    Advertising
        Planning promotions
        Producing materials
            Selecting production house
            Writing copy
            Designing layout
            Preparing for printer
        Buying media
        Measuring results
    Qualifying suspects
    Calling on prospects
    Specifying deliverables
    Negotiating terms
    Closing the order
Fulfilling orders
    Scheduling production
    Producing deliverables
    Packaging
Supporting customers
    Taking service calls
    Providing on-site service
    Solving problems
Managing the business
    Managing HR
    Keeping financial records
    Informing shareholders

Why so much emphasis here on defining what processes are? It is because most managers *have not* clearly defined the processes they utilize to produce the results they deliver to customers. The processes are there, and they are cranking out the results, but many managers have not defined them as such and, therefore, don't know exactly where to start to change and improve the results they want. Defining processes is at the heart of the responsibilities that management has to close Gap #3 of the CPV Delivery Cycle.

CONTROLLING PROCESSES

Michael Hammer suggests four things the manager must do to manage processes:[10]

IDENTIFY AND NAME PROCESSES
IDENTIFY WHERE AND HOW PROCESSES DELIVER CPV
TRAIN EVERYONE
MEASURE PROCESS PERFORMANCE

Identify and Name Processes

Identifying the processes that exist in an organization and are currently producing what the customers see is not a trivial undertaking for most companies. Although the processes exist (or else nothing would be getting done), they have often not been thought of in this way. Rather, the traditional functional organization overshadows the concept of processes and sometimes managers mistakenly view a function such as accounting or shipping as a process. The reality, however, is that processes generally cross functional boundaries and are, therefore, very different from those functions. The shipping department, for example, cannot do its work properly unless production provides the goods to be shipped, Accounting confirms that the credit check has been completed, Sales has input the customer's shipping address properly, and Purchasing has set up the arrangements for the trucking companies to take the load. Looked at this way, it is easy to see that a cross-functional process exists and that managing it, rather than the individual activities of the shipping department alone, is the only way to effectively manage the results produced.

Identify Where and How Processes Deliver CPV

It is not quite enough to say that the shipping department delivers CPV because the customer would not receive anything if that department failed. That is too general to help much in the management of improved performance. What is needed is to thoroughly understand what constitutes CPV and then connect those attributes with where they are produced in the process.

In the new e-commerce environment, for example, next day delivery is often an important benefit attribute on the customer's CPV balance scale. When that isn't happening with sufficient regularity, the manager must analyze the poor performance and trace that back to the offending process. Perhaps, in this example, it is found that the "transferring orders to the warehouse" process is failing. Or, it might be the "picking orders" process. Or, any of probably a dozen other possibilities. Identifying this link between CPV and the related process is the very point of "process management."

Methods have been developed, primarily in the field of new product development, that are applicable to the issue of managing for improved CPV through processes. The larger topic here is Quality Function Deployment (QFD) – a set of analysis techniques developed in the TQM movement. A thorough exploration of QFD is beyond the scope of this book. It is sufficient for our purposes, however, to illustrate the approach with the diagram in Figure 10.2.

As can be seen here, the objective is to trace the attributes that are perceived by customers as CPV to the processes or activities that produce them. In most cases, it will be multiple processes and activities that produce each of the components of CPV – a fact that properly reflects the complexity of managing any large business organization. This simple matrix, however, when accurately developed, provides management with a very clear direction on where to go to solve problems in delivering CPV and where to go to build the capability for delivering superior CPV.

Figure 10.2 - Tracing CPV to Processes

BUSINESS PROCESSES	Unit Price	Brand Awareness	Easy to do business with	Ease of use
Designing products	✔			✔
Producing products	✔			
Answering customer calls			✔	
Solving customer problems			✔	✔
Resolving warranty claims	✔		✔	
Buying advertising		✔		
Managing website			✔	

Train Everyone

Understanding the role that she plays in the entire process will not necessarily change the task that a worker performs, but it will profoundly change the way she thinks about performing that task. Training the entire organization about processes – from senior manager to frontline employee – is a fundamental step toward refocusing that entire organization on delivering superior CPV.

Training people about processes is also one of the first steps toward redefining the way they, or the organization, think about their "jobs." Viewed in the context of processes, jobs automatically become "bigger." No longer is it the assembly line worker's job to simply tighten ten fasteners; that worker is now seen as contributing to the assembly of a product destined for use by a customer. Like so many of the issues raised in this book, this is not a new idea, but it is a profoundly important one that still escapes the attention of many otherwise sophisticated managers.

In a major financial services company, the credit scoring function was an autonomous group within the leasing department. They were very good at applying the various tools available for determining a lessee's credit worthiness, but they were not contributing very much to getting the lease paperwork out the door to the customer. When the "originating the lease paperwork" process was identified as such, and all of the functional groups involved in that process were given the responsibility of improving the process, the credit scorers began, for the first time, to evaluate their own impact on the overall business activity. Very early in the work, they suggested that certain credit checking work on small deals should be eliminated altogether. Their attention had moved from doing their "task" to delivering the greatest possible CPV.

Measure Process Performance

There is no question that "you can't manage it if you can't measure it" is an accurate aphorism. So, if management is to address performance by managing processes, certainly it must be those same processes that are measured. Because most organizations are still functionally organized, measuring processes rather than people or functions does not come very naturally.

Most people find, however, that they *prefer* measuring processes over measuring people. Because the performance objective of processes is to deliver superior CPV, that objective becomes the basis for establishing measurement systems. No longer is it "Danny screwed up that job," but rather it becomes, "The final packaging process failed." This depersonalization, with its attendant shift in focus from *who* did what to what *results* are produced, becomes almost a liberating realization for both manager and worker.

Effectiveness

Every process should be measured against four parameters. The first is *effectiveness*. This parameter evaluates how well the result of the process meets the customer's needs. At first, it can only be measured by getting feedback from the customer as a part of understanding CPV. Later, internal metrics can be identified that can help to track performance according to what is learned about CPV.

At a pharmaceuticals testing company, early research work identified the most important benefit attributes its customers placed on their CPV balance scale. The most important of those was "credibility of test results," so the company worked to understand what that actually meant to customers and which of its processes produced those results. They decided that one of the most important measures of test result credibility was the number of participants that dropped out of the test before completion. They established an acceptable ratio, say 95 percent, of completing participants to the total starting the test as a measure of process *effectiveness*. This enabled management to focus on the subprocesses impacting this ratio (such as "recruiting participants" and "giving directions to the test site" and "calling to remind participants") to maintain the best possible level of CPV delivery.

Efficiency

The second parameter for measuring processes is *efficiency*. Efficiency is calculated as the amount of output produced for an amount of input. Most companies are more proficient at this type of measurement than any other because it is the closest to traditional accounting, The unit of measurement of efficiency is usually dollars, and the ultimate measure is generally "cost per unit produced." Much has been realized recently, however, about the fallacies of traditional cost accounting in connection with measuring unit costs of production and, as a result, the practice of Activity Based Costing has become more common.

At the pharmaceuticals testing company described above, labor costs associated with the people administering the tests was identified as the major issue in efficiency and profitability. Rather than simply looking at time cards, however, the company identified the various activities involved in test administration. Each of those activities was then costed, and it was these activities as compared to the number of test participants processed that was established as an *efficiency* measure to be actively managed. This approach led to a better understanding of how the company was making its money and helped managers improve profitability dramatically.

Cycle Time

Third, processes should be measured for *cycle time*. Although perhaps a subset of efficiency, we suggest that cycle time is important enough to be considered a separate measurement parameter. Cycle time is, of course, the elapsed time from beginning of the process to its completion – measured from the customer's perspective.

A primary objective of the claims department of a major insurance company was to minimize the time an insured customer waited for his reimbursement check to arrive. This was causing a great deal of consternation among the managers responsible for this performance, because the measured time from receipt of a claim to the issuance of a payment was averaging about 26 days. That was not good, because the actual work involved usually took only about three hours. Their investigation revealed that, although the daily output of their department was about 350 claims, there were approximately 9,000 claim forms accumulated in piles on desks throughout the office. Working on a first-in-first-out basis, then, it was taking a long time to get three hours worth of work performed on a new claim. Efficiency wasn't the problem here, but the piles had created a significant cycle time problem.[11]

Adaptability

Finally, processes should be measured for *adaptability*. This parameter indicates how well the process adapts to changing inputs and conditions while still delivering the required CPV. To a large degree, this measurement relates to the conformance-to-quality issues that were the predominant focus of the TQM movement.

Many customer call centers measure not only the "time to problem resolution" required to answer a customer's question (a cycle time measure) but also, among other things, the "number of calls escalated" to a telephone agent's supervisor or manager. This "number of calls escalated" is an adaptability measure because it is attempting to identify when the process is failing to work well because of special circumstances encountered in the process.

Clearly, the four process measurement parameters are highly interrelated. Jack Welch, the renowned CEO of General Electric, emphasized, for example, the cycle-time measure over all others. His theory was that it was easier to focus on only one thing, and that one thing should be getting every thing done quickly. Groups of employees often met in "Work Out" sessions that were designed to focus solely on shortening the cycle time of GE's various processes. Welch assumed that shortening cycle time would also produce better results for customers (efficiency), cut out waste (efficiency), and reduce variability (adaptability).

REENGINEERING PROCESSES

So, when processes have been identified and named, and performance objectives developed and measured, how should a manager go about improving how well a process works? A debate around this has raged since consultant Michael Hammer wrote his most notable book, *Reengineering the Corporation*, in 1993. The TQM movement of the 1980s first introduced the ideas of process management to the U.S. and, in doing so, emphasized the importance of *continuous improvement*. Advocates of TQM taught us that processes should be identified, defined, stabilized, and then gradually improved upon. Useful techniques for analyzing the root causes of performance problems, such as Ishikawa fish-bone diagrams and Pareto charts, were emphasized. Teams of workers, including those directly involved in performing the process activities themselves, were the primary participants in the continuous improvement approach.

Then Michael Hammer published his book and, in it, suggested that continuous improvement wasn't enough. He introduced the concept of *reengineering*. In his words, this means "the radical redesign of business processes for dramatic improvement." Going well beyond continuous improvement, Hammer's approach started with "throwing out" the old process and designing a new, and better one, from scratch. Assuming that the workers involved in the current processes would be biased against major changes in those processes that might put their own jobs in jeopardy, reengineering was usually conducted by staff experts or outside consultants.

This approach fit well with management's sense of urgency in that era, when America was trying to catch up with new, international competitors in basic issues of product quality. In practice, reengineering became associated with highly automated solutions and large reductions in workforces. The euphemism "downsizing" came directly out of the reengineering movement.

So, which is better? Continuous improvement or reengineering? Predictably, the answer is probably "neither and both." We suggest that the choice between the two approaches, or something in between, is too specific an issue to generalize about for all business performance issues. The two approaches are simply points on a continuum of management styles or techniques for managing processes.

The importance of considering the two approaches is to recognize their commonalties. First is the importance of using processes as the point at which performance can be managed. The second is the objective of delivering superior CPV through those processes.

VALUE-ADDED ACTIVITIES

Certain parts of the TQM movement had problems. Its sole focus on "continuous improvement" over "reengineering" was probably one of them. Another was Quality Circles, where largely unsupervised employees were asked to come up with their own solutions for self-defined problems. We encountered some cultural problems with this approach in the U.S. that were not of concern in other parts of the world. One TQM principle, however, proved to be right on the mark and has survived well to date. That is the focus on delivering CPV.

The TQM people called it "managing processes for *value added*."

A method for managing processes to improve their performance is to examine each of the work activities taking place in the process and categorize the activity into one of three types: value-added, non-value-added, and waste. Value-added activities are to be encouraged, non-value-added minimized, and waste eliminated.

Value-Added Activities

These are the activities in a process that contribute features or attributes of an offering that lead directly to a customer placing a benefit on their CPV balance scale. Assembling a machine for delivery to a customer is a value-added activity. So is securing it to a pallet for shipment. Both of those activities lead directly to the receipt and use of the product itself by the customer. Receiving goods in the returns department is also a value-added activity because it directly leads to the warranty service that the customer would put on the left side of his balance scale.

Sometimes, of course, the distinction is more difficult to make than that. An activity that takes several tries to get it right, for example, isn't all value added. The unsuccessful attempts to deliver a package to an obscure address are not value-added. Only the final, successful attempt can be put into that category.

The most difficult aspect of using the value-added concept for managing process performance is defining the "customer" of the process. The original TQM movement introduced the concept of an *internal customer* as the immediate recipient of the process' output. This made it easier to define the process output requirements by simply asking the receiver of that output about it, even if that was only another department of the same company. For example, who should be considered the "customer" of the process of completing a salesperson's expense report? Most people would probably say it is the accounting department, because that is where the expense reports are sent and where they are processed. There is a problem in this, however, when the principle of "value added" is applied. If, for example, the customer is the accounting department, then "neatness counts" in connection with completing expense reports. It is much easier for the accounting department to do its work when those reports are printed from a personal computer instead of hand written. It would make sense, if the accounting department is the customer, to prohibit handwritten expense reports.

If the company's end-user customer is considered in this simple example, however, the value-added analysis is different. If printing out expense reports takes more of the salesperson's time than just writing it out, that salesperson has less time to spend with prospects and customers delivering value to them. Whose expenditure of time delivers greater value to the end-user customer, the salesperson or the accounting clerk? Considered in this light, it is probably not a good idea to prohibit handwritten expense reports.

At the level of managing individual processes, there is no simple answer to the issue of "internal customers." Sometimes the connection to the end-user customer is so many steps away that it is difficult to base specific management decisions on that basis. Still, the danger of expending resources only to make internal customers happy without adding value to end-user customers is significant. The management of processes requires that *all* of a process's customers be considered in identifying value-added activities – both internal and end-user customers.

Non-Value-Added Activities

These are the activities that do not directly contribute CPV but are necessary for the performance of those that do. Maintaining machinery, supervising operations, cleaning offices, and putting gasoline in the delivery trucks are examples of non-value-added activities. These activities can't simply be eliminated because the value-added activities would fail if they were and CPV would be diminished. However, they can and should be minimized to every extent possible. Doing so will increase the efficiency, cycle time, and sometimes the effectiveness of value-added processes.

All of the usual administrative activities of a company are categorized as non-value-added activities. Some of those are important, even essential, of course, such as preparing the employee payroll and filing tax returns. The most that can be done with those is to maximize the efficiency with which they are performed. Others represent greater potential for process improvement, however, such as checking document accuracy and approving management decisions. These should be evaluated closely and, where possible, eliminated through process redesign.

A large insurance company was looking at its process for reimbursing expense reports of its field sales representatives. The "customer" of this process was primarily the sales representative because the objective was to get the reimbursement payment to the employee before his personal credit card bill arrived and required payment. While examining the current process, it was determined that three different managers were required to approve each expense report. This made the cycle time for payment of the expenses quite long, because the report usually sat on each manager's desk for at least one day until it reached the top of the stack and was signed and forwarded on. By declaring that two of those three managers needed "information only" copies of the reports to be kept informed about the sales representatives' activities and only the third needed to actually sign the original document, several days were easily eliminated from the typical cycle time of this process.

Waste Activities

Waste activities are good targets for elimination to improve the performance of all processes. The trick, however, is to find them.

Most processes in companies today were not "designed" but have simply "evolved" – that is, they grew over time into what they are now. This means that waste activities probably arose and were made a part of otherwise good processes for what, at the time, probably seemed like good reasons. Typically, they have now outlived their usefulness and should be eliminated as quickly as they are identified.

Many clerical functions can be found to have outlived their usefulness and could now be considered "waste" activities. We found, in a small company we were helping, that an assistant was taking every outbound piece of correspondence to the copy machine, copying it, punching three holes in it, and placing it in a notebook on a shelf near her desk. This was probably an important practice 20 years ago when "hard copies" of correspondence were the only record of it available, but now all of this correspondence was already on a hard disk somewhere, and copies in a notebook were certainly no longer required. This realization freed up a significant amount of time for the assistant to perform more "value-added" tasks.

Well, everybody knows about "value-added" and "non-value-added" and "waste" activities by now, right? So why waste a few pages of this book on something as old as TQM itself? The reason is simple – most managers aren't yet doing very much about it. Every time the dictum comes down from above that "everyone has to cut their budgets by 10 percent" or "we're freezing all hiring until further notice," management is announcing that it doesn't understand the difference between "value-added" process activities and those that cause "waste." This old concept of "value-added" provides management with a powerful tool on which to prioritize its allocation of resources. It isn't easy, because it requires a thorough knowledge of the organization's processes, and it requires performance measures aligned with those processes to track progress. Nonetheless, today's competitive business environment demands it.

PROCESS OWNERS

At the heart of the "process view" of an organization is another principle of TQM that has survived the last 20 years – *employee involvement*. Frederick Taylor's preoccupation with "job specialization" and "command and control" management has largely been replaced with the realization that most workers have the capability to significantly contribute to the design and execution of the processes in which they are involved. No one is probably more knowledgeable about Customer Perceived Value than the employee who interacts directly with the customer everyday. No one is more expert on how to perform a production activity than the employee who has been struggling to get the right results from it for many years. Clearly, most jobs have become "bigger" during the years, as the benefits of employee involvement have been realized.

Nevertheless, given our existing organizational cultures and until we invent a better organizational structure than the options provided earlier in this chapter, someone ultimately has to be in charge. Traditionally, that person has been called the *process owner*. The title is probably not the ideal, because the use of the word "owner" implies that others are nonowners and therefore have less stake in the performance of the process. That is not true, of course. But, the term "process owner" is well enough established that we will use it here to represent the remaining management responsibilities that must be discharged to get the most CPV possible out of each process.

Hammer organizes process owner responsibilities into three categories: design, coaching, and advocacy.

Design

Because the purpose of every process is to deliver CPV, the first responsibility of the process owner is to identify the attributes of CPV for each market segment served by the process. A thorough understanding of CPV is essential for process design.

We described earlier a medical services company that successfully reduced the cycle time for delivering medical reports to its customers by eliminating a few redundant activities and using private courier services, where appropriate, instead of the U.S. mail. These actions came as a result of significant time and effort on the part of its staff and, interestingly, increased costs connected with using private courier services. Unfortunately, the company hadn't done much effective customer research into CPV until after they measured the results of their process improvement efforts. When they finally did that, they found that their customers were not nearly as concerned about the speed with which they received the reports as they were with their opportunity to interact with the doctors preparing the reports in the first place. That was a different matter, from a process improvement viewpoint, and made the earlier efforts concerning cycle time frustratingly insignificant.

When customer CPV needs are completely understood, the current process must then be defined and documented. It is the process owner's responsibility to see that this is done. Usually, groups of employees or consultants perform the work (interviews, observation, performance data collection, etc.), but the direction and leadership comes from the process owner.

Finally, performance measures for ongoing tracking of performance must be established. Process measures have been discussed earlier in this chapter, so it only remains here to remind that it is the process owner's responsibility to see that the measures are in place, the resulting performance information is made available to those who can make use of it, and that changes in process objectives or activities are reflected in updated and corrected performance measures.

Coaching

The process owner position is truly different than that of traditional functional managers. Borrowing from information and terminology in Chapter 8 about relationships between marketing channel members, business process owners can be said to possess *expert* power. That is, they are in a leadership position because they hold a higher level view of the process and are the most knowledgeable about how the process works and how it relates to other important processes in the organization. In most organizations today, the process owner does not carry *legitimate* power as "the boss" of the people working in the process.

The process owner is *not* the most expert at how the activities within the process are performed. Unlike traditional management structures, the process owner need not be able to perform the activities within the process better than any of the workers, as the factory foreman or the sales force manager usually does.

The process owner in her role as "coach" provides information and training to all concerned about the workings of the process. Usually, the emphasis is on coordination of activities at those points where the horizontal process crosses the vertical boundaries of the traditional functional organization. Most organizations and people are not very skilled at working across functional boundaries, so it is the process owner's responsibility to facilitate doing that.

Advocacy

Because most businesses today have retained their functional structure and manage processes as an overlay structure across those functions, an important role of the process owner is to obtain resources for the process. Without the process owner, there is no one to represent the process at senior management levels (where resources are allocated) and the process would either starve from lack of sustenance or strangle on the disproportionate wealth of resources concentrated at the point where a particular function (the traditional source of resources) intersects with the process.

The allocation of resources is an easier task when the organizational focus is on delivering superior CPV. When this is the case, the arguments for increased budgets is based on how CPV is created in the organization, how to prove that with valid measurements, and how to determine that the CPV, in fact, is delivered and is perceived as such by the customer. That is exactly what every business organization should be working on.

SUMMARY

This chapter, differently than the previous six, focuses on the last two gaps of the CPV Delivery Cycle – Processes and Management. These gaps are concerned with implementation rather than strategy. Implementation requires attention to processes, because processes are what produce all results including those that the customer perceives as CPV.

Implementation is also the point at which the marketing function is sometimes at odds with the other functions of the organization. Because of their respective perspectives on the business, functions such as engineering, R&D, manufacturing and operations, and administration sometimes mistrust and misunderstand the role of marketing. A common focus on delivering CPV provides the best hope for eliminating these differences.

Meanwhile, the structure of the marketing function itself continues to evolve as the "work of the customer" becomes, more and more, the work of all parts of the organization. From simple sales departments to horizontal, process-oriented structures, the line between the traditional marketing role and those that directly deliver CPV to customers continues to fade.

Cross-functional processes have become the focus of management's efforts to deliver superior CPV in an increasingly competitive and customer-driven environment. While some companies have turned their entire organization on its side to manage processes, most are still experimenting with ways to overlay the management of processes across their traditional, functionally-oriented structures. The first step in doing so is to clearly identify the processes that are currently producing the results that customers see.

When the company realizes that results can only be managed through processes, the real work begins. Specifically, management must (1) identify and name processes, (2) identify where and how processes deliver CPV, (3) train everyone about processes, and (4) measure process performance. In the course of doing this, improving processes can take either, or both, of two forms: reengineering (the radical redesign of processes) or improvement (from TQM's continuous improvement). In either approach, the objective is to emphasize "value-added" activities, minimize "non-value-added" activities, and eliminate "waste."

Process owners are the invention of the TQM movement to reconcile the conflicts of the traditional, functional organizational structures with the new, horizontal nature of processes. While process owners need not be better at performing the activities in a process, as traditional functional managers usually have been, they are responsible for design, coaching, and advocacy in connection with their process. Fortunately, delivering superior CPV resolves most conflicts that may arise between contending functions or processes.

REFERENCES

[1] www11.toysrus.com, February 2, 2000.

[2] From Toys "R" Us press release, dated April 27, 1999.

[3] From Toys "R" Us press release, dated November 2, 1999.

[4] Ellen Simon, "Christmas Delivery Problems Continue to Haunt Toyrus.com," *Knight-Ridder/Tribune Business News*, January 18, 2000.

[5] Philip Kotler, *Marketing Management: The Millennium Edition,* (Upper Saddle River, Prentice-Hall, 2000), pg. 689.

[6] Helen L. Richardson, "Must You Meet All Customer Demands?" *Transportation & Distribution*, June 1998, pg. 55.

[7] Joan O. Fredericks and James M. Salter II, "Beyond Customer Satisfaction," *Management Review*, May 1995, pg. 29.

[8] For additional resources on managing business processes, see H. James Harrington, *Business Process Improvement: The Breakthrough Strategy for Total Quality, Productivity, and Competitiveness*, (New York, McGraw-Hill, 1991); Geary A. Rummler and Alan P. Brache, *Improving Performance: How to Manage the White Space on the Organization Chart*, (San Francisco, Jossey-Bass, 1990); Rohit Ramaswamy, *Design and Management of Service Processes: Keeping Customers for Life*, (Reading, Addison-Wesley, 1996).

[9] Charlene B. Adair and Bruce A. Murray, *Breakthrough Process Redesign*, (New York, AMACOM, 1994).

[10] Michael Hammer, *Beyond Reengineering: How the Process-centered Organization is Changing Our Work and Our Lives*, (New York, Harper Collins, 1996).

[11] Adair and Murray, pg. 152.

SECTION THREE

Listening for Customer Perceived Value

CHAPTER 11

Monitoring CPV

The early 1990s brought dramatic change in health care. HMOs began to dominate the industry. Consolidation among health-care providers was taking place at a tremendous pace resulting in the emergence of a small number of huge vertically integrated cooperatives of health-care providers. As a result, fewer and fewer individual hospitals and health-care facilities handled their own purchasing. Instead, they relied on their network organization to leverage the purchasing power of the entire network to secure preferred pricing.

This was good news for the health-care providers but potentially bad news for their suppliers. In effect, the number of customers in the health-care supply market was dwindling rapidly, and the stakes were high for securing and retaining customer relationships. Baxter Healthcare, a leading medical products firm, saw the handwriting on the wall. It needed to come up with an offering that would clearly provide superior customer value or risk losing one or more major clients. Baxter business strategy executives proposed a unique solution to this dilemma: Provide clients with an information management system that would closely link the health-care network facilities with that of Baxter, allowing Baxter to provide superior products and services and a guaranteed savings to the customer.

Baxter approached Columbia/HCA, one of the nation's

largest health-care providers, with its proposition: allow Baxter to develop an information management system and operate the system in Columbia's member facilities, and Baxter would guarantee several million dollars in savings during an 8-year period. If the specified savings were not realized, Baxter would write Columbia a check for the difference. Not surprisingly, Columbia accepted the offer. Now all Baxter had to do was develop and implement a system that delivered on its promises.

Chuck Smith, a Baxter product systems manager and point man for this initiative, enlisted Ken Kauppila, a strategic applications development manager in Baxter's IT department, to make the dream a reality. A system, referred to as the Managed Care Tracking System (MCTS), was soon under development. Designed to draw and provide information across a wide range of computer platforms, the system allows Baxter and Columbia/HCA facilities to effectively manage their relationships with each other. The bottom-line benefit for the customer is reduced costs and additional information that can be used to more effectively run the facilities. Baxter benefits by having invaluable customer information at hand to support management decision making and by gaining long-term customer commitment.

How effective was Baxter's unique approach to using information management as a tool for providing superior customer value? In 1996, Baxter spun off Allegiance Corporation, which was immediately recognized as America's leading provider of health-care products and cost management services – another example of the results of focusing on Customer Perceived Value.

DEVELOPING A CPV LEARNING SYSTEM

Development of a system that provides a continuous stream of useful information about Customer Perceived Value (CPV) does not occur by accident. Collecting and managing CPV information requires the same commitment companies give to managing financial information or manufacturing processes, for example. Making a CPV Learning System a reality requires a systematic development and implementation process that includes the steps shown in Figure 11.1. Specific considerations for each of the phases in developing a CPV Learning System follow. As you will see, attention to these considerations is necessary to ensure optimum returns from the system.

Figure 11.1 - Steps to a CPV Learning System

1. Define information needs.
   a. Determine the information needs of individuals in the organization.
   b. Identify attributes customers use to judge CPV.
   c. Link CPV attributes with the business processes used to deliver them.
2. Obtain data.
   a. Identify appropriate existing internal information sources.
   b. Design customer research to gather additional information required.
3. Manage the information and its outputs.
   a. Obtain or develop a data compilation and access platform using information management software.
   b. Specify appropriate protocols for analyzing data.
   c. Specify protocols for regular reporting of results.
   d. Analyze and reports results on a regular basis. Provide the organization with access to information necessary for ad hoc investigation.

Defining Information Needs

In the search for the "holy grail" of management, corporate America has become accustomed to gurus presenting the new management approach *du jour*. Each new approach is typically based on sound logic, and one or more major companies have demonstrated its effectiveness. Still, when others seek to implement the approach, the results usually fail to meet expectations.

An excellent example of this is the use of the Balanced Scorecard approach developed by Norton and Kaplan.[1] The approach was designed to help companies rapidly and effectively implement business strategy. Mobil Oil, CIGNA Property and Casualty, and Brown & Root Engineering are companies that reported phenomenal results thanks, in part, to implementation of the Balanced Scorecard. We have experience, however, in working with other companies that have attempted to implement the Balanced Scorecard and have seen little results from their efforts.

Why are some companies successful at adopting and using management tools like the Balanced Scorecard, or Knowledge Management (KM) systems, or Customer Relationship Management (CRM) programs, while others have little or no success? More often than not, failure can be attributed to the lack of involvement by middle management, staff, and line personnel in the early design stages of the process or approach. Senior management dictates "here's what we're doing and why" and those responsible for executing the process or system go through the motions. Lacking is any compelling evidence of how the result of the process or system will make life better for the manager, or staff member, or line employee. Consequently, there is no commitment to make the initiative work as it should "in the trenches."

Developing a CPV Learning System that will be used – and used effectively – requires that those with a stake in the potential benefits of the system, namely managers and customers, have input into its design. This initial step is the first key to ensuring that the CPV Learning System is able to accomplish its purpose.

The Business Side of the Equation

Development of any information collection and management system is generally assigned to a specific functional unit. For example, Accounting gathers financial information, Marketing gathers customer-related information, and the MIS Department gathers operational process information, etc. Each group proceeds with the design of its system based on the general understanding of its purpose, knowledge of the group's own needs as a functional unit, and perhaps some consideration of the needs of other functional groups in the organization. This approach fails to lay the groundwork needed for a system that can benefit the entire organization.

It can be argued that nearly all organizational functions have a role in delivering CPV – more apparent to certain groups (e.g., Sales, Marketing, Product Development, Customer Service) than it is to others (e.g., Legal, Maintenance). A company's requirements for a CPV Learning System should be based on the information needs of all functional groups that have some impact on CPV.

Individuals within the groups impacting CPV have specific responsibilities and concerns. Consequently, their information needs differ. Design of the CPV Learning System should take these information needs into account. Figure 11.2 provides some of the questions that help to identify stakeholder requirements of a CPV Learning System. Learning the information needs of the system users not only lays the foundation for developing an effective CPV Learning System, it goes a long way toward achieving buy-in to use of the system after it is in place.

**Figure 11.2 - Questions to Determine
CPV Stakeholder Requirements**

- How do the individuals' responsibilities relate, directly or indirectly, with generating CPV?

- What types of customer-related information do they currently receive that are valuable & not valuable?

- Ideally, what customer-related information would they like to have?

- How will they use that information?

- When do they need the information? With what frequency?

- How should the information be provided to best suit their needs?

The Customer Side of the Equation

It was noted earlier that an effective CPV Learning System will facilitate communication between a company and its customers. The simplest way to learn what information customers want is to ask them in the same way that internal stakeholders are asked, but that is not very practical and it is not likely to be very effective. The challenge, then, is to make the CPV Learning System work for the customer as well as for the organization, even though it is unclear exactly how the customer could best benefit from the system.

The solution lies in a thorough understanding of CPV attributes – the customer-perceived benefits and costs associated with a specific product or service offering (see Chapter 2). The CPV Learning System must gather data concerning those attributes that customers place on their CPV balance scale. This means that data must be gathered on the performance of the company and competitors in providing CPV on each of the attributes customers use to weigh value provided. Factors that can change how customers perceive the value delivered through specific attributes must be monitored as well.

How does this approach benefit the customer? It allows them to learn areas in which the company is able to provide superior value. More importantly, it provides customers the opportunity to specify offerings that provide greater CPV.

From Parts to the Whole

The third key to developing an effective CPV Learning System is to link customer perceptions of value with the business processes used to deliver this value. At the most basic level, businesses take inputs, manipulate them, and typically generate an output, or product, that has a value greater than the sum of the inputs. This capability is a prerequisite to making profits. Generating value is not a magical occurrence. Understanding what the company does to generate value is fundamental to improving the CPV that its customers perceive.

Jan Carlzon took over Scandinavian Airline System (SAS) in 1981, the year it lost $20 million. Carlzon focused on identifying and attending to more than 50,000 "Moments of Truth" – those instances when passengers had an opportunity to judge value. This market-driven perspective, along with initiatives launched by Carlzon to make SAS "the best airline in the world for the frequent business traveler," resulted in SAS returning to profitability within one year and being named World Airline of the Year in 1983.

The mechanics of linking CPV to business processes were discussed in the previous chapter. Establishing linkages between process owners and customers who judge the value generated by their processes makes the CPV Learning System a tool for continual, widespread, management decision making.

Sources of Information

Any information system – which is what the CPV Learning System represents – is only as good as the data it gathers and analyzes. Based on the examples presented in this chapter thus far, it is apparent that there is a variety of information sources that companies can, and should, draw upon to monitor performance in providing CPV.

Multiple sources of information are important. Each information source has inherent strengths and limitations. A comprehensive approach allows companies to capitalize on the strengths of multiple information sources and compensate for their weaknesses. Another reason why information must be captured in several ways is because there is no single approach or information source that can answer all of the questions a CPV Learning System will be designed to address. For example, if a manager wants to determine market share, it would be unusual to survey or interview individual customers to gather that information. On the other hand, if the objective is to understand what customers do and do not value in a specific offering, that information is best gathered through direct customer research.

Practical issues involving information gathering and use also support the idea that multiple data sources are preferable. Companies have learned that "one-shot" customer measures – typically represented by a single comprehensive customer survey every couple of years or so – don't work. The effectiveness of changes made to improve what customers are offered, and what they experience, cannot be evaluated in a timely fashion. It is also becoming increasingly difficult to secure from customers detailed information that is both valid and reliable. If the "what's in if for me" is not clear, people are increasingly hesitant to provide feedback out of the kindness of their heart. Even those inclined to provide feedback are granting less "air time" to respond to inquiries.

So, the bad news is that there is a clear need for multiple sources of information to effectively monitor CPV. The good news is that a myriad of sources do exist – many of them often unnoticed or untapped. These information sources fall into three general categories:

INTERNAL SOURCES
PRIMARY RESEARCH DATA
SECONDARY RESEARCH DATA

Internal Sources

Internal information sources are used by most companies, primarily to manage financial and operational aspects of the business. They are not designed, and are seldom used, with the thought of the customer in mind. The information sources can, however, contribute to the overall picture of CPV delivered by a company. Figure 11.3 lists and describes several available internal information sources.

The primary advantages of using internal information sources are that they are readily available and are typically well understood by most employees. From a customer learning standpoint, the main disadvantage of internal information sources is that most are surrogate rather than direct measures of performance in delivering CPV. Some are based on little, if any, direct customer interaction and are not always representative of experiences of all current or potential customers. Additionally, internal data sources seldom provide any indication of competitor offerings and relative performance. Consequently, use of internal information alone to monitor CPV would not be appropriate.

If internal information sources are so readily available, why aren't they used more frequently in the context of understanding CPV de-

Figure 11.3 - Internal Data Sources

Information Source	CPV Learning System Use
Data captured via other customer transactions (e.g., inquiries, complaints, field service reports, etc.).	Represents direct source of customer feedback.
Order to payment cycle transaction records.	Provides surrogate measures of performance in areas, such as order acceptance, fulfillment, delivery, and invoicing.
Sales information – sales figures, sales call reports.	Indication of success in offering CPV. Call reports can provide information concerning CPV attributes and competitors.
Supply chain partner feedback.	Conduit for gathering indirect end-user feedback on value of offerings.
Prior research reports.	Often includes information on specific aspects of CPV provided (e.g., new product tests, needs-based segmentation research, etc.)
Enterprise Resource Planning (ERP) information	Provides indication of effectiveness in producing outcomes critical to customers, particularly concerning product- and service-related feedback.

livered? Typically overlooked are the identification and systematic capturing and analysis of these data. Some companies have realized the benefits that internal information can provide. For example, Xerox Webmaster Bill MacLain has created a knowledge base derived from all queries he receives. Since 1996, Xerox Corporation's U.S. Customer Operations has developed a "customer connections tool" that gathers data from a variety of internal sources – verbatim responses gathered on three customer satisfaction surveys, write-ups of site visits to and from customers, and write ups from other meetings with customers. Xerox has found that gathering, analyzing, and using this information has produced documented improvements in both customer satisfaction and loyalty.[2]

Customer Research

While internal information sources can be useful in helping to monitor and manage the delivery of CPV, there is no getting around the fact that effective measures must involve the true judges of value delivered – customers. Customer research encompasses the processes of proactively securing data to meet your CPV information needs, rather than relying solely on various sources that are already at hand.

Criteria for Effective Research

The characteristics that Kotler uses to describe good customer research also help to distinguish the difference between customer research and the use of internal information.[3] Effective customer research meets the following criteria:

Follows the Principles of the Scientific Method. Most of us learned the principles of the scientific method in a middle school or high school science class and promptly forgot them. Good research is based on establishing a hypothesis and testing that hypothesis with systematic collection and analysis of data. Unfortunately, much research being conducted fails to meet these most basic criteria.

Employs Multiple Methods. It was noted earlier that every research method has some inherent flaws. Good research uses multiple approaches to test hypotheses, thereby increasing confidence in the results.

Is Cautious about the Application of "Marketing Myths." All managers have assumptions about the way that their markets work and their customers make decisions. Research should not accept these assumptions as fact. A classic example is the development of surveys to measure customer satisfaction, or loyalty, or CPV, without any input from customers.

Is Ethical - Benefits the Company and the Respondent. Noted earlier as a characteristic of an effective CPV Learning System, mutual benefit to the company and respondent is also essential to the research that feeds into the CPV Learning System as well. Resentment to involvement in research continues to grow in the U.S. because this tenet has been and continues to be frequently violated.

Weighs Value of Information versus Cost. Some would argue that good research must be "bulletproof" by providing virtually certain answers to the research questions posed. The fact is that there is typically a direct correlation between the level of investment required and the level of certainty that research results are able to provide. Good research provides the most "bang for the buck" by considering what the results are worth to the users of the resource results.

Appropriate Research Techniques

In addition to demonstrating the above characteristics, good customer research builds on empirical knowledge. Selection of appropriate customer research techniques is a function of what one has learned through previous research and what one wishes to learn.

Those "starting from scratch" to address specific CPV issues require the use of exploratory research techniques. The purpose of exploratory research is to become more familiar with an issue, to gain new insights, and to help formulate more specific research questions or hypotheses. This type of research tends to be qualitative in nature, typically focusing on gathering responses to open-ended questions. Constraints on the nature of the data gathered are few. Customers are allowed to express and explain their perceptions as they choose. Exploratory research is done using the majority of secondary research and primary qualitative research techniques described in the following section.

Exploratory techniques lay the groundwork for confirmatory research that provides the accurate and generalizable results sought by most managers. Confirmatory research answers – with a known degree of precision – the who, what, when, where, and how questions. Confirmatory research is also used to describe correlations, or relationships, among factors. Ultimately, confirmatory research can explain or predict how customers perceive CPV. It is more quantitative in nature and typically involves primary research techniques (e.g., descriptive survey research, experimental research), which are also described below.

Confirmatory research of some type is usually necessary to meet most management information needs. So while it may be apparent that confirmatory research should be done, those with limited research experience too often overlook the need for exploratory research to guide the development of the confirmatory research. This is one of the major reasons why customer research fails to generate the type of information desired. A fundamental tenet of good research is overlooked.

With an appropriate combination of exploratory and confirmatory research, there are few questions concerning CPV that cannot be answered. The research techniques that allow the accomplishment of this feat can be grouped into three general categories:

- *Secondary Research* - Using data from existing, outside sources
- *Primary Qualitative Research* - Gathering nonstatistical data directly from customers.
- *Primary Quantitative Research* - Gathering numeric or statistical data directly from customers.

Secondary Research. Secondary research relies on existing sources of information. Instead of gathering data "from scratch," the research questions are answered with data or information that has already been gathered by another party.

There are several advantages to using secondary research.[4] Secondary research provides a means for clarifying or redefining the definition of a problem as part of the exploratory research process. It also has the capability to answer some research questions without the investment and effort required to do primary research. In instances where primary research is not practical (e.g., short time frame, limited budget), secondary research may offer an alternative approach to securing needed information. Secondary research can provide necessary background information on markets to enhance the interpretation of findings from other sources and it can alert researchers to potential problems that might be encountered in moving forward with primary research.

There are several constraints that secondary research typically faces. The most critical is a lack of available data. However, research questions are specific in nature so that their answers can be actionable. As data specificity requirements increase, the probability of locating the data needed from secondary sources decreases. Assuming appropriate data exist to be gathered from secondary sources, these data may also be limited in scope or have only marginal relevance to the research question. While these constraints present another argument for the use of multiple data sources, secondary research clearly offers valuable data sources for development of the CPV Learning System.

Secondary research can be conducted using either internal (to the company) or external data sources. Secondary research using internal data is commonly referred to as *data mining*. Data mining differs from the process of gathering and analyzing internal data described earlier in that data mining is guided by specific research questions or hypotheses. Obviously, the more data on customers and customer transactions, the richer the opportunities for data mining research. This explains why companies with a wealth of customer information, such as financial institutions and catalog retailers, are leaders in the use of data mining as a customer learning tool.

The key to the effective use of data mining is tying customer behavior indicators to measures of transactional experiences (e.g., frequency and types of purchases, use of services). Data mining will continue to increase in popularity, practicality, and effectiveness with the development of information management systems such as data warehouses. These information management systems will be considered in depth later in this chapter.

Secondary research using existing external data sources provides a cost-effective means for monitoring developments and trends that impact entire markets or specific market segments. Figure 11.4 lists a variety of secondary data sources that are readily accessible and can provide a wealth of general customer information. Government data sources offer market demographic information and trend data at little or no cost. Periodicals offer insight into changes within industries – what issues and challenges customers are focusing upon and how they are dealing with these issues. Several companies offer industry- or market-specific information on a commercial basis. A variety of public and commercial information can also be secured via the Internet, offering immediate information access. In fact, entire books have been published as guides to using the Internet for secondary marketing research.

Primary Qualitative Research. Qualitative research is best described as research that is not quantitative, or numerical. As noted earlier, qualitative research usually is exploratory in nature. It is used to provide a general understanding of issues or topics that we want to learn more about and is a necessary prerequisite for good quantitative research. But, the precision that quantitative research can provide means nothing if one is measuring the wrong thing. Qualitative research ensures that the proper things are measured.

Qualitative research has other strengths as a part of a CPV Learning System besides providing direction for and improving the efficiency of quantitative measures. Qualitative research provides the tools necessary to effectively understand the feelings and emotions that drive customer behavior. Understanding why customers buy, or don't buy, is at the crux of providing superior CPV. Qualitative research also supplies an organization with the "voice of the customer." Hearing directly what customers have to say carries as much, if not more, weight than statistical facts in driving change in a company. The "voice of the customer" helps to remove the distance that typically exists between customer and many company personnel.

Figure 11.4 - Secondary Data Sources*

Government Data & Publications
- *Statistical Abstract of the United States.*
- *County & City Databook.*
- *Industrial Outlook.*
- Other demographic data compiled by the U.S. Census Bureau (www.census.gov).
- Other economic data compiled by the U.S. Dept. of Commerce, Bureau of Economic Analysis (www.doc.bea.gov).

Periodicals
- General business magazines (*Business Week, Fortune, Forbes*).
- Trade magazines (*Industry Week*).
- A complete list of general and trade publications can be found in *Business Periodicals Index.*

Commercial Data
- Industry-specific study results (J.D. Power survey results in automotive & air travel; Greenwich study in banking; TQS study in electric utility industry).
- Dun & Bradstreet (www.dnb.com); Bloomberg Personal (www.bloomberg.com); Hoovers (www.hoovers.com); Company Link (www.companylink.com) – company-specific financial, demographic, news-related information, and SEC data.
- Roper (www.roper.com) - Syndicated research results on consumer perceptions of companies and brands; youth lifestyles, attitudes, and marketplace influence; consumer attitudes and behaviors related to environmental issues.

Internet-based Sources
- Newsgroups.
- Search engines.
- Public Register's Annual Report Service (www.prars.com/index.html) - Database of 3,200 public companies that can be searched by company name or industry. Offers annual reports via e-mail.
- National Trade Data Bank (www.stat-usa.gov) - 18,000+ market research reports of trends and competitors for hundreds of products in scores of industries.
- EDGAR (www.sec.gov/edgarhp.htm) - Public company financial filings.
- Commercial sources noted above.

---

* The commercial information sources are presented only as examples. This is not a complete list of these sources, and recommendation of only these sources listed is not implied.

Qualitative research does have some notable weaknesses. It is rarely safe to assume that qualitative results provide a highly accurate representation of the customer group of interest, so there is inherent risk in making decisions based on qualitative research results alone. Many managers view nonstatistical data as being "too soft." The link between what the manager can do and how it will impact what the customer thinks is often unclear. A third problem with qualitative research is that it looks easy to do – just ask some open-ended questions. This makes it easy for almost anyone to claim that they can conduct qualitative research. In actuality, simply asking questions no more makes one a qualitative researcher than being able to operate a microwave makes one a chef.

Figure 11.5 presents some of the commonly used qualitative techniques that can be integrated into a CPV Learning System. The most commonly used are customer interviewing approaches, including one-on-one interviews and focus groups. Qualitative research is certainly not limited to conducting interviews, however. Some techniques involve very nontraditional approaches, including observation of customers "in their natural habitat" (a.k.a. anthropological approaches) and gathering perceptions completely outside of the context of the product and/or service being offered (projective techniques).

When we consider the various qualitative research tools available, it is usually not as simple as directly asking the customer the question for which one is seeking an answer. For example, health-care giant Kaiser Permanente has developed a web site designed to support a mutual learning process between Kaiser and its members. At www.kponline.org, members are offered the unique opportunity to take part in moderated discussions on a variety of specific medical topics. Kaiser doctors and psychologists read every posting, and offer advice or correct misinformation as warranted. These forums not only provide members with easy access to information, they also provide Kaiser with a wealth of information about its members, including their concerns and any potential medical challenges.[5]

Some qualitative research can even be done without the active participants feeling like they are involved in research. The Jeep Division of Daimler-Chrysler holds an annual event called *Camp Jeep*.

Figure 11.5 - Qualitative Research Techniques

- One-on-one interviews (in person, by phone, by web - depth interviews) - for CPV Learning System, used to identify CPV attributes for small or important targeted customer groups.
- Focus-group interviews (small group & focus group) - For CPV Learning System, used to identify CPV attributes for larger populations (e.g., market segments). Can be traditional or web-based.
- Nominal group sessions - Small groups of customers independently generate ideas about a subject and then discuss these ideas as a larger group.
- Customer feedback (customer advisory panels, performance review evaluations) - Structured customer interactions to periodically gather feedback directly from customers.
- Web-based interactive - Provides opportunity to share information, identify major issues & concerns.
- Customer role-playing & shadowing (mystery shopping) - Systematic evaluation of the customer's experience in dealing with a supplier.
- Customer events - Informal customer gatherings focusing on ownership and use of specific products.
- Sentence & story completion - Technique to study customer reactions to situations.
- Zaltman Metaphor Elicitation - A projective technique. Customer creates a collage representative of their experiences and feelings about a product. They then meet with researchers to explain the connection between the images selected and their experiences with the company and its products.

Chrysler invites Jeep owners to get together for a couple of days of off-roading enjoyment. Engineers spend time with the participants, not to formally interrogate Jeep owners, but to learn how they feel at a deeper level about their Jeep products and the Jeep brand.[6] The Saturn division of General Motors has also sponsored similar events since that division was launched.

Primary Quantitative Research. After qualitative research identifies how customers perceive value, a company's performance in delivering CPV must be monitored with a reasonable degree of accuracy. This is where primary quantitative research is necessary. Primary quantitative research is best described as statistically-based research that gathers data directly from customers and generates numerical (quantitative) results with a known degree of accuracy.

Quantitative results having a known degree of accuracy allow managers to reduce the risk in making decisions based on these results. The same does not hold true when considering qualitative results alone. Another key advantage of quantitative research is that it can accurately describe a situation or identify causal relationships. From a practical standpoint, this is invaluable information for managers, because linkages between actions that managers take and the impact of these actions on customer perceptions become much clearer.

While quantitative information has very desirable characteristics, its weaknesses should not be ignored. Quantitative results are usually assumed to be representative, valid, and reliable. Unfortunately, the rules that must be followed to ensure these qualities are often ignored. For example, it is common practice among many researchers to report that a sample provides results that are accurate to within plus or minus 3 percentage points (or 5 points, or whatever) based on the size of the sample. However, they ignore that the sample may not be representative because the respondents were not randomly sampled or nonrespondents were ignored. If the sample is not representative, one should not expect the results of a survey to be any more representative of a population's perceptions than the performance on a single monthly P&L statement is representative of financial performance for a full year.

One technique to encourage responses from a representative group of customers is to ask a limited number of simple questions. Contact cards are a common example of asking questions that are "short and sweet." However, a small number of more generalized questions can only provide nonspecific feedback and rarely are results the type that managers can use to improve the delivery of CPV.

Another major weakness of quantitative research is that it can be, and often is, misinterpreted. Misinterpretation can sometimes be attributed to the use of improper statistical procedures, but more frequently it is the result of misinterpreting the statistics themselves.

Even those who have endured the rigor of a battery of statistical courses often fail to test the assumptions that underlie many statistics and profoundly impact their proper interpretation.

Acceptance of quantitative research results should be based on evidence that the researchers have made every effort to ensure that the data are valid, reliable, and representative. Evidence that appropriate analysis and interpretation of the data are being performed should be examined as well.

The most common type of primary quantitative research is survey research. Figure 11.6 lists a variety of survey methodologies. The appropriate type, or types, for use in a CPV Learning System are largely dependent on the types of customers and customer contacts being targeted. For example, while mall intercept surveys may make perfect sense for a clothing retailer, it is difficult to imagine a case where an industrial equipment manufacturer would use this technique. E-mail and Internet-based surveys are increasingly popular, but obviously require that all potential respondents have Internet access and/or researchers have a valid e-mail addresses.

Figure 11.6 - Types of Survey Research

- Executive interview (with quantitative component)
- Door-to-door
- Mall intercept
- Direct computer - used in mall environment
- Point of service touch-screen
- Self-administered - comment cards, captive audience surveys (e.g., classrooms, airplanes)
- Telephone interviews
- Interactive Voice Response (IVR) surveys
- Mail surveys
- Mail panels
- Computer disk by mail
- Fax surveys
- E-mail surveys
- Internet surveys

It is generally best to use multiple survey approaches in the development of a CPV Learning System. The ability for companies to gather all of the customer information they need through a single survey conducted by mail or telephone is quickly becoming an impractical dream. Brief, targeted surveys designed to gather data at or near the time that customer value judgments are made should serve as key data sources for the CPV Learning System. The decision as to what approaches to use should be based primarily on what is most comfortable and convenient for the respondent.

While survey research is likely to play an important role in any effective CPV Learning System, it is not the only primary quantitative research approach available. Experimental research is an option that goes beyond the basic description of customer perceptions provided by survey research. Experimental research offers a means of clearly measuring the relative importance and worth of value attributes to customers. This makes it a particularly appropriate research methodology to use when designing new products and/or service offerings when CPV attributes are already defined and validated.

The conjoint analysis methodology, where customers indicate relative preferences among combinations of value attributes at a variety of levels, is an example of a powerful experimental research approach for understanding CPV. The reason this approach is not more commonly used is the practical challenges and costs associated with data collection. As the number of levels of value attributes to be considered increases, there is an exponential increase in the time required of customers to evaluate and respond to the available options. This makes experimental research more expensive to conduct than survey research. Note, however, that additional investment results in additional accuracy in the research results.

Information Management

The previous section demonstrated that a myriad of data sources are available to learn about customers and, in turn, deliver superior CPV. Selection of the appropriate sources for the development of a CPV Learning System is based on the information needs of the company and its customers. The challenge, however, does not end with identifying what data are needed and simply gathering that data. Realizing the true value of assimilated data requires the development of a platform to access data and the establishment of protocols for ongoing data analysis and reporting.

Development of a data access platform for a CPV Learning System involves the same issues that surround the development of any information management system. These include resource commitment, hardware and software selection, and information source characteristics. For companies with limited resources and an interest in using existing hardware and software platforms, the technology base for a CPV Learning System can be quite simple – relying on input of all data into an existing, commonly used data management program (e.g., Microsoft *Excel* or *Access*). For example, a GE Capital business unit in the early 1990s designed and implemented a simple and effective system for gathering customer feedback from multiple sources. A process manager compiled data on an ongoing basis and reported quantitative trend data and current performance on a monthly basis. Qualitative data were distributed internally to appropriate contacts. Customers were also kept informed of process changes made and documented improvements as a result of their feedback. All of this was accomplished without additional investment in information management technology.

While the use of a simple data management platform offers the advantage of minimal investment, it typically does not provide easy, immediate access to all managers who require information provided by the system. Additionally, the gathered data are typically limited to critical customer inputs and measures of performance.

To capitalize on the wealth of available data that exists, some companies have invested in more complex data management platforms. These platforms are developed as data warehousing and/or customer relationship management (CRM) information systems. The function of these systems is to provide a common interface to a variety of data sources that may reside on multiple platforms in multiple computer languages. These systems not only provide tools to access data – they also have data capturing, querying, and analysis features that allow both ongoing and ad hoc reporting of information.

Development of a comprehensive customer information management platform does require a substantial commitment. CAP Gemini reports that the mean total investment for the development and full implementation of typical CRM information systems is currently $3.1 million. However, they also found through ROI analysis that this investment is recouped within 28 months, on average. It is normal for companies to realize double-digit sales increases attributable to the benefits provided by the system by the second year it is in place.[7]

Whether the information management system used for the CPV Learning System is simple or complex, the quality of information generated can be enhanced – or constrained – by the protocols used for ongoing data analysis and reporting. These protocols must take two critical factors into consideration. First, analyses must be appropriate for the type of data that is available. The rules guiding the appropriate analysis for quantitative and qualitative data must be applied. Second, the information needs of users must be met. The following section considers this factor in greater detail.

OUTPUTS FROM A CPV LEARNING SYSTEM

Recall that the first step in development of a CPV Learning System is to determine what management information it should provide. Often, these determinations are forgotten as a company gets into the nuts and bolts of selecting data sources and an information management platform. In the end, outputs are driven more by information system platform capabilities and the nature of the data available than the original management information requirements specified. It is critical to guard against the tendency that the information system drive its own outputs, leaving managers to "take what they can get." To ensure that this does not occur, the outputs of a CPV Learning System should meet the following criteria.[8]

Results are Relevant

The CPV Learning System outputs should directly respond to management information requirements. Results should focus on customer segments of interest, particularly in response to the needs of sales, marketing, service, and new product development management.

Results are Useful and Precise

Results must provide a degree of specificity that allow a manager to act on the information provided. Information that is general in nature is seldom useful for taking action. For example, an overall satisfaction score does nothing to tell a manager what a manager should do to improve from the customers' perspective. As researcher Brian Lunde notes, "One of the worst criticisms that could be made by a line manager about a company's … information is that it is 'interesting.' 'Interesting' is a code for 'useless.' The information simply must be specific enough that executives … can take action – make decisions, set priorities, launch programs, cancel projects."[9]

Results are Presented in Context

Lacking a point of comparison for interpreting customer feedback or a company's performance ratings seriously detracts from the value of the information. Qualitative results should note, at a minimum, the characteristics of the customers providing the feedback and the questions or situations to which they were responding. Contexts for the presentation of quantitative data should include change over time or comparisons to some basis of reference (e.g., competitor ratings).

Results are Credible

Reporting of results should include evidence of steps taken to ensure that the information presented is based on valid, reliable, and representative data, such as the use of multiple methodologies and data sources, appropriate sampling, and data collection instrument validation by managers. The easiest way for a manager to dismiss lackluster performance ratings by customers is to challenge the quality of the data. Information users should be assured that results are not erroneous because of poor data quality.

Results are Understandable

Output of the CPV Learning System should be information – not statistics or data used to generate the statistics. Information is presented so managers can review results and interpret them appropriately. The basis for quantitative results (the measurement scale and its range) should be clear. Meaningful differences between current results and their points of comparison should be apparent.

Results are Timely

Results must be readily available to management for making decisions. Reporting should support decision making and planning cycles.

CPV Learning System results generated should not remain static. The value to managers of specific types of customer information changes as management challenges change. The usefulness of specific CPV Learning System outputs should be monitored to make certain that time and effort are not wasted in collecting data that are of minimal value to management. Most people know of at least one company that has been doing customer research the same way, using the same survey, for several years even though use of the results are minimal. The desire not to lose the investment in data from previous years overrides the primary purpose of the customer research in the first place – to assist in management decision making. So companies keep on surveying their customers, but doing little with the results. The CPV Learning System should not be set on "auto pilot" and allowed to follow this course.

BENEFITS OF A CPV LEARNING SYSTEM

Much of this chapter has reflected on the challenges of developing an effective CPV Learning System. However, the potential benefits provided by a CPV Learning System make these challenges pale in comparison. In the Age of the Customer, knowledge and information management has become the basis for maintaining a competitive advantage. A CPV Learning System offers the tools necessary to manage that knowledge.

Understand What Customers Value

From a management perspective, a customer learning system provides the key to understanding what customers truly value, and for what they are willing to pay a premium. What company would not find this information to be priceless? This fundamental understanding of CPV allows management to guide its prioritization of resources and efforts to realize maximum value generation. The 3M Company lives this philosophy. Its customers benefit from the additional value they receive, but maximizing value generation also benefits 3M by providing an opportunity to recapture more value from the customer.

Monitor Performance in Delivering CPV

A CPV Learning System allows companies to track, over time, the customer perceived value they are providing. Efforts to provide greater value to customers can be effectively evaluated. Practices that are known to generate superior value are identified and fostered. Practices that do not support the creation or addition of value can be modified or eliminated to make more effective use of available resources. In essence, the CPV Learning System provides the information necessary to drive and reward value creation.

Competitive Advantage

Development of a CPV Learning System offers a clear competitive advantage as a result of having a more in-depth understanding of customers than does one's competitors. Inherent in the CPV Learning System are measures of how customers view a company's offerings compared to alternatives to those offerings. This presents a clear picture of how a company stacks up against its competition on the only factors that count – those that cause a customer to choose or reject an offering.

Improve Management Effectiveness

An in-depth understanding of CPV also has positive implications for management of critical customer interactions. Clearly understanding prospects' specific perceptions of the value of specific offerings allows companies to prepare marketing materials that are targeted directly at those perceptions. More effective materials and sales presentations result in both reduced costs and, more importantly, an improved "hit rate" for the selling process. Increasing the selling close rate by just a modest amount typically translates into substantial revenue gains. Even understanding which prospects place a lower value on specific offerings and why they do is of immense value. This knowledge allows companies to prioritize prospects and, thereby, shorten the selling cycle and increase "close" rates.

Reduced Risk

A CPV Learning System also provides benefits that are less tangible, but certainly just as important as improved positioning with customers. Information generated by the CPV Learning System reduces the uncertainty, or risk, associated with most management decisions. If managers know that their decisions might positively, or negatively, impact how customers perceive the value of a company's offering, the risk in making an incorrect decision is reduced. Consider the product development function. In the past many companies would make most of their product development decisions based on little, if any, understanding of what customers value. Products would be launched and fail miserably in the marketplace, resulting in wasted time, effort, and financial investment. Product developers have learned that consideration of CPV early in the product development process significantly reduces the risk associated with development of an offering that customers will reject.

Improved Return on Information Assets

Finally, companies that have developed customer information management systems have realized more effective return on their own information assets. Rather than limiting information use to specific functional areas, these companies have found that linking and providing management access to a company's full wealth of information has resulted in returns that quickly recoup information management investments and provide them with a competitive advantage.

The benefits of adopting a disciplined approach to learning and monitoring what customers value are clear. Ask yourself this question: Can your company clearly distinguish its product and service offerings from those alternatives available to your customers? Often the answer is "no." Superior product and service quality are rapidly becoming "givens" – necessities just to have the opportunity to survive in the marketplace. The only way companies can ensure their long-term success is through understanding and providing superior CPV.

SUMMARY

As markets change and customers gain power, effective use of information is becoming increasingly important to the long-term success of companies. Most companies have a myriad of readily available information from which they are realizing only a fraction of its potential value. More often than not, a means for clearly understanding CPV and monitoring value provided to customers is lacking as well. When these situations exist, it is difficult for a company to deliver customer value, no matter how committed they are to that objective.

For a company to be proactive in generating and delivering customer value, it must provide its people with the information necessary to make this happen. A CPV Learning System is designed to capitalize on existing company information and capture additional data from customers and other sources to provide the information necessary to effectively deliver CPV.

Developing a CPV Learning System that will be used – effectively – requires that those with a stake in the potential benefits of the system have input into its design. It can be argued that virtually every functional position within a company has some impact on the CPV delivered by the company. Individuals in these functional positions have specific responsibilities and concerns, so their information needs differ. The CPV Learning System must also work for the customer. This is accomplished with a thorough understanding of customer perceived value attributes – the customer-perceived benefits and costs associated with a specific product or service offering.

Any information system – which is what the CPV Learning System represents – is only as good as the data it gathers and analyzes. There are a variety of information sources that companies can, and should, draw upon to monitor performance in providing CPV. Using multiple sources of information is an important feature of a CPV Learning System as each information source has inherent strengths and limitations. Fortunately, an extensive array of information sources do exist – many of them often unnoticed or untapped. These sources fall into three general categories: internal sources, secondary research data, and primary research data.

Selection of the appropriate information sources for the development of a CPV Learning System is based on the information needs of one's company and customers. The challenge does not end with identifying what data are needed and then gathering those data. Realizing the true value of assimilated data requires the development of a platform to access data and the establishment of protocols for ongoing data analysis and reporting.

From a management perspective, a customer learning system provides the key to understanding what customers truly value and for what they are willing to pay a premium. This fundamental understanding of allows management to guide its prioritization of resources and efforts to realize maximum value generation.

REFERENCES

[1] David P. Norton, "Using the Balanced Scorecard to Implement Strategy," Proceedings of the 10th Annual Customer Satisfaction and Quality Measurement Conference, March 1-3, 1998, Atlanta GA, American Marketing Association and

American Society for Quality.

[2] Thomas A. Stewart, "Customer Learning is a Two-Way Street: E-commerce at Dow, GE, Kaiser, and Xerox," *Fortune*, May 10, 1999, pg. 158.

[3] Philip Kotler, *Marketing Management, The Millennium Edition*, (Upper Saddle River, Prentice-Hall, 2000), pg. 104.

[4] Carl McDaniel, Jr. and Roger Gates, *Contemporary Marketing Research: Fourth Edition*, (Cincinnati, South-Western College Publishing, 1999).

[5] Stewart, *Ibid.*

[6] Barry Sheehy, "Are You Listening?" *Across the Board*, April 1999, pg. 42-43.

[7] Rachel Miller, "Holistic Approach to Keeping Clients," *Marketing*, July 29, 1999, pg. 22.

[8] Leonard L. Berry and A. Parasuraman, "Listening to the Customer – The Concept of a Service Quality Information System," *Sloan Management Review*, Spring 1997, Vol. 38, No. 3, pg. 65-76.

[9] B.S. Lunde, "When Being Perfect is not Enough," *Marketing Research*, Winter 1993, Vol 5, pg. 26.

CHAPTER 12

Payback on CPV

In the late 1960s, Bob Walter graduated from Harvard Business School and then moved to Columbus, Ohio to go into business. He didn't know what kind of business he wanted to be in, only that he wanted to make money. He looked around at opportunities and, in 1971, purchased a small food distributor called Cardinal Foods. The business was relatively simple – food distributors had been operated the same way for generations.

The company grew steadily but Walter decided it wasn't enough. Food distribution was a low margin business that met its customers' needs only by keeping costs low. He couldn't find a better way to deliver CPV, so he decided it was time to diversify. In 1979, the company bought a small drug distribution company located about 60 miles up the interstate highway in Zanesville, Ohio. He changed the name of the company to Cardinal Distribution, and embarked on a strategy to deliver superior CPV to both sides of the health-care industry – manufacturers and providers. In 1988, Cardinal sold its food distribution business.

Those decisions, to build a business on delivering high CPV and to select a market that would permit that strategy to succeed, were the basis of one of the most successful business stories in the last several decades.

From the beginning, the company has found ways to de-

liver more CPV to its customers. In addition to its break bulk-and-ship function, Cardinal helps its merchant customers keep their books. It sets up electronic ordering systems so customers can manage their inventories. It provides training and material in merchandising to help these merchants sell more product. In other words, it continues to find ways to deliver value-added services around, and in support of, its basic distribution function. Last year, the company went into the Internet website development business for its customers, helping them get set up with e-commerce capabilities. For its chain drugstore customers, this service is called Chain Online, and with it Cardinal develops and manages a complete Internet presence. This service is provided by Medical Strategies, one of many different Cardinal subsidiaries that delivers CPV in different ways to different customers.

Now known as Cardinal Health, Inc., the company was recently added to the S&P 500, confirming its stature as one of the nation's most successful companies. Total revenues for its most recent fiscal year were more than $25 billion, with gross profits at 11.3 percent, and earnings of $1.26 billion. The company employs more than 36,000 people and was, by far, the fastest growing company in its industry.

All of this was based on understanding CPV and implementing a strategy to attain competitive advantage by delivering that CPV better than anyone else can. Walter, his original partners, and all of his shareholders, realized a handsome return on their investment in understanding CPV.

WHY INVEST IN UNDERSTANDING CPV?

By now we're hopeful that the reader is persuaded that there is nothing more important in business than delivering superior Customer Perceived Value (CPV). Fundamentally, there is nothing more important because CPV is the basis on which customers hand over cash to a supplier. And without that cash, a business starves to death. That is what it's all about.

But there are many things that a manager must worry about to successfully deliver superior CPV. We've dealt with some of them here, such as developing and communicating strategy. That's Gap #2 on our CPV Delivery Cycle. Closing that gap has much to do with such intangibles as leadership and vision in addition to the mechanics of "making strategy." Then there's Gap #3, which is about designing and managing business processes. As discussed in Chapter 10, that looks much easier than it really is. And Gap #4 represents the hard work of management follow-through. Some very difficult issues, including performance measurement and reward systems, fall into this gap.

And there are many other important management issues that are well outside the scope of this book, including capital acquisition and financial management, motivating and managing personnel, organizational knowledge management, and corporate culture. All of these things are the responsibility of top management and require time, energy, and organizational resources to deliver superior CPV.

We want to end this book, however, with the proposition that the absolutely most important thing that any business can do in striving for competitive advantage is to understand how customers define CPV. Close Gap #1 – the Research Gap.

Why is this most important? It is a relatively safe and easy investment that promises a greater financial return to the business than any other. Understanding CPV is a great business investment.

Of course, this investment cannot be made *instead of* all of the other things that top management must accomplish. Every business operates with limited resources and each investment decision involves trade-offs against all of those other demands. But understanding CPV deserves to be a *top priority* among those investment choices because of its potential financial return.

Is measuring the financial return on just one aspect of management's responsibilities difficult? Sure it is. But measuring the return on understanding CPV is easier than for some of the other things on which top management spends resources. Let's take a look at this by reviewing each of the subject areas covered in the chapters in Section Two of this book.

Business Strategy

A leading American consumer products company introduced its successful suntan lotion product into the European market.[1] The introduction landed with a loud "thud." Despite heavy investments into packaging, logistics, and marketing communications to support this product introduction, it was clearly a dismal failure. Although details remain confidential to the company, it can safely be assumed that several million dollars were lost in the unsuccessful efforts to gain market share in Europe for this product.

Then, someone decided that perhaps some customer research might be useful. In fact, several efforts at research had been attempted, but each of them was flawed in some way. This time, an innovative psychodrama approach to the research was used. Several French women were given a scenario that placed them in a damaged airplane landing on a remote desert island. They had only 60 seconds to select from their purses what they would take ashore with them. They were permitted to choose from a variety of American and French suntan lotions, other lotions, and moisturizing creams. The results led to a better understanding of CPV for this European market.

All of the women chose to take the moisturizing creams with them and none of the suntan lotions. Why? It was their perception that the worst danger of the sun was that it dried out their skins, and dried out skin was the worst sign of aging skin. The copper-skinned American models that portrayed the results of using suntan lotion were symbols to these women of damaged, aged skin. Marketing communications that worked in America didn't work in Europe. The people in these two markets defined the benefits and costs resulting from use of this product very differently. Until this research was conducted, management didn't understand the difference in CPV.

What did the research cost to conduct? We don't know, but we'd guess that it couldn't have been much more than, say, $100,000. If the failed product introduction cost only $1 million (surely it was more than that), the return on the customer research was almost 900 percent! The reader is free to adjust our dollar estimates however she would like. The return on investment will remain huge.

This example is not isolated. Unfortunately, the total cost of most major strategic decisions – entering a new market, introducing a new offering, building a new plant, acquiring another company, raising additional capital, etc. – rarely adds up to one number. If it were, the cost of understanding its impact on CPV would seem trivial in comparison. We believe the error of failing to conduct good customer research occurs simply because management fails to recognize the tremendous return on investment that understanding CPV offers.

Segmentation

A well-known Japanese manufacturer of forklift trucks had a decision to make.[2] It could target all users of forklift trucks and strive to be the dominant supplier in every category. Or, it could concentrate on only a portion of that total market and try to establish a competitive advantage in the markets it entered. This company chose to segment the available markets according to differences in CPV.

The company identified two basic segments. The first was the light industrial market consisting of the retailing and construction industries. The second was the heavy industrial market, which included harbor and logging applications. CPV was very different between these two segments. The light industrial market was cost conscious at the time of purchase, and needed machines that ran without much maintenance or downtime. The heavy industrial market was more focused on lifting capacity and durability.

By identifying these segments, and targeting the light industrial one, the company chose to develop a line of trucks that carried a 20 percent cost advantage over the competition. These trucks wouldn't serve as well in the heavy industrial applications, but those represented only about one-fifth of the total market for forklift trucks.

So what were the savings this company enjoyed by taking this route? For one thing, they avoided the cost of developing an entire heavy-duty product line to serve a relatively small segment of the total market. What would that investment have been? One million dollars? Ten million dollars? In addition, the company reduced the cost of penetrating a new market with their light industrial product by entering it with a lower-cost product than currently existed. What was the financial benefit from more sales, sooner? Certainly, more millions of dollars.

By understanding how different customers define CPV, companies are able to segment markets according to what causes them to make purchasing decisions. That's something worth investing a lot of money in – and certainly more money than a dose of good customer research costs.

Product Innovation

3M is among the most famous of all product innovators. Its programs to encourage creativity and innovation among all of its people are legend. By the mid-1990s, though, top management was concerned that few breakthrough ideas were being produced and that most of the new product revenue was coming from less rewarding changes to existing products. Among other actions it took, top management set an organizational goal that fully 30 percent of sales should come from products that did not exist for more than four years. That challenge spurred some 3M employee groups to look for new ways to come up with new, breakthrough product ideas.[3]

One group was charged with finding a breakthrough in the area of antiseptic surgical drapes. Surgical drapes are the materials used to cover the area surrounding the site of surgery with the purpose of preventing the spread of infection. 3M was the dominant supplier in this high technology business, but its position was beginning to stagnate. Changes were continually occurring in the surgery field, such as in the use of catheters or tubes, but little had changed about the surgical drapes. If some breakthrough wasn't found to revitalize sales growth, 3M would sell off the product line. A task force was formed to address the problem.

In this case, the team developed an aggressive program of meeting with "lead users" to explore for product innovation ideas. The cross-functional group consisted of six members who dedicated half their working hours to this effort. For six months, they "networked" their way into discussions with the world's leading authorities on surgical procedures and bacterial and viral infections. As a result, the team recommended four new product thrusts for 3M, all of which were accepted and implemented by top management. These innovations were directly the result of moving outside of this very creative company to talk to customers. The results were spectacular.

What did this cost? Let's estimate that the salary costs of the project team on this work amounted to almost $150,000. Add that same amount for travel expenses and support, and the total investment in this customer research must have been around $300,000. Now compare that investment with the total cost of developing and introducing four new products. Let's say at $1 million each (a nice round number), the product development costs totaled $4 million. That's what the company is putting at risk in introducing four new products. If the customer research increased by only 10 percent the likelihood that these four products will be successful, that increased the expected value of the product introduction investment by $400,000. Already 3M is ahead!

Is a 10 percent improvement in new product success probability a reasonable figure? It is probably too conservative. On a broad basis, surveys indicate that nearly 80 percent of all new products will fail to meet commercialization criteria within one year. And experts point out that the leading cause of new product failure is lack of input into the development process by the intended market.[4] So good customer research doesn't have much trouble improving success rates by only 10 percent.

And that doesn't consider the lifetime of profits from new products that wouldn't have been conceived except by good customer research. The return on investment for that level of success with product innovation customer research is embarrassingly high.

Pricing

The Loctite Corporation launched a product, called RC-601, that was a paste-like substance used to repair worn or broken metal machine parts.[5] Molded to the required shape, it could then be cured to a steel-like hardness. It was a new concept for machinery repair and so, to encourage trial usage, the product was priced at a modest $10 per tube. The company knew that production engineers might be skeptical, so they prepared marketing materials that provided detailed technical specifications. Nevertheless, the product failed miserably.

Within less than a year of introduction, the product was recalled and withdrawn from sale. Distributors were reimbursed for their unsold inventory. We don't know the magnitude of this recall, but if only 500,000 units were returned, at a $5 manufactured cost per tube, almost $2.5 million would have been refunded.

Only then was the appropriate customer research conducted to determine what went wrong. It was discovered that the production engineers weren't the correct target market. They resisted new, unproven solutions and the low price per tube of RC-601 probably added to their fears. Instead, Loctite decided to target the maintenance workers with this product, and renamed it Quick Metal. They simplified the instructions for its use and *raised* the price to nearly $20 per tube. This price was still within the budget authority of the maintenance workers, but better conveyed the value of the product. The newly introduced product was, and is, a huge success.

In attempting to calculate the return on investment of this customer research, we should include the profits from this product during its market lifetime as the major part of the "return." But let's remain conservative and look only at the original, failed product introduction. To make arithmetic easy, let's add a mere $500,000 to the amount of refunds given in the recall to reflect the other costs involved, such as marketing, distribution, and administration. We'll omit any possible damage done to the company's image in the marketplace and consider that the first product introduction failure cost Loctite at least $3 million. Theoretically, any investment in customer research that would have avoided this mistake up to the amount of $3 million would have been justified. If that research cost only $300,000, the return on it would have been 900 percent!

Surely that estimation appears incredible to some people. But it is not. Those are the kinds of returns often realized when good customer research is applied to important management decisions. The reason they are so large is because understanding CPV goes to the heart of the business objective: Getting customers to buy the product. If one can be just a little more successful at doing that, the returns on investment are substantial indeed.

Channels

Mobil Corp.'s commodity product is distributed through a network of 8,000 independent gasoline dealers. So, most of the competitive advantage the company can gain in CPV has to come at that point in the marketing channel. Fortunately, it is gaining the cooperation of almost 85 percent of those dealers in pursuing an innovative, aggressive campaign based on important customer research it conducted.[6]

In a study of nearly 2,000 gasoline buyers, Mobil found that many are much less sensitive to the price of gasoline than would have been expected. From their research, they divided gasoline buyers into five types: Road Warriors, True Blues, Generation F3, Homebodies, and Price Shoppers. Road Warriors drove 25,000-50,000 miles per year and used a gasoline outlet as a rest stop on the highway. True Blues were brand or dealer loyal and often bought premium grade gasoline. Generation F3 (for Food, Fuel, Fast) was younger, and most liked the convenience store aspect of the stations. And Homebodies were low mileage drivers who stopped for gasoline at the nearest station. Only the Price Shoppers based their gasoline purchases on price. This segment constituted only 20 percent of the total gasoline market, so Mobil chose to target the other 80 percent who would pay a couple of cents more per gallon for a gas station they preferred.

The new service, called Friendly Serve, had a careful roll-out. Participating sites, however, have already realized sales increases of up to 20 to 25 percent. Simply cleaning up the property and adding lighting increased sales by 2 to 4 percent, and well-stocked stores, concierge services, and friendly sales personnel have accounted for the rest. Participating stations are realizing these volume gains despite posting prices of almost $.02 per gallon more than nearby competing gasoline stations. They're accomplishing this because they better understand CPV.

What was the customer research that framed this strategy worth to Mobil? Well, an extra $.02 per gallon on all of the 650,000 barrels of gasoline that Mobil sells each day would provide the company with almost $118,000 million in increased annual profit. Cut that in half (even though, as we said, 85 percent of their dealers expressed interest in participating) and cut that in half again to provide for the increased expenses for providing the extra service, and it still means Mobil is better off by nearly $30 million. If the research cost as much as $300,000, the return is nearly 10,000 percent.

We will even admit to being skeptical about returns on investment that appear so high. Then we remind ourselves that we're talking about better understanding the key reasons that customers buy things. That is worth a lot, which is why the return on investment of a piece of customer research could be astronomical.

Marketing Communications

The glass for smooth-top kitchen stoves was originated by a German company named Schott. The product, called Ceran, was an immediate hit when it was first introduced in Europe, based on its technical performance. It was nonporous, stain resistant, easy to clean, very durable, and contained the heat of each burner to the small area above it very efficiently.[7]

But, when Schott's American sales rep approached the 14 appliance manufacturers in the U.S., the reception was lukewarm at best. Most ordered a few samples to try out, but no one put the glass tops into production. So, the company engaged in some extensive customer research to determine the problem.

It turned out that American appliance buyers defined CPV for these products differently than did the European market. While the Europeans were enamored with the technical features of their stoves, Americans were more interested in how they *looked*. So, Schott's advertising agency embarked on a new promotional program for Ceran in the U.S. Targeting both consumers and the middlemen (dealers, designers, architects, and builders), they pitched the aesthetic beauty of the smooth-top stoves. Advertisements for designers and remodelers used the theme, "Formalware for your kitchen." Another ad pitched the theme that Ceran was "More than a rangetop – a means of expression." To reinforce this slant, print advertisements featured visuals of the product.

Schott, a privately-owned company, doesn't disclose sales figures, but all 14 North American appliance manufacturers now offer multiple models using the Ceran smooth-top surface. And smooth-top stoves now account for more than 15 percent of the electric range market. Schott built a new plant in Indiana just to produce the Ceran product for the U.S. market.

Could we conservatively say that a dedicated production plant must represent at least a $100 million business? If Schott's margin was only 20 percent on this product, that represents an annual profit of $20 million that was created by the manufacturer's ability to understand CPV and communicate the benefits of their product accordingly. If the customer research cost $200,000, then, the return on that investment would be 9,900 percent in just one year!

Are all customer research and resulting promotional campaigns this successful? Of course not. Several other elements went into this particular success story, such as the underlying technology of the manufacturer and the creative capabilities of the advertising agency that executed the program. Still, it couldn't have happened until the realization occurred that American stove buyers define CPV differently than buyers elsewhere do.

Operations

The American unit of Roche Diagnostics is headed by Carlo Medici, a longtime member of the senior management team of the parent company, F. Hoffmann-La Roche. Roche Diagnostics provides diagnostic chemicals and instruments to clinical and drug testing facilities. Product lines include drug testing kits, blood cultures, hematology and chemistry instruments, pregnancy tests, and tumor-monitoring assays.[8]

When Medici took over in 1991, the division was an also-ran. Not satisfied with this performance, he initiated a campaign to focus on the needs of the customer and to deliver greater CPV. He started by conducting a series of focus groups, first with customers and then with frontline employees. These groups helped determine which were the most critical interactions – from the initial sales call to the follow-up call after installation – between the company and its customers. From this exploratory work, a "customer satisfaction" survey was designed and implemented to provide a regular means of reporting the company's performance in the eyes of the customer.

As information was gained from the customer research, processes were developed or improved in response. For example, much attention was devoted to improving the performance of the customer call center, which customers used to place orders, report problems, and seek help. Among other things, the automated voice response system was eliminated during normal office hours in favor of live operators to serve the customers. This action was taken because that is what customers told the company they wanted.

Although operating profits for this division are not publicly available, the company reported "profit index" results for the time that process improvements were implemented. During this 5-year period, the percentage of *very satisfied* respondents to the customer surveys nearly doubled, and the profit index increased almost 4.5 times. The division moved from a "low-growth division" to the "fastest growing competitor within its industry and in the F. Hoffmann-La Roche worldwide health-care group."

How can we turn that kind of information into a return-on-investment calculation? It's not easy with the limited information available, but we can take a broad brush approach to it. Let's consider what a 4.5 times improvement during five years would mean to any company that started with, say, an annual profit of $10 million. If the earnings gains were realized smoothly each year, that would be $7 million in additional profits per year. If the comprehensive customer research program described above cost $350,000 (for arithmetic simplicity), the profit improvement represents a return of nearly 2,000 percent per year. Clearly that is a very rough approximation, but the point is only that the resulting number is very big. And it is very big because these examples illustrate the power of converting an understanding of CPV into actions that increase that CPV. The return on this kind of investment is, indeed, significant.

ARE THESE ROI CALCULATIONS REALISTIC?

These examples represent dramatic successes based on better under-standing CPV. We don't have enough information about the details to be precise with the calculations of return on investment. But, we believe these examples legitimately make the point that gaining a better understanding of CPV, and then incorporating that into the important decisions that management makes nearly every day, has huge potential for improving business performance. It doesn't mat-ter whether the return is calculated as 10,000 percent, 1,000 percent, or even 100 percent. Those kinds of returns are huge compared to any other investment that management can take.

We said earlier that none of this is rocket science. Because the objective is to get more customers to buy more, using information about *why* they buy will improve results. Nevertheless, many man-agers still lurch forward making strategy, developing new offerings, setting prices, and so on, without really understanding what their target customers are likely to think about the results of their actions.

We believe the problem is that most managers are never able to slow down enough to think about the logic we've presented here. We hope this book, in some small way, contributes to correcting that error. Understanding how customers define CPV, and then integrat-ing that into everyday actions, is clearly the safest and surest way to increase sales and profits. We hope our readers find that to be true through firsthand experience.

SUMMARY

Management has several different things to worry about, including closing all of the four gaps in the CPV Delivery Cycle. However, we believe that there's nothing more important than closing Gap #1, the Research Gap. We believe that is the case because the financial re-turn on an investment in good customer research has the potential to be greater than any other kind of investment that management can make. Understanding CPV is simply a "sure bet."

Many examples demonstrate that understanding CPV makes a huge difference in the performance of the business. Usually, detailed numbers are not available to make precise calculations of ROI, but approximations indicate that the returns are very large indeed. No matter how many times the estimates are pared back and rounded down, the calculated return on good customer research exceeds any other kind of investment of business resources.

The premise here is quite simple. A better understanding of how customers think about their buying decisions can help management make better decisions to influence those decisions. The cost of attaining that better understanding, through good, ongoing customer research, is not very much when compared to the potential for gain. That gain, in increased sales and profits, can be huge.

REFERENCES

[1] Tony Siciliano, "Creating brand equity for U.S. goods in international markets," *Marketing News*, June 19, 1995, pg. 11; Tony Siciliano and Michael Amoroso, "The Increasing Importance of Strategic Research," *CASRO Journal*, 1993, pg. 65-68.

[2] Kenichi Ohmae, *The Mind of the Strategist*, (New York, Penguin Books, 1982), pg. 43-46.

[3] Eric von Hippel, Stefan Thomke, and Mary Sonnack, "Creating Breakthroughs at 3M," *Harvard Business Review*, September-October 1999, pg. 47-57.

[4] Robert G. Cooper, "From Experience: The Invisible Success Factors in Product Innovation," *Journal of Product Innovation Management*, March 1999, pg. 115-133.

[5] Roger J. Best, *Market-Based Management: Strategies for Growing Customer Value and Profitability*, (Upper Saddle River, Prentice-Hall, 1997), pg. 171-172.

[6] Allana Sullivan, "Mobil Bets Drivers Pick Cappuccino over Low Prices," *Wall Street Journal*, January 30, 1995, pg. B1, B8.

[7] Nancy Arnott, "Heating up Sales," *Sales & Marketing Management*, June 1994, pg. 77.

[8] Timothy L. Keiningham, Melinda K.M. Goddard, Terry G. Vavra, and Andrew J. Iaci, "Customer Delight and the Bottom Line," *Marketing Management*, Fall 1999, pg. 57-63.

About the Authors

David C. Swaddling is president of Insight·MAS, a research-oriented management consulting firm. Insight specializes in helping companies understand their Customer Perceived Value and how to use that to increase sales growth and profitability. Prior to consulting, Dave practiced with KPMG Peat Marwick and then was a senior corporate executive in the information services industry, including eleven years as CFO and senior planning officer of CompuServe. He holds a business degree from Northwestern University and an MBA from Ohio University. He is a member of the Society of Competitive Intelligence Professionals and an officer of the Product Development & Management Association. He is also a CPA and a certified New Product Development Professional.

Charles Miller, Ph.D., is Senior Vice President and Research Director of Insight·MAS. In addition to countless Customer Satisfaction and Customer Perceived Value studies, he has conducted numerous CPV Learning Systems audits, in-house educational programs, and major research projects for companies throughout the U.S. Before consulting, Charles was a faculty member at The Ohio State University, where he taught research, statistics, and data analysis. He holds B.S. and M.S. degrees from Louisiana State University and a Ph.D. from The Ohio State University. He is a member of the American Marketing Association and the American Society for Quality.

insight·MAS

4230 Tuller Road, Suite 200
Dublin, OH 43017
voice: 614-932-9690 - fax: 614-932-9691
www.insightmas.com

Index